PENTAGRAM

A.

Pentagram Book Five

THE MONACELLI PRESS

First published in the United States
of America in 1999 by
The Monacelli Press, Inc.
10 East 92nd Street
New York, New York 10128

Library of Congress
Cataloging-in-Publication Data
Pentagram book five.
p. cm.
Fifty case histories of Pentagram Design projects.
ISBN 1-58093-003-4
1. Pentagram Design.
2. Design – History – 20th century – Themes, motives.
3. Group work in art. 4. Group work in architecture.
I. Pentagram Design. II. Title: Pentagram book 5.
NK1535.P39A4   1998
745.4'4922 – dc21   98-31114

Printed and bound in Singapore

Designed by Pentagram
www.pentagram.com

Contents

Global Warming
The Multinational Interdisciplining
of Pentagram Design

Randall Rothenberg

It is raining. Naturally.

I am in London, where earlier in the 1990s I'd spent a glorious year being wet and misunderstood. In Notting Hill, to be exact – one of those neighborhoods where many American tourists, delighted by the Georgian housing and over-whelmed by the Portobello antiques market, tend to coo and fuss and wonder why life stateside can't be as civilized. Well! Just let them try to find a decent meal without curry in it for anything less than . . .

But I digress. This is not a worry for me today. For I am inside the sedate and eminently dry office of Pentagram Design, certainly one of the Western world's more prestigious design organizations, where every day at 1 p.m. lunch is served gratis to staff and visitors.

Why am I here?

Well, they are paying me, of course – the sort of thing that tends to concentrate a writer's mind. I've just been fired by *Esquire* magazine, so I certainly have the time. I also have high hopes that, if I acquit myself well, Pentagram partner Michael Bierut might show me the jacket he'd designed for my last book, which the publisher had rejected. Perhaps it would have sold better; I want to know.

But my curiosity extends beyond the pecuniary and the selfish. Before my ignominious bouncing, for the first time in my checkered career, I (who have written about design before) got to work closely with the art director on the redesign of *Esquire*. It was fascinating – far more interesting than working with writers (whiny and selfish, speaking from personal experience) – and I found myself wondering, first, "Where does he get these ideas?," and second, "How does he come up with so many ideas in the time it takes me to come up with maybe one?"

Needless to say, when after my firing Pentagram offered to pay me to go to London, give me access to my rejected book cover, and quench my curiosity about where designers' ideas come from, I leapt at the chance – and into this room. Where, it seems, not much is going on. A lot of not much, frankly. One Pentagram partner, a graphic designer, from New York, is tapping away at his Powerbook, answering e-mail. Another, a product designer based here in London, is standing and holding forth at the front wall. In a scene eerily reminiscent of the old "Dr. Kildare" television show, he is scrawling male and female symbols, a square and a circle, and the words *rational* and *emotional* in Magic Marker on two large pieces of paper tacked to it. The dialogue seems aimless and desultory.

"We want them to start addressing a problem that every large organization confronts at some point – the parts do not work together," suggests one partner. There is no response.

"We need something that illustrates easy and cost-effective," suggests the other partner. There is another pause. Through the glass wall, I can see the cast and crew of Pentagram London gathering their food (today the menu includes spicy stuffed peppers, salad, and, as usual, fruit and good cheeses) and assembling at the long tables in their lunchroom. I am hungry.

"We'll use a black tray to illustrate ease," the second partner posits.

"I'll just play devil's advocate," says an assistant. "Why is a black tray any 'easier' than a blue tray?"

Nearby sits a trolley well stocked with gin, Campari, scotch, and bourbon. I am thirsty.

"We have got to be careful of over-branding," the first partner says.

"Using color is over-branding?" the second partner reacts.

Must I listen to this?

"Yes. You brand the experience."

And then it dawns on me: I've never heard designers talk this way before.

Maybe I ought to pay attention.

Actually, maybe I ought to confess. For truth be told, I do have a motive for trying to understand Pentagram that extends far beyond the personal. Most who write about media and marketing, whether in the academy or the mainstream press, tend to concentrate their attention on – no surprise – the words. But long before my trip to London, time and technology had conspired to persuade me that the pictures were at least as important. With the multiplication of television channels, the proliferation of magazines, the development of the Internet, with advertising evolving into the search for holistic "brand experiences," it struck me that as the millennium turned, context – not just pictures but the design of spaces, places, products, events, brands – was becoming far more important than text.

Of the world's leading design firms, few have managed to insert themselves as successfully into this full range of contextual disciplines as Pentagram, the prestigious Anglo-American partnership, now spread beyond the original London office into New York, San Francisco, and Austin, Texas. The evidence lies between the covers of this, Pentagram's fifth, weighty collection of designs – and thoughts thereon.

While highly notable for the work, Pentagram is special for other reasons. Most great design, the sort that helps define or even fashion an era, derives from a particular vision. For this reason, most great design firms tend to die with their founders or evolve into corporate entities more skilled at making money than actually reshaping the visual world. Pentagram has defied the traditions of its industry by making the transition to a second generation of individualistic designers. "None of the companies we think of as leading design firms have done that yet," says William Drenttel, president emeritus of the American Institute of Graphic Arts. "Pentagram has."

More importantly, with that generational transition has come a realization of an ideal that was advanced by the founders but until now honored mostly in the breach: multidisciplinary collaboration. Today, Pentagram's graphic designers routinely work with its architects and product designers to craft integrated solutions to increasingly complex communications problems – a style of work increasingly necessary, I submit, if the cacophony of words and images that engulf us are to be turned into clear, purposeful, and delightful communication.

"Collaboration was very key to what Pentagram was supposed to be about, but when I joined, it wasn't like that at all," John McConnell, who entered the partnership in 1974 and is now one of its elder statesmen, told me. "It really changed when the new partners came in. And now I can absolutely say without any hesitation that collaboration is not only real, but colossal. And Pentagram is actually closer to its original concept than ever before."

The evolution of Pentagram matters because many in the design community have long seen the firm embodying a pure merger of art and commerce. In Pentagram, neither ideal serves the other. The client is neither the platform on which an artist heedlessly performs nor the ogre to be placated at the expense of the work. Here, client and designer come together in order to satisfy one master: public communication.

Pentagram's success at advancing this philosophy led the *Financial Times* to call it "the Rolls-Royce of design." No less a competitor than Milton Glaser has publicly wondered whether the firm is a "designer's Eden." If that is a lot of pressure to place upon an enterprise of sixteen fiercely autonomous partners and several score associates and employees, it is a burden that Pentagram invites. From its prehistory – first as Fletcher/ Forbes/Gill, then as Crosby/Fletcher/ Forbes, with Kenneth Grange Design

and then Mervyn Kurlansky, making the original five – the firm self-consciously opposed the orthodoxies of Swiss modernism, arguing instead that graphic communication meant allowing a thousand flowers to bloom. Yet it also resisted the excesses of eclecticism. Communication had to be about something, its founders argued – something more than the designer's own self-fulfillment.

Their timing was good. While industrialization faded into postindustrialism and goods started giving way to services, corporate culture began to be supplanted by communications culture – one in which everything informs. As Alfred Sloan's world slowly evolved into Michael Eisner's, a new design ethic was required. Pentagram represented it.

This ethic – it was strong enough to be called an ideology – was idea-based design. It asserted that design communicated both viscerally and intellectually – that it gratified the soul at the same time it satisfied the mind. As such, communication through design could not be achieved by the imposition of a strict set of rules or by the intrusion of an artistic vision. Idea-based design posited that each communication opportunity – or "problem," as the firm referred to it – was unique and therefore invited a singular solution, one that could be intellectualized and elucidated. In a formulation usually attributed to one or another of Pentagram's original partners, "an idea isn't an idea unless it can be explained over the phone."

At Pentagram, the ideology took specific form in the way design problems were sought, approached, and solved.

Designing stationery for a friend or a logotype for a multinational corporation could be equivalent challenges, hence the appearance on the firm's account roster to this day of clients large and small, penurious and rich. And whatever a client's specific need, the partner in charge of the account would invariably develop a structure for resolving it – a structure that would lead to the resolution. Hanging ominously over the whole creative process, John McConnell says, is "that fear of being found out by the other partners that you've done something frivolous."

The ideology of conceptual design defines Pentagram's newer partners as much as it did their predecessors. Michael Bierut, who joined in 1991, remembers his Uncle James receiving in the mail the legendary *Esquire* with a cover depicting Andy Warhol drowning in a can of Campbell's soup. "The idea that those things could be put together and add up to something more – and work on all those levels – just seemed so thrilling to me," said Bierut when I asked him why he became a designer.

Such rationalism can come as a shock to clients more accustomed to designers who traffic in magic. When an editor of a magazine Pentagram partner David Hillman was redesigning questioned his rejection of one photograph in favor of another, Hillman, one of the world's top publication designers, responded with a disquisition on context, composition, and relationships. "I've never heard anyone talk about pictures like that," said the editor when he was through.

Such rationalism, replicated times sixteen partners, actually undergirds the institution's character. The partners are acutely articulate – sometimes endlessly so. They love to debate – their industry, in the pages of *Print*, the *AIGA Journal*, *Eye*, and *I.D.*; and each other, in the partners' meetings held twice-yearly at exotic locales around the globe. (It is a standing joke in the organization that Hillman cannot abide Paula Scher's lauded branding campaign for New York's Public Theater, which he bemusedly considers "a perfect solution for a typesetter.")

But for years, there was one thing the ideology of conceptual design could not override. Although it presupposed the organization's involvement in a variety of visual disciplines – after all, if everything communicates, then the firm should involve itself across a full range of design endeavors – it could not force people into working together to solve communications problems. They talked a great deal about their "collective commitment . . . to make collaborative designing work," cofounder Colin Forbes has said. But for much of their first two decades together, Pentagram's partners usually worked alone.

It was not an issue that could be forced. Pentagram's system – each partner in charge of a team, all teams independent – precludes forcing anything. Indeed, other than the insistence on the partners' independence, the Pentagram management handbook, such as one exists, consists of two principles. The first: equality. From the day the partnership was created, the members agreed they would take equal salaries and equal bonuses. No point system, no seniority system, no counting one partner's good year more than another partner's bad year: in each office, Pentagram partners were to be compensated equally.

The second principle: generosity. Simply put, older partners continually make financial sacrifices to enable younger designers to buy into the firm. Not only has that required Pentagram to make different accommodations for virtually every new principal to enter the partnership, but it has actually required the firm to do something inimical to most businesses – hold down its asset value. This situation – individual responsibility, individual control, individual expression, and individual accomplishment within a minimally structured group environment – has been confusing to many who have been approached about joining. Most are accustomed to a binary world of employers and employees, designers and clients. "I assumed that they were going to do this, and they were going to do that," said Paula Scher, who fretted for months about the loss of her independence before she decided in 1991 to accept Pentagram's invitation. "They were going to set up rules. This is going to happen to me from them. Then you find out: there is no them. When you join Pentagram, there is only us."

The partners talk enthusiastically about the joys of collectivization. The provision of a basic corporate infrastructure enables each to pursue a career without the fear that failure lurks behind every inappropriate font choice. "You can actually control your own destiny," Michael Gericke, who became a partner in 1993, explained to me. "You don't have to report to anyone else, you don't have to worry too much about what someone else thinks, or how much business you generate. You really only have to worry about what your contribution is to making this whole big thing happen."

This Three Musketeers–like unity has not gone unnoticed by other designers, who reach far and wide for metaphors to describe Pentagram. Design historian and *AIGA Journal* editor Steven Heller likens the firm both to an orchestra ("each unit can play a part of the piece beautifully, and then come together to make it into a symphony") and to a military operation ("one squad may be better at demolition than another squad, but they come together as a unified force to advance the strategic goal of the mission"). Yet a more apt comparison may be to the Japanese keiretsu, in which titularly independent but financially and emotionally interdependent companies operate, often in undefinable ways, to mutual advantage.

Even Shangri-la is not without tensions, of course. Because Pentagram's "us" defiantly remains a collection of "me's," competitiveness characterizes the enterprise. Money, respect, ego, and control – subjects that creative types often conflate – continually collide inside Pentagram. Because the firm's utopian "equality principle" removes compensation from the open list of competitive issues, it forces partners to evaluate their self-worth against their colleagues in other ways. One is the continual judgment they pass on each other's work. "They look at each and every thing you are doing, and you worry that if it's not quite right, they're not going to think as highly of you," said Kit Hinrichs, who opened the San Francisco office in 1986. "It's a lot of internal pressure."

At times, it boils over – no small component of Pentagram's intercontinental expansion. "We grow by fight," Paula Scher likes to say. "Two partners will go to dinner, they'll have an argument, and the next day, we'll have another office."

The emotional pressure can be particularly tough on new partners, especially those raised up from associate level. Pentagram's original, informal rules of operation stated that associates – senior designers in the employ of a partner – could not accede to partnerships. That rule was amended in 1989, when John Rushworth, who had earned his colleagues' admiration during four years working under John McConnell and another two years essentially running his own business, was invited to join. His success cleared a path for others; Gericke in New York and Justus Oehler in London also began at Pentagram as senior designers.

All told me it was one of the most difficult life transitions they've ever had to make. "When I started – and it's the same for everyone – I had to learn to do everything myself," said Oehler. "You have never even worked with an accountant, and suddenly you are required to run a company. You need a lot of strength and thick skin."

John Rushworth agrees. "Changing from employee to employer creates its share of insecurity," he said. "I honestly would not recommend it to anybody to do it the way I did it."

Pentagram's evolution and growth has added to those pressures. Partners continually debate the wisdom of working for big, bureaucratized clients. During my sojourns in the firm's offices, the subject was raised constantly. Many of the partners want to prove themselves and the ideology of idea-based design on fields provided by the world's largest corporations. Yet some worry that such clients' demands – for market research and meetings and coddling – coupled with the undeniable allure of their large fees, might subtly lead Pentagram to stray from the craft of design. "Because of the way we are structured, with individual partners insisting on doing the work with small dedicated teams, we're not equipped to handle the large projects that the more corporate corporate-identity firms are," John McConnell told me.

True to the Pentagram spirit, others tend to disagree. "Because of the way we are structured, we can actually put multiple partners and multiple teams on any given project at the same time," says Lowell Williams. "This enables the partners to still be responsible for the actual designing, yet we have the network and the backdrop that all of the larger, more market-driven firms claim to have."

Pentagram's two largest offices seem to represent physically the two poles of this art-versus-commerce debate. The London headquarters, designed by late partner Theo Crosby and located on a quiet street in fashionable Notting Hill, resembles nothing so much as an academic institution. Starting at the reception room, a covered outdoor walkway leads to a main building whose soaring ceilings, carefully arranged posters, sculptural displays, and rolling-stock archives recall a college library. By contrast, the New York office, hard by Madison Square, hums with activity. Vertically stacked around a central atrium, partners and associates are constantly peering up or down at each others' chaotic workspaces, their conversations reverberating off the walls. The place, designed by partner James Biber, is redolent of commercial Manhattan, still leaking hints that it was once a bank.

In fact, though, Pentagram is an amalgam of art and commerce – as any truly inspired design enterprise must be – and while the issue is debated, the debate itself assures that the firm will become neither institutionalized nor marginalized. In the design of the two newest offices (which differ markedly from their predecessors) there is an almost palpable sense that it is time to move beyond this discussion, already. Peeking through the big, open San Francisco headquarters, in a converted warehouse in the chic SOMA district, are enough unfamiliar techie toys to remind a visitor that this place abuts Silicon Valley, where the future of communications is being invented. The Austin headquarters, fashioned after the traditional Hill Country ranch house, also conveys the notion that there is life beyond both art and commerce – as does its e-mail address, "howdy@texas.pentagram.com."

In fact, it is in the features the four offices share, notably the open congre-

gating rooms, dining areas, and glassed-in conference spaces, that Pentagram's true character – solipsistic and conversational – shines through. "We are," says Woody Pirtle, who came up from Texas to join the New York office in 1988, "an ongoing therapy session."

If there was one thing therapy alone would never resolve, it was the early lack of interest among the principals in collaboration. Joining a "club of stars," as Pentagram construed itself, was not only emotionally difficult for younger partners; it persuaded the older partners that they were the centers of their own universes – something their peers reinforced in the accolades that showered down on their work. David Hillman, who was happy and successful and living in Paris, the design director of *Le Matin*, when he accepted Pentagram's partnership invitation in 1978, remembers being surprised by the place's atomization. "When I first came here," he told me, "I sat in the old office surrounded by everybody, and I'd never been so lonely in my life."

However, the tide would start to turn at about that time. Partly out of a desire to attempt to "reprogram" the firm, partly out of a fascination that derived from a late 1950s summer vacation in New York, Pentagram cofounder Colin Forbes in 1978 persuaded his colleagues to let him try to start an office in the U.S.

The task was far from easy. The New York design community does not take easily to outsiders; Forbes and Peter Harrison (also an expat Brit), his first partner, had considerable difficulty getting work other than annual reports. They survived in no small part due to the indulgence of their colleagues in London, whose continuing success served to provide the financial and emotional wherewithal to see the U.S. experiment through.

An incessant networker, Forbes continued to spread the Pentagram gospel in American design circles, trying to persuade others to join their club. He eventually worked his way to San Francisco, where he persuaded Kit Hinrichs to become a partner. Hinrichs – who had long believed that "design doesn't begin and end on a piece of paper" – committed himself along with Linda Hinrichs and Neil Shakery to Forbes's primary goal of growing and expanding the capabilities of the partnership.

His presence did more than extend Pentagram geographically. It also caused Woody Pirtle, a deeply respected designer from Dallas, to take a second look at Pentagram. Pirtle had spurned a 1981 offer to join the firm, which he considered a "colony" in the U.S. Seven years later, though, with the Texas economy in the doldrums and his personal life prodding a change in venue, he was more receptive – as he told his friend Kit Hinrichs. Within a month, the deal was done and Woody Pirtle was a Pentagram principal in New York.

Pirtle's reputation made others in the insular American design community take note of the "colony." In 1991, while on a business trip to San Francisco, Lowell Williams, another Texas designer, found himself jogging past the Pentagram office. Acting on an impulse, he called Hinrichs and invited him to lunch. That in

turn led to conversations with Pirtle and Forbes. And soon, like Pirtle, Williams found himself closing a good business and resettling in another city, driven by the idea of joining – and becoming – something larger than he had been.

At the same time, Pirtle was scouting for designers to augment the New York office. Rather quickly, he targeted Paula Scher and Michael Bierut. Scher, who had established her eclectic bona fides at CBS Records in the early 1970s and later on her own, was also a frequent contributor to design publications and a presence within design organizations. When Pirtle asked her about joining Pentagram, "I felt like I was being asked to the prom by the football captain," she told me.

She was, however, deeply worried about subsuming herself to the group. So, for advice, she called her friend Michael Bierut, with whom she was co-chairing the following year's AIGA national conference. Like her, Bierut was a visible figure within the design world, known as much for the intelligence of his work – from Alfred A. Knopf book covers to large architectural signage projects – as for the contentious positions he would stake out in the pages of *I.D.* and other publications. He was also restless. So Pirtle called him, and in 1991 Bierut and Scher joined Pentagram New York.

Scher then introduced her new partners to an architect she thought would complement the group, James Biber. Biber had run his own studio since 1984, but he possessed a temperament that distinguished him from others in his field. As he told me: "The graphic designer's whole job is to communicate something –

to get an idea from their brain to somebody else's gray matter. They're about visual literacy. You could say that architects do exactly the opposite. Most tend to enshroud themselves in an obfuscation of ideas, a declarification of reality. They communicate in an arcane language that protects their sense of ownership of a thing. It's arrogant, it's a big mistake, and I resent it. I like making an impact on people that has richer depth than surprise or shock." In 1991, Biber, too, accepted an offer to join as a principal.

And while most of the attention in the early 1990s was being focused on new partners, Michael Gericke, who had joined Pentagram in 1985, was quietly and methodically building a significant style of his own. First as a senior designer, then as an associate on Forbes's team, he produced a body of work that earned the respect of his peers and led to his invitation to become a partner in 1993. Pirtle recalls that "it was difficult to tell exactly where Forbes left off and Gericke picked up, all of which is a testament to Gericke's abilities."

The timing could not have been more inauspicious. The New York economy was in the process of bottoming out, and the new partners, far from taking the city by storm, found themselves struggling to make ends meet. But the financial pains accomplished a goal that had previously eluded Pentagram. It actually forced partners to guide work each other's way. "If ever there was a time to refer back to our founding principle of generosity, this was it," said Bierut.

Even after the American economy emerged from its trough, other developments conspired, however inadvertently, to inculcate an atmosphere of collaboration across geographic boundaries. The new New York office space, where the company moved in 1994, was designed so that all partners, while in continual vertical contact with their teams above and below them, nonetheless sit together, in tight bays on the middle level. "Sitting with my partners and overhearing what they said and being part of that group meant that we bonded," Biber said.

After two years in San Francisco, Lowell Williams returned to Texas, setting up a Pentagram office in Austin. Now spread among four outposts with a continent and an ocean separating them, the firm's principals had no choice but to strive actively to maintain constant contact. "If I had moved to Austin and never said 'hello' to anyone else in the company, then that would have failed," Williams said. "But if the commitment is there to keep the culture intact, then you will keep the culture intact."

With Williams's departure, Hinrichs redoubled his efforts to find new partners for the San Francisco office. One day, he attended a presentation about the development of Apple Computer's brand identity. The forty-five-minute talk – about the quest to define the visual vocabulary and the Apple brand through product design – gave Hinrichs the intellectual jolt he would often get while attending Pentagram partners' meetings. When he approached the presenter for names of designers with a similar acuteness about their work, he was surprised when the fellow said, "How about me?"

The presenter, Robert Brunner, was one of America's better-known product designers. As head of design for Apple for six years, he had been responsible for some of the world's more talismanic pieces of technology, including the Macintosh LC line, the Powerbook, and the cultish Newton MessagePad. He was intrigued by Hinrichs's overture because of the reputations inside Pentagram. (As a student, Brunner had been inspired by Kenneth Grange's designs for Kenwood, the home-appliance manufacturer.) What finally persuaded him, though, was his and Pentagram's mutual commitment to idea-based design. At Apple, Brunner had developed a system for problem solving that involved developing scenarios about how a product might be used, then writing and illustrating stories that would explain and describe it, and only then beginning to design it. The approach was pure Pentagram. In 1996, Brunner joined the firm.

As the 1990s drew on, Pentagram U.S. seemed to grow into its reputation. Multidisciplinary projects, once rare, became frequent. Cleveland's Rock and Roll Hall of Fame and Museum and New York's Fashion Center teamed Bierut and Biber for, respectively, an exhibit on the psychedelic 1960s and an identity campaign. Geographic boundaries were crossed: Biber in New York and Williams in Austin collaborated on the design of retail environments and packaging for Gianfranco Lotti, as well as the Taco Bueno fast-food chain. Biber and Hinrichs met midway to design a genetics exhibition at the Chicago Museum of Science and Industry.

All of this because Forbes talked to Hinrichs talked to Pirtle talked to Williams talked to Scher talked to Bierut talked to Biber talked to Brunner. "We kind of realized Colin's plan," Scher told me, "but accidentally."

The same process was taking place in London – although it was even more arduous, because the partners had to battle against their own success, not the mind-focusing problem of financial failure. Some felt the place was drifting. "There were a number of early years when we did quietly admit in dark corners that allowing Colin to go was a terrible mistake," John McConnell told me. "His going to America left a vacuum here, which none of the other partners would ever allow anyone else to fill."

Yet if Pentagram's founders' collaborative dream went unrealized, the ideal remained intact. What eventually turned that ideal into action was the arrival of a non–graphic designer who needed work.

Daniel Weil, from Argentina, joined the London office on the day cofounder Alan Fletcher left Pentagram in 1991, with little immediately to suggest that he would do anything other than strive to build his own accounts. An architect, product designer, and at the time professor at the Royal College of Art, Weil had been introduced by Kenneth Grange, one of his postgraduate examiners.

But he shared certain characteristics with New York's "3-D man," James Biber. Like Biber, Weil was thirty-nine, an age at which graphic designers are considered seasoned but at which architects and product designers are just coming into their own; mature personally, they are still capable of professional exuberance. Like Biber, Weil opposed the "black box" theory of design – the notion that design is something mysterious that occurs within the unfathomable soul of the designer: "Believe in the process," one of Weil's favorite phrases, was also a fine summary of Pentagram's idea-based design ethic.

The next significant addition was German–born Justus Oehler. He joined Pentagram in 1989 and was made an associate in 1992. Since becoming a partner in 1995 he has gone on to design corporate identity programs for the U.K.'s National Grid Company, the World Economic Forum, and the Star Alliance.

Before too long, the London partners found themselves working together, crossing disciplines on project after project. For TSE Cashmere, Weil and Oehler teamed to create retail spaces and collateral graphics; for the Granada service areas, Weil and McConnell collaborated on a top-to-bottom redesign of the physical and visual environments; for the Boots retail chain, McConnell supervised a host of different designers, including Weil (who designed a new exterior for the stores) and Grange (who designed a new shopping basket complete with curved surfaces and comfortable handle encapsulating Boots's new, friendly image).

In an even more fundamental realization of Pentagram's founding vision, various partners began collaborating across national boundaries. Weil and Biber together helped design the Swatch watch company's flagship store on Fifty-seventh Street in Manhattan. Weil and

Bierut teamed to redevelop the corporate identity of United Airlines. Rushworth and Williams have worked together for two American high-technology companies, Hewlett-Packard and Intel.

Pentagram was transformed yet again in mid-1998 with the election of two new partners in London, Lorenzo Apicella and Angus Hyland. By temperament and skill, both promise to extend Pentagram's multidisciplinary efforts. Hyland, a graphic designer with his own studio in Soho, had already collaborated with Pentagram on numerous projects, most memorably the promotional material for Shakespeare's Globe Theatre in London. Apicella, an architect, who for a decade had run an award-winning architecture and design practice, had earlier been a key player at Imagination, perhaps one of the world's leading creators of integrated brand experiences.

The two new partners evened the trans-continental balance: the partners are now divided equally between Europe and North America. But London has added three partners since 1995, the U.S. only one. The New York office, particularly, is feeling some heat. "We are now the older office," Paula Scher said shortly after the partners' meeting at which the decisions were made. I could not tell whether it was rue or pride in her voice. "Now we are going to have to work harder to make sure we hold up our end of the generational bargain."

The need is not a competitive one, for generational transition has been instrumental in fulfilling the real dream of Pentagram's founders: collaboration beyond borders, the real theme of this book. But Pentagram would not be what it is without its partners' equivalent dedication to their own singular visions, and to the craft of design itself. Accordingly, among the fifty projects illustrated, photographed, diagrammed, and described herein are a full range, from extra small to extra large. Whatever the scope, however long the duration, whatever the structure, these projects all emerged from the principals' fierce devotion, against long odds, to the idea that they are without a doubt made better individuals by working together.

"When I joined the company, there were two myths about Pentagram, which we consciously perpetuated, to our public and to our benefit," James Biber said. "One was that we were an international company, when in fact we were a series of national companies. The other was that we were interdisciplinary, when really we were a series of small teams, each operating more or less independently. Those are no longer myths."

But it should not have been a surprise. Many years before, at a partners' meeting in Arizona, the partners – some reluctantly – engaged in a group-therapy exercise. They had called in an industrial psychologist, who provided them a scenario. They were on a plane that crashed in the wilderness. They could salvage only a few artifacts. What strategy would they develop and refine in order to survive?

First, they worked out their options individually. Then the therapist assembled them in teams. And they quickly realized that the most important judgment had nothing to do with the tools.

"We realized," remembered David Hillman, "that we were stronger as a group than as individuals, although we could operate as individuals as well. And we knew that that had always been the philosophy of Pentagram."

It is late, and I am once again eying enviously the drinks trolley outside the glassed-in conference room at Pentagram London, where I have been trapped for most of this day. And unbelievably, the two partners are still contemplating, debating, justifying, rationalizing their efforts to "rebrand" a client. "What's the clear explanation of why and how this is used?" one demands.

"I don't think we're doing irreparable harm here," the other responds.

John McConnell, who has been observing the waving hands and furrowed brows through the glass wall, allows a wry smile to creep up his lips as he saunters over to the drinks trolley and mixes himself a gin and tonic. No one but me appears to notice him as he cracks open the door and listens to the debate.

"This is one of only two options we have to establish the logo," maintains the second partner.

"What's the logic?" insists the first.

McConnell takes a sip from his drink, looks at one colleague and the other, then interrupts. "Well," he says, a glint in his eyes, "have you solved anything yet?"

American writer Randall Rothenberg, a contributing editor to *Wired* magazine and former media reporter and columnist for the *New York Times* and *Esquire*, is the author of *Where the Suckers Moon: An Advertising Story*.

Allowing a visually seductive art form to speak for itself, through type and photography, across a broad range of printed materials and interior spaces, creates an identity for a cultural organization and introduces it to a new public.

The Crafts Council

It was the end of the 1980s, and the Crafts Council faced a problem . . . and an opportunity. A government-financed body whose mission was to encourage public support for British craftspeople and purchases of their work, the council, like other public organizations during an era of budgetary scrutiny, had to strengthen its reason for existence or face the prospect of elimination. What's more, the council was about to shift its offices and galleries to a building outside London's West End, where visibility and tourist traffic, at least, had been assured. The timing was clearly right for the council to reassess who constituted its "public," and the ways in which it presented itself to them. In support of men and women who make silverware, ceramics, jewelry, textiles, furniture, and glass, and engage in hundreds of other activities, the Crafts Council mounts exhibitions, conferences, and workshops; tours throughout the U.K. an always growing national collection of the best of contemporary crafts; markets the crafts; and educates the public through its grants, publications, shops, fairs, and visual archives. Nevertheless, for all its work, the council was barely even known.

Since its founding in 1971, it had used different graphic designers to fashion the promotional campaigns for its six annual exhibitions, two yearly fairs, and a multitude of other works, internal and external. In seeking to unify through design the council and its activities, Pentagram recognized immediately that the craftworks featured in the organization's exhibitions, fairs, and archives were so strong that they could brand the body itself and, at the same time, sell its various activities to the public.

Strong, punchy photography of crafted objects was the first component of the campaign. Featured works were unabashedly selected for their appeal to a broader audience. Exhibition posters, the most regular and visible aspect of the council's promotion, each included an enlarged, cutout photograph of a single, handmade object to highlight the elegant classicism of craftwork. Other elements of the design work supported this robust approach. The design team frequently used bright colors – offbeat acids as much as primaries – for both lettering and backgrounds, as in the "Flexible Furniture" exhibition catalog and poster. The goal was to draw back from the sepia tones and other folksy associations with which craft is too frequently saddled. Even the council's new logotype was a piece of craft. It consisted of a lettercutting, done in stone, by Tom Perkins, one of a dwindling number of typographers to abjure the use of the computer in favor of older traditions. The logo embodies and symbolizes the two sides of the organization's work: in combining hand and machine techniques and contrasting letterforms, it conveys both the "soft" qualities of cre-

In the late 1980s the Crafts Council's national center for crafts relocated from near Pall Mall to Islington. The new location, away from central London and the passing visitor, meant the council had to raise its profile through a more synergistic identity to continue to meet the exhibition program's visitor targets.

ativity and handwork with the "hard" pragmatism of an organization that must make decisions about the distribution of public money.

With similar reasoning, we reduced the multiplicity of typefaces the organization had used to two. To underscore the lively, expressive side of the crafts, we chose Joanna, an Eric Gill serif face about fifty years old, which retains a craftlike appearance. To emphasize the council's administrative role, we chose a sans serif, Futura, an exemplar of modernist efficiency whose strong, clean lines would, we believed, also help signal the urbanity and toughness underlying the lives of contemporary craftspeople. The initial, image-led phase of the identity program evolved to include pictures of creators along with their wares, notably in the series of four posters designed for the "Visions of Craft" exhibition, which showcased the council's national collection of contemporary crafts. In using full-bleed,

grainy, black-and-white photography, the integrity, devotion, and hard work demanded by the lifestyle was conveyed alongside the splendor of the objects.

Pentagram has designed some exhibitions and played a supervisory role in others. For the 1992 "Silver Show," a display of historical and contemporary European silverware, we developed a refined infrastructure combining white space, clearly articulated forms, and glamour through light to highlight the beauty and the value of the objects. By contrast, the exhibition and catalog for "Works for '94" – a show featuring a series of makers who had just left college and established businesses in the midst of a recession – emphasized the grittiness of a craftsperson's life. The catalog was a broadsheet newspaper in sepia, black, white, and red that fused huge type headings with bold text dominated by atmospheric photographs of participants and their works.

Pentagram initiated an approach in which leading architects were asked to design the Crafts Council's five to six annual exhibitions. This provided an additional incentive for the individual crafts' natural audiences to visit each show. The "Silver Show" (below) was designed by architect Zoka Skorup.

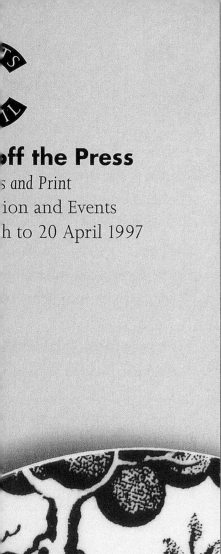

off the Press

s and Print

ion and Events

h to 20 April 1997

CRAFTS COUNCIL C

**New Times,
New Thinking:
Jewellery in Europe
and America**
19 September to
24 November 1996

CRAFTS COUNCIL C

**Photosto
Picture Li**

CRAFTS COUNCIL

How to borrow
works from the
**Crafts Council
Collection**

Elizabeth Fritsch Vase 1979

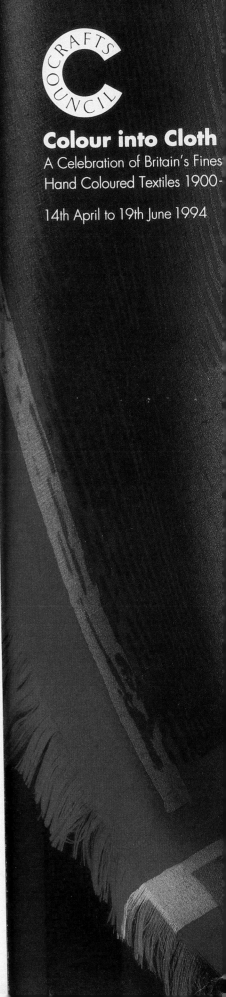

CRAFTS COUNCIL

Colour into Cloth
A Celebration of Britain's Fines
Hand Coloured Textiles 1900-

14th April to 19th June 1994

nd
y

Literature (previous pages) for many of the council's activities follows a repetitive, formatted approach for the position of the logotype and typography. This reinforces the authority of the council while the imagery and colors promote the particular event.

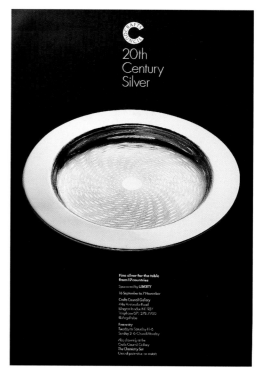

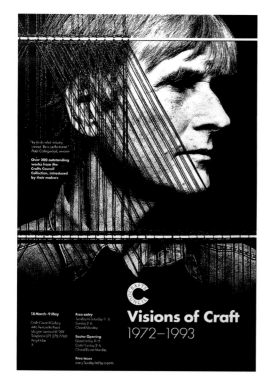

The exhibition poster program has evolved through two distinct phases. Initially, the posters were strongly image-led. Later this evolved into an information-driven solution that naturally made the posters even more synergistic.

The identity is managed through Pentagram rather than through a documented rule book. Occasionally exhibition themes demand a less "council"-authored promotional approach that can be managed within the overall basic identity palette.

"Works for '94" was an exhibition featuring the experiences of craftspeople who had recently left college and established businesses in the midst of a recession. The format and style of the exhibition catalog was a gritty, urban-style broadsheet newspaper.

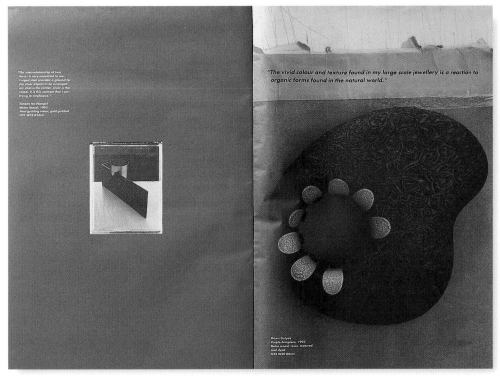

"My work uses a variety of non-precious and evocative materials in new contexts such as chairs made from industrial recycled felt, bubblewrap, recycled plastic and a range of storage furniture using off-cuts of heavy duty corrugated cardboard."

Jane Atfield
RCP Chair 2, 1993
Recycled plastic (originating from plastic shampoo bottles)
H81 W30 D37cm

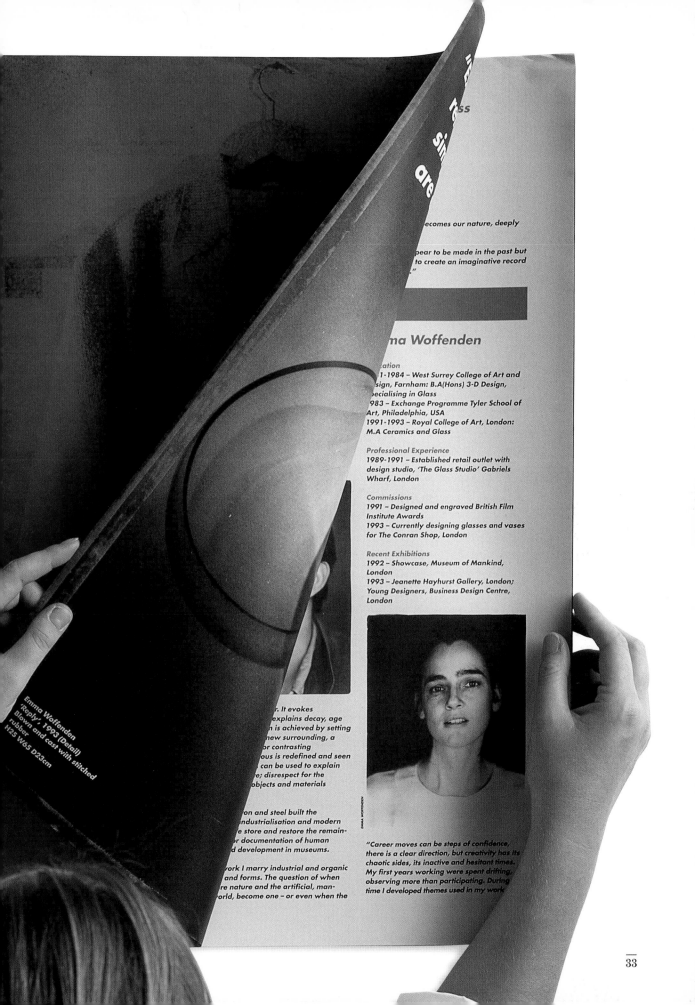

To evoke the late 1960s – for those who lived through it and for others too young – in an otherwise gray museum interior, an exhibit uses spaces, not cases, and sounds, not walls, to create an environmental experience.

Rock and Roll Hall of Fame

Take a stack of pulsating concert posters, Janis Joplin's letters to her mom, a sampling of flavored rolling papers, and Wavy Gravy's Woodstock sleeping bag. Add some historic guitars, Tom Wolfe's manuscript for *The Electric Kool-Aid Acid Test*, and a pair of platform shoes once worn by Jefferson Airplane's Jorma Kaukonen. For color, throw in the Merry Pranksters' Thunder Machine. Now arrange this eclectic collection to tell a coherent story about some of the most incoherent years of the twentieth century. This was the task facing Pentagram when we joined forces with the Rock and Roll Hall of Fame and Museum in Cleveland to design that institution's first special exhibition, "I Want to Take You Higher: The Psychedelic Era, 1965-69." An exhibit on psychedelia could easily have devolved into a decadent blur of throbbing guitars, oozing light shows, and stinking incense. Pentagram took a very different tack.

Faced with over five hundred artifacts, the design team avoided the obvious themes – sex, drugs, and rock and roll – and gave the exhibit a strong organizational identity that emphasized the unique character of the individual years.

The show takes the form of an abstract, six-petaled daisy, with one petal – "she loves me" – already plucked. The remaining five petals are each devoted to the story of one psychedelic year, 1965 through 1969. The daisy shape, while symbolically associated with 1960s "flower power," also provided an appropriate template for our chronological arrangement and made excellent use of existing circulation patterns within I. M. Pei's Hall of Fame building.

At the entrance, the twin cities of psychedelia, London and San Francisco, are immediately introduced with two of the most impressive artifacts in the show: John Lennon's rococo Rolls-Royce, set against a zebra-striped Abbey Road crosswalk, and Janis Joplin's equally audacious butterfly-painted Porsche, "parked" on a steep Haight Street ramp.

The poles of London and San Francisco are reflected, too, in the graphic components of the exhibition's design, which hover between the high contrast style of a "Bill Graham Presents" poster and the more elegant look of British psychedelia. The design team created a language that is one or two steps removed from the graphic design of the 1960s but not so far distant that it becomes ironic. The display descriptions are set in a single typeface, Cooper Black; although it dates to the turn of the century, the font, with its blobby character and overall zaniness, is particularly associated with the 1960s. In designing the interior walls, we used contrasting colors, manipulated foregrounds and backgrounds, and played with positive and negative space – a conscious effort to pay homage to two of the leading poster artists of the period, Victor Moscoso and Rick Griffin, and an effect that also mimicked one of

The exhibit title and identity were an homage to the psychedelic style created in San Francisco in the 1960s by artists like Victor Moscoso and Rick Griffin. The introductory signage, the book cover, and the fifty-foot-high banner in the main atrium share this design.

the architectural traditions of the time, supergraphics.

After the elaborately painted cars, the road and a series of sinuous, hanging beads lead visitors to the center of the flower: a twenty-foot-wide spiraling disk of song titles, set in the floor like Day-Glo grooves on a black vinyl record album. The songs listed were dubbed "The Psychedelic 100" and are those considered most quintessentially mind-expanding by the museum's curators. Played in their entirety in a continuous, chronological loop, these songs consti-tute the soundtrack of the exhibition. As visitors browse the years from 1965 to 1969, they always return to the cen-ter, where they are reminded that this body of music was both the fuel for the psychedelic era and its most important legacy. The designers' decision to place song titles at the heart of the show sends a strong message: this music still may be the best record of the period.

Around this central point, the five display areas that form the petals are defined by plywood-sheathed cases arranged as an open horseshoe. This design gives the visitor a sense of enclo-sure and immersion in each year with-out cutting off views to the rest of the show. The design of each display care-fully amplifies the essence of the mater-ial it houses and the year it covers. For instance, the black and white stripes of 1965 allude to the simple, sometimes amateur beginnings of the psychedelic look, but the circular cut outs and acrylic discs in the 1968 display suggest the lusher Barbarella-style futurism that took hold that year.

Another element central to the design is the exhibit labels: the explana-tory text is printed on plastic buttons or, in some places, on a fat, splashy six-petaled daisy. This symbol (a close cousin to the bright rubber flowers still stuck to so many bathtubs) appears everywhere, becoming the de facto emblem of the show and linking the big picture with the little ones, in the spirit of the best psychedelia.

Flowers figure in the slogans, the imagery, and the self-labeled culture of the psychedelic years in San Francisco. The flower, abstracted and reinterpreted, forms the five-petal main exhibit, with each petal displaying artifacts from one year in the exhibit's 1965–1969 scope.

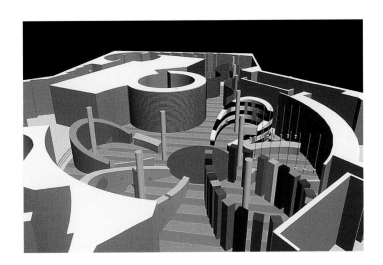

"I went to the first Family Dog concerts at the Longshoremen's Ha...

"The London Undergrou...

5 6 5 6 5 6

Spring 1969 * Electric S...

The Nice * July 1969* * Jug...

Old Turkey * Big Boy Pe...

Jimi Hendrix E...nce * ...nuary 1969 *

UNDERGROUND PRESS

"We were college-educated,
bored white children who were
disenchanted with the nature
of the times around us.
And we spoke to that,
in one way or another."
— Paul Kantner,
Jefferson Airplane

96 97 98 99

In a program repositioning J.P. Morgan's private-client business, intended to reach beyond the company's traditional markets, a literature program appeals to a younger, more contemporary audience of high-net-worth individuals and families.

J.P. Morgan

Few industries have faced the wrenching changes confronted in recent years by the banking sector. What was for centuries a staid undertaking has been transformed by consolidation, technology, and globalism into an intensely competitive business. J.P. Morgan & Co., one of America's oldest, largest, and most powerful financial institutions, has met this challenge by expanding beyond its original role. Originally a bank that focused largely on lending to the giants of industry, it has become an international financial services group offering finance and advisory services, sales and trading, and asset management to individuals and families as well. Pentagram began working with J.P. Morgan in 1994, assisting in the design of marketing tools aimed at high-net-worth clients outside its existing and typically long-standing client relationships. The challenge put to the design team was to help the bank dispel a perception that it felt could hinder its growth in the future.

07

06|1998

05|1998

04|1998

03|1998

02|1998

01|1998

For almost a century and a half, J.P. Morgan, a name synonymous with established influence and wealth, had conveyed an image of elitism; it was known, not incorrectly, as an institution that catered to the wealthiest, most powerful members of society and industry. In today's financial marketplace of grassroots wealth creation, however, this history is at once a strength and a weakness. As it had for generations, the bank continued to draw the financial elite. But for younger entrepreneurs, the generation to whom trillions of dollars in wealth will be transferred over the next ten to fifteen years, this image also carried with it a perception that J.P. Morgan & Co. was out of their reach, unapproachable.

The new program's primary responsibility was to help attract these newly affluent private clients without abandoning Morgan's heritage, culture, or traditional client base. Another objective was to capitalize on J.P. Morgan's reputation for its depth of services in a manner that clearly signaled to private clients that there was a point of personal access to these vast resources.

Pentagram designed and produced a package of materials to help market a wide range of products and services – from asset accounts to investment management and brokerage services – to this growing group of private clients.

To give the services their own unique voice within today's broadly sophisticated financial markets, the materials were formulated to be functional, emphasizing informational content, but within an unexpected context. In contrast to the prior marketing materials, for example, which had tended toward a more conservative style, abstract imagery and a vivid palette of primary colors were used to convey contemporary elegance as well as a degree of personal warmth. This helped to distance the program from the more institutional style of J.P. Morgan's corporate identity. At the same time, by tempering design boldness with the addition of blacks and grays and maintaining an allegiance to corporate standards in the form of logo use and typeface (Bodoni), the materials communicated the right level of seriousness and provided the appropriate measure of compatibility with the rest of the institution.

Using nontraditional imagery and vibrant, forceful colors, the program introduced a distinct personality to a newer private clientele by being less institutional than the style that had personified J.P. Morgan throughout the century.

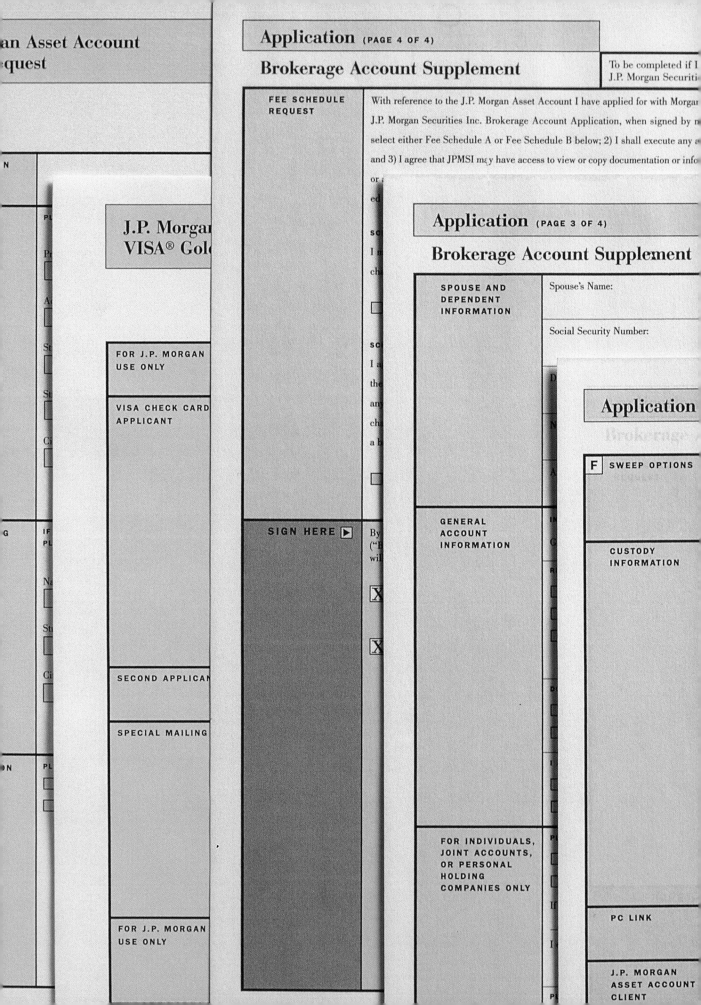

an Asset Account
quest

N

PLA

Pr

Ac

St

Sp

Ci

IF
PL

Na

St

Ci

ON

PL

J.P. Morgan
VISA® Gold

FOR J.P. MORGAN
USE ONLY

VISA CHECK CARD
APPLICANT

SECOND APPLICAN

SPECIAL MAILING

FOR J.P. MORGAN
USE ONLY

Application (PAGE 4 OF 4)

Brokerage Account Supplement

To be completed if I
J.P. Morgan Securiti

FEE SCHEDULE
REQUEST

With reference to the J.P. Morgan Asset Account I have applied for with Morgan
J.P. Morgan Securities Inc. Brokerage Account Application, when signed by n
select either Fee Schedule A or Fee Schedule B below; 2) I shall execute any a
and 3) I agree that JPMSI may have access to view or copy documentation or info
or a
ed

SC

I m
ch

SC

I a
the
any
ch
a b

SIGN HERE ▶

By
("
will

X

X

Application (PAGE 3 OF 4)

Brokerage Account Supplement

SPOUSE AND
DEPENDENT
INFORMATION

Spouse's Name:

Social Security Number:

D

N

A

GENERAL
ACCOUNT
INFORMATION

I

G

R

D

I

FOR INDIVIDUALS,
JOINT ACCOUNTS,
OR PERSONAL
HOLDING
COMPANIES ONLY

P

I

Application

Brokerage

F SWEEP OPTIONS

CUSTODY
INFORMATION

PC LINK

J.P. MORGAN
ASSET ACCOUNT
CLIENT

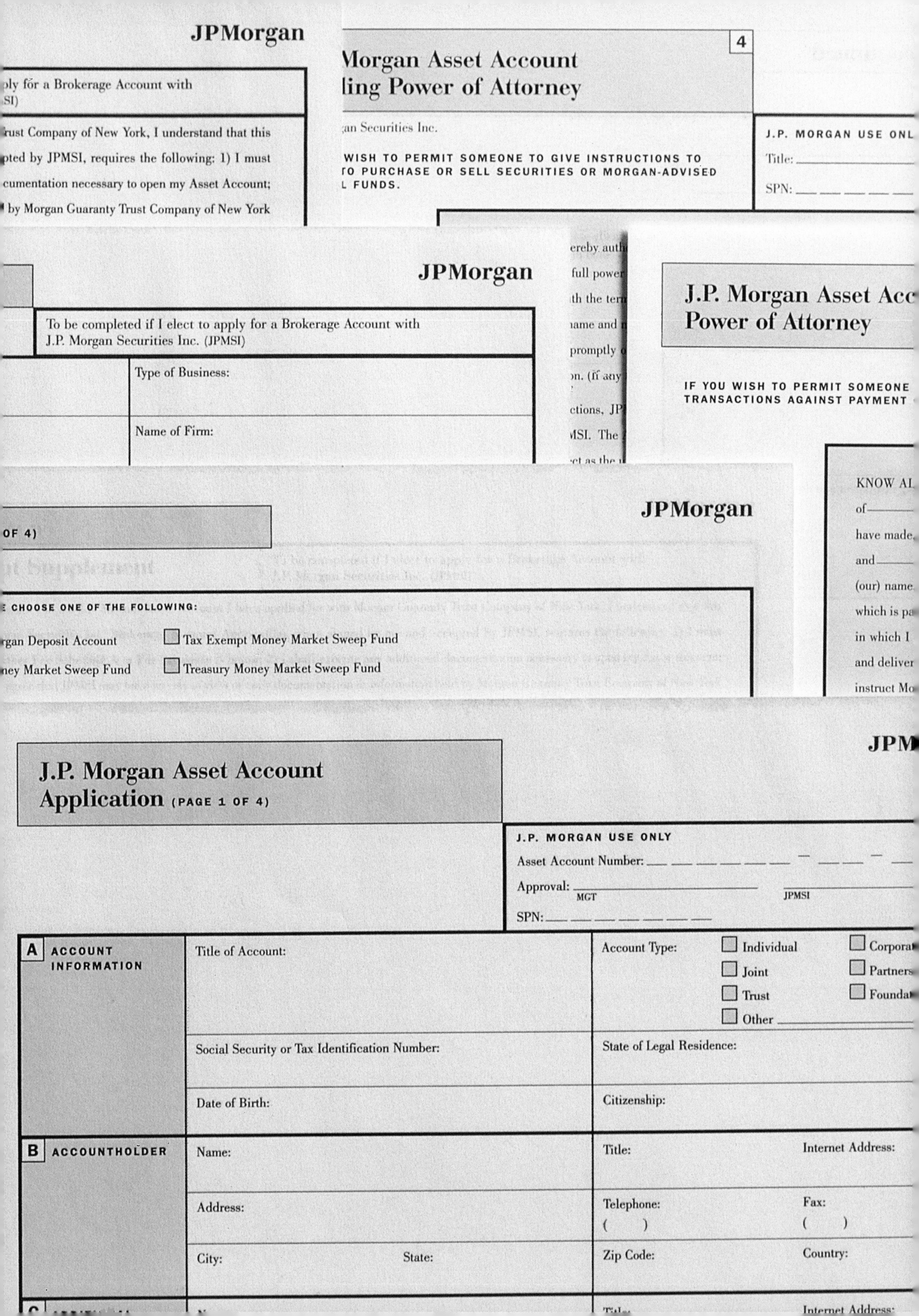

JPMorgan

Morgan Asset Account
ling Power of Attorney

gan Securities Inc.

WISH TO PERMIT SOMEONE TO GIVE INSTRUCTIONS TO
TO PURCHASE OR SELL SECURITIES OR MORGAN-ADVISED
L FUNDS.

ply for a Brokerage Account with
SI)

rust Company of New York, I understand that this
pted by JPMSI, requires the following: 1) I must
cumentation necessary to open my Asset Account;
by Morgan Guaranty Trust Company of New York

J.P. MORGAN USE ONL

Title: _____

SPN: __ __ __ __ __ __

JPMorgan

To be completed if I elect to apply for a Brokerage Account with
J.P. Morgan Securities Inc. (JPMSI)

Type of Business:

Name of Firm:

hereby auth

full power

th the ter

name and

promptly o

n. (if any

ctions, JP

MSI. The

t as the

J.P. Morgan Asset Acc
Power of Attorney

IF YOU WISH TO PERMIT SOMEONE
TRANSACTIONS AGAINST PAYMENT

KNOW AL

of_____

have made

and_____

(our) name

which is pa

in which I

and deliver

instruct Mo

JPMorgan

OF 4)

CHOOSE ONE OF THE FOLLOWING:

rgan Deposit Account   ☐ Tax Exempt Money Market Sweep Fund

ney Market Sweep Fund   ☐ Treasury Money Market Sweep Fund

JPM

J.P. Morgan Asset Account
Application (PAGE 1 OF 4)

J.P. MORGAN USE ONLY

Asset Account Number: __ __ __ __ __ __   __ __ __ __ __

Approval: _____   _____
                MGT   JPMSI

SPN: __ __ __ __ __ __ __

A	ACCOUNT INFORMATION	Title of Account:	Account Type:	☐ Individual ☐ Corpora ☐ Joint ☐ Partners ☐ Trust ☐ Founda ☐ Other _____
		Social Security or Tax Identification Number:	State of Legal Residence:	
		Date of Birth:	Citizenship:	
B	ACCOUNTHOLDER	Name:	Title:	Internet Address:
		Address:	Telephone: ( )	Fax: ( )
		City: State:	Zip Code:	Country:
C		N	Title	Internet Address:

**Brokerage Services for
Private Clients**

so many choi

strategy ∘ obtai

and research

portfolio that w

assets ∘ who can

investment prog

**Investment Management
for Private Clients**

so many choi

returns ∘ minin

∘ crafting a por

your other asse

your investment

when you build your own portfolio

○ a tool for holding your securities and Pierpont Funds ○ conveniently managing your cash needs ○ and keeping track of it all through one easy-to-read statement

JPMorgan

A working relationship spanning more than twenty years and an uncompromising belief that design must serve the needs of sound nurture a family of audio equipment with a look as distinctive as the performance.

B&W Loudspeakers

How extraordinary it is that in the huge world of home electronics, and stereo in particular, the British still have a reputation for making the very best loudspeakers. Given Japan's virtual ownership of the world's audio and video technology, it seems against all logic that this pocket of engineering excellence should remain in the United Kingdom. That it does is a tribute to the peculiar leadership of a few unusual people like John Bowers – the B in B&W. What started in a modest stereo shop in an English seaside town has through his vision grown to a £60 million business, exporting 90 percent of what it makes. In the rankings of sound quality, B&W loudspeakers are by any account among the world's very best performers. John Bowers lived for his loudspeakers – always trying new ideas, always spending the profits on new equipment, always investing in talented people. He died in 1987 but his spirit lives on, in a free-thinking creative culture that is driven by one mission: acoustic excellence. Industrial design is an integral part of that mission.

John Bowers was first introduced to Pentagram in 1974 by his friend Tony Armstrong Jones (Lord Snowdon), himself a music enthusiast and a friend of good design. From this first meeting grew a professional relationship that continued for twenty-four years.

The key to the relationship is the close link between technical and industrial design. The form of a B&W speaker is derived from its acoustic principles; and if the principles are radical, then so too is the shape. It might even appear a bit eccentric.

This is evident in Pentagram's first assignment, the DM6. In that instance, John Bowers had concluded that in order to focus the sound, bass drivers and midrange units should be set at different distances from the listener's ears. So the DM6 acquired a peculiar belly shape that placed one driver forward of the other. It also stands on uncommonly skinny feet, to minimize anything below the bass driver that might discolor the sound. The final design is in effect a visual statement of acoustic theory, and that is what gives B&W speakers their recognizable style.

Many other speaker designs followed the DM6, each one testing a new sound theory and design. Most significant of all was the famous 801. In any venture, there is probably some key event that is the turning point in its fortunes. For B&W it was this loudspeaker, launched in 1979 and a market leader to this day. The technical basis of the 801 is sound-driver separation, with individual enclosures for each of the three sound "territories." Each enclosure is a different design in different materials, tailored to that particular range of frequencies. Uncompromising technical performance rules every aspect of the design, and the quality of sound it delivers is a benchmark standard.

This is the loudspeaker that all of the main recording studios now choose as their recording monitor. Many other loudspeakers have since been modeled on the principles established by the 801, but the original, it seems, is still the best.

It takes many different people to deliver a product of this status, and sometimes that includes an industrial designer. When it does, the designer is most fortunate. To have a part in something as important as this is what all who live by selling creativity most hope for.

To be associated with a British product of such rare quality is an enormous privilege.

The distinctive bass-forward design of the DM6 (above) was Pentagram's first assignment. Tweeters first appeared on top of the main cabinet in 1977. This one belongs to the Matrix Series of 1990 (right), so named for the elaborate pattern of baffles that stiffens the main cabinet.

The 802 (left) and the 801 (below) have three different enclosures for the three sound territories. The bass driver is enclosed in a massive twenty-two millimeter MDF; the mid-range enclosure is a compound of resin and concrete; the high-frequency tweeter is housed in plastic. The overall style may be somewhat eccentric, but the sound is an industry leader.

The very lavish Signature Series was introduced in 1996 to mark the thirtieth anniversary of the company. While embellishments like the spun bosses in the center of each speaker have no great acoustic significance, they do not harm the sound – and that in itself is an acoustic achievement.

S&P

plus reinvested dividends
...estment on 12-31-83.
...ough 1993, the Company's
...erformed the S&P 500
...to-1.

$1,286

$298

$100

| 1983 | 1988 | 1993 |

KO

In its annual reports, The Coca-Cola Company wanted to say something that only it could say; Pentagram responded, avoiding any temptation to invent a graphic designer's "New Coke" by making innovative use of The Coca-Cola Company's visual iconography.

The Coca-Cola Company

Roberto Goizueta was dissatisfied. Even though The Coca-Cola Company's newly published 1992 report had been cited as top-notch, the chairman of the world's largest beverage company wanted something different. He wanted a report that compelled investors by truly capturing his company's uniqueness. For The Coca-Cola Company, generically good was actually bad. The discontent prompted immediate soul-searching among company staffers, who soon engaged several firms in heavy conversation. Four designers were asked to submit detailed concepts showing they could deliver the required breakthrough, with Pentagram earning the call. So what would take the Coke® report beyond generic excellence? What made The Coca-Cola Company unique? Well, most obviously, it had an enviable stable of powerful visual icons, including the familiar white script, the Coca-Cola contour bottle, and, yes, the color Coca-Cola red. It also had a good story to tell, having created more wealth for its shareholders over the previous decade than almost any other company.

Consequently, the 1993 report took a simple yet powerful approach – use the unique Coca-Cola® iconography to tell The Coca-Cola Company's unique story as an investment. The result? Coke got what it viewed as a true Coca-Cola annual report, and research said readers recalled key messages like never before. Invigorated by the progress, the team immediately began to think about how to make the same sort of leap in the 1994 report.

In the early stages, the company's then president, now chairman and CEO, Doug Ivester, issued a provocative challenge: "The cover needs to be something no other company can do." At first, the challenge seemed severe. After all, virtually any clever design concept or luxuriant production values could be copied by any company willing to spend the money. So the team realized it had to go deeper in asking itself again what was unique to Coke. The solution was so basic and so whimsical it initially seemed impossible to consider. During the year, the company had used simple, black-and-white Coca-Cola contour bottle silhouettes in a billboard campaign. Why not showcase the simplicity of the silhouette against a virtually nondescript landscape?

In fact, why not put the idea to the ultimate test? Why not run it without any identifying copy? After all, if it truly was something that only The Coca-Cola Company could do, wouldn't it be able to stand on its own without being labeled? Wouldn't the lack of such a label make the point even more dramatically?

It would, and it did. The majority of investors actually had fun pointing out the fact that the cover did not include the company's name. Others, while instinctively identifying the report as belonging to The Coca-Cola Company, did not even notice the absence of the company's name.

In 1995, the company asked itself and us, "How many times can we communicate an idea that powerfully in a single report?" The question was particularly relevant, given that the objective of the 1995 report was to remind investors of the company's fundamental strengths, a story told many times before. The result was a series of five graphics-driven riddles, each playfully leading readers to a new understanding of a well-worn idea. Readers showed a remarkable ability to recall the five key ideas.

What's the lesson in designing for one of the world's best-known companies? Don't get intimidated by familiar icons. Just have fun putting those icons to work in telling a story that nobody else can tell in a way that nobody else can tell it.

The 1993 report (previous page) initiated a movement to simple graphs, each attempting to make a single point clearly. Using Coca-Cola iconography to "brand" those facts, the report implicitly asked investors, "Wouldn't you rather buy Coca-Cola stock?"

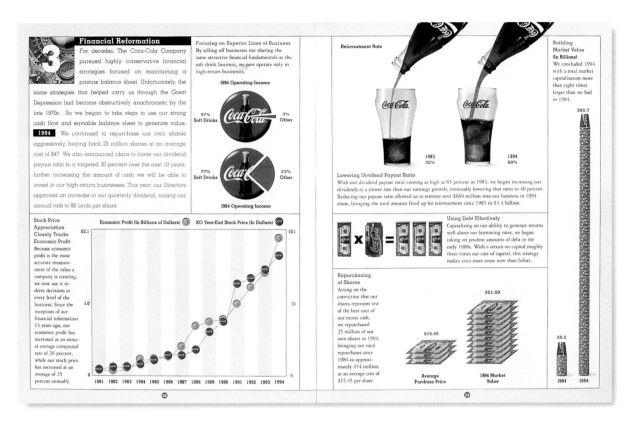

The 1994 report didn't just tell investors it was putting the Coca-Cola brand to work, it showed them. It also reminded them of the rich heritage of the Coca-Cola contour bottle design, which was being extended very successfully to larger plastic packages.

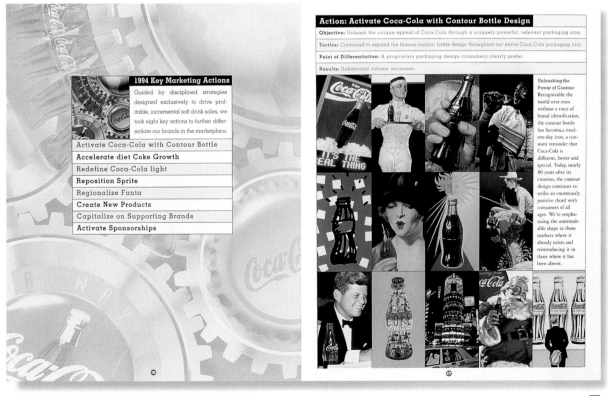

Our 1994 Annual Report

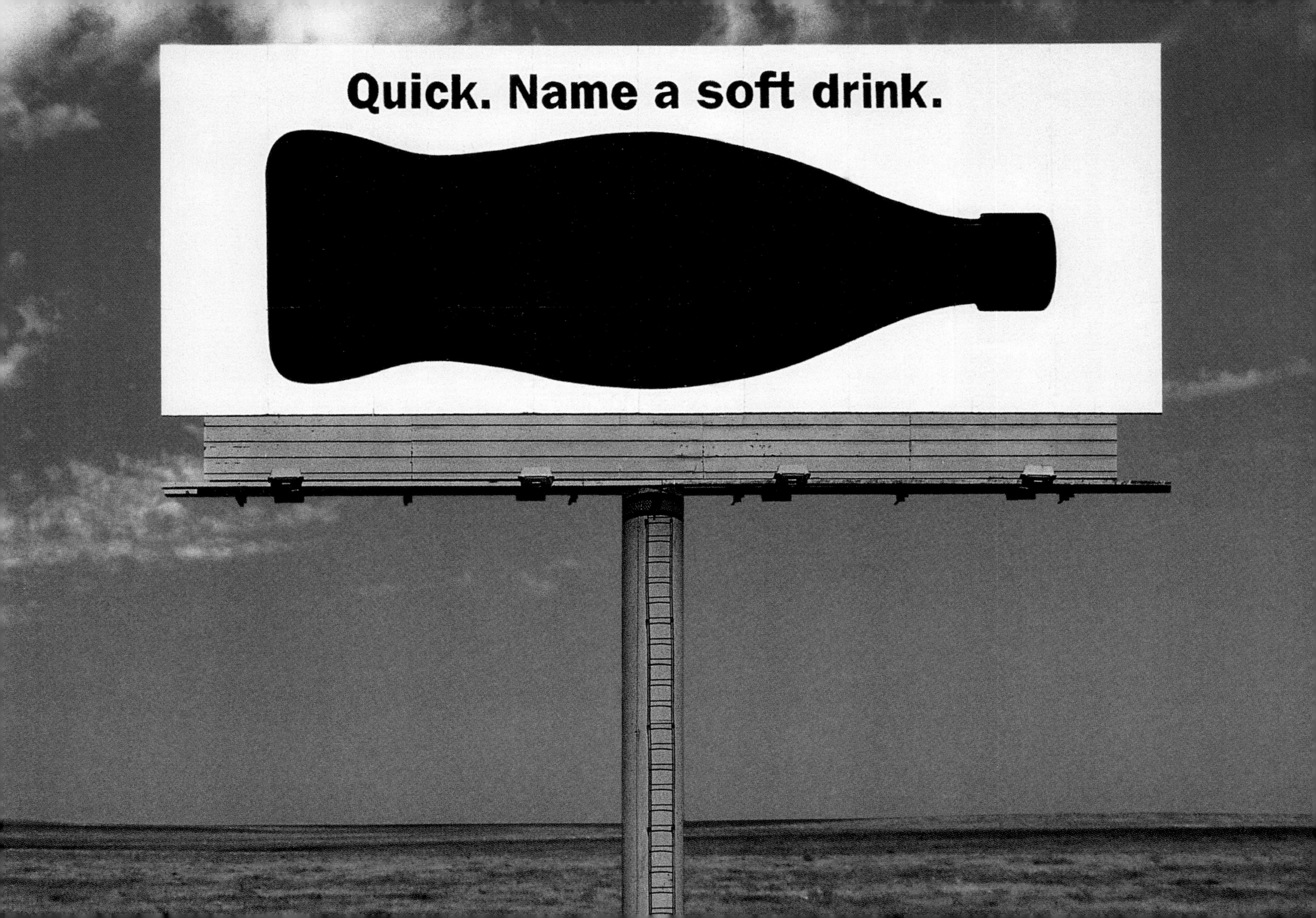
Quick. Name a soft drink.

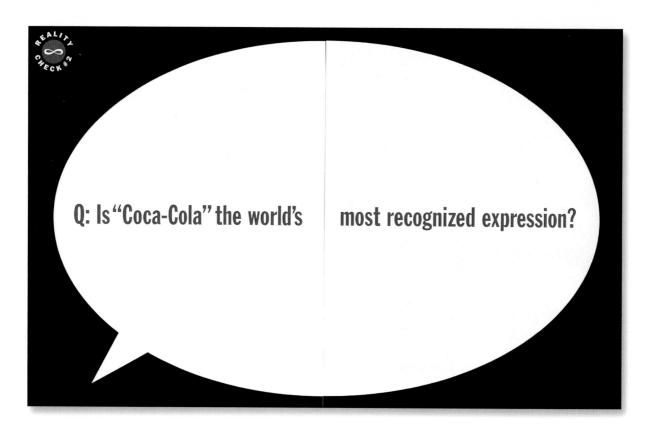

The Coca-Cola brand is so pervasive worldwide that it is difficult for people to gauge its scope. Hoping to make it easier and more interesting to think about, the 1995 report asked a seemingly preposterous question, and then responded with a very interesting answer.

We're rapidly strengthening the world's strongest brand.

So people buy Coca-Cola because of its name recognition? Partly. Name recognition offers us the opportunity to make our case. It's up to us to make that case relevant and compelling enough to win people over. For brand Coca-Cola, we're doing that in at least three ways. First, we're focusing renewed energy on marketing the taste of the product itself – its unparalleled ability to refresh and the uniquely satisfying sensation at the back of the throat that Coca-Cola provides. Second, we're cultivating and perpetuating the brand's personality and heritage – its mystique, its magic and its special ability to connect with consumers. And third, we're re-igniting the symbols that encapsulate the essence of the brand – including the curvy shape of the contour bottle, the instantly recognizable Coca-Cola script, the familiar Dynamic Ribbon device and, of course, the color red.

Then it all comes down to good advertising? No, it comes down to the total value offered by the brand. In fact, the reintroduction of our contour-shaped bottle did as much to directly drive our volume growth in 1995 as any of our advertisements. In the U.S., for example, our 20-ounce plastic contour bottle racked up 40 to 90 percent growth rates over prior-year packaging in markets where it was launched in 1995, while sustaining a strong 20 percent growth rate among all markets that have launched the package since 1994. The package, which is now available nationwide, has also sparked increases in the frequency and quantity of consumer purchases, which bodes well for our future growth.

The Coca-Cola trademark must be worth billions, right? Actually, it's worth $1 – from an accounting standpoint, that is. According to some valuation sources, however, its real value is closer to $39 billion. We don't really know how much it's worth. We do know this: If our Company burned to the ground, we'd have no trouble borrowing the money to rebuild, based on the strength of our trademarks alone.

But aren't "alternative" beverages where your real future lies? No. Coca-Cola is our engine of growth – past, present and future – a fact clearly evidenced by its more than 425 million unit case volume increase in 1995. Alternative beverages, by comparison, represent a tiny portion of our overall sales, and that's not likely to change. We're determined never to get caught in the trap of chasing the fad of the month, but we will put the full weight of our resources behind any emerging trend that will contribute positively to our overall growth. Fruitopia, for example, continues to excel, as does POWERaDE.

Q: What do we produce with our secret formula?

The task was to find a fun way to say "our financial fundamentals are strong and reliable." By teasing the reader with a tiny piece of the seemingly familiar logo script, the report then offered a very telling surprise.

A: Superior cash flow.

With a return on capital that's more than three times the average cost of that capital, we've built a track record for consistently delivering enviable financial results.

Our financial fundamentals are superior and reliable.

What makes your cash flow so strong? Three factors contribute to our ability to generate superior cash flow. First, our capital requirements are low for a business our size. Second, our business is not labor intensive; we employ just 32,000 people worldwide. And third, unlike products such as wine, our beverages can go from production to consumption in a matter of hours.

What do you do with your cash? We reinvest our operating cash flow in three ways: by channeling it back into our own business, by paying dividends and by buying back our own stock. And because virtually all of our investment opportunities worldwide offer potential returns well in excess of our cost of capital, we have more choices than you might think.

Why don't you just put it all into dividends? Everybody likes dividend checks, but the fact is, our strong return on capital creates an extremely efficient vehicle for reinvesting our share owners' resources. Our total return to share owners – 46 percent in 1995 – clearly reflects this.

So why do you buy your own stock? Because investing in our own stock offers our share owners the potential for a significantly higher long-term return than other investment alternatives and is clearly superior to maintaining excess cash, which provides a relatively low after-tax return.

Is there ever a time when you wouldn't consider buying your own stock? Yes – whenever securities laws say we can't. Otherwise, we've yet to encounter a time when we felt our stock wasn't a long-term investment bargain for us.

How can there be any place left to invest when you're already nearly as global as the United Nations? That's just "horizontal" expansion. The real growth opportunities come from "vertical" expansion. As we continue to strengthen our global business system and step up the pace of our marketing efforts, our investment opportunities continue to multiply. In 1995, for example, we invested nearly $940 million in capital projects and another $3.8 billion in aggressive marketing initiatives.

Isn't it risky to be operating in so many markets? No, because the more we're in, the less risky it generally becomes. If one market falters, we have dozens more that can take up the slack. In 1995, for example, robust growth in Brazil and China helped offset the impact of economic difficulties in Mexico and Argentina.

Can you really keep generating such attractive cash flows with such simple, inexpensive products? Actually, the simplicity of our business and the affordability of our products are two of the reasons we are able to generate such consistently attractive cash flows. After all, billions of people can afford our products every day, a fact few other companies can claim.

21

The quintessential Swiss product of the twentieth century came to the table carrying its unique and multifaceted reputation and image. The response was not to embalm these but to help them to grow.

Swatch

Design as a linear process – brief, analysis, development, execution, production – tends to give less room to the lateral jumps and discoveries that can spawn new and relevant opportunities. Design as an organic process – with each stage redefined by the previous one – requires the designer to maintain great clarity of purpose and greater concentration on ideas. This is where the designer, rather than the process itself, takes the strain of driving the project. Working with Swatch has resulted in new packaging, products, and shops. The chronology is less important than the fact that each new step fed backward, forward, and sideways. Thematically, the basic notion of time has given a discipline and direction to the design thinking. Image and culture were also constant references in the particular mechanics, engineering, materials, and aesthetics being employed. The open approach – with the emphasis on beginnings, not endings – has allowed Swatch itself to identify and understand new opportunities for developing its business, the perception of its market, and its brand image.

Swiss culture is eternal. Just as the Swiss cuckoo clock defines its eccentricity, the Swiss watch defines its conservatism and obsessive sense of order, as well as its enduring qualities. But suddenly the traditional Swiss watch, one of the finest possessions to be aspired to, to be venerated and handed down from generation to generation, was confronted with a watch that the wearer could want to and afford to change regularly. And it wasn't Japanese – it was also Swiss. It was Swatch.

Built on the idea that cultural rules and notions are made to be challenged, Swatch curiously did not undermine the cultural perceptions that fed it but, by parodying them, redefined them as it defined itself. From an industry that was associated with history, great craftsmanship, expense, and precision came a range of inexpensive, plastic, colorful watches with design appeal that, although often verging on the silly, was always smack in the middle of street code, fashion, and trend. Switzerland itself quaked and entered the new order of world mass markets. All the right harmonies and chords were struck, and Swatch – the generic name for the products themselves and for the company – became a cult.

Swatch had gone into a market where standing still means sliding backward. Inevitably there came a time when the original idea, however radical, needed refreshing. Not forgetting their defining rule – rules are there to be broken – they decided to produce watches that pandered less to the whim of fashion, watches that were more permanent, more grown-up. "Here is a Swatch – a metal Swatch – you are meant to keep." This was ironic. And Irony became its name. The new Swatch system – five formats in all – has become one of Swatch's biggest sub-brands, doing its job as intended by taking up the slack caused by the gentle decline of the original Swatch concept.

If Irony was a challenge to the Swatch brand image, its packaging was equally so. "Express greater permanence, a little more luxury, a gift perhaps, but still inexpensive, maybe useful in its own right even, complement and add to the function, enhance the image" – these were the initial thoughts that occupied the designer's mind.

The packaging is a box made of laminated card finished to feel like leather and edged with crimped metal. A green-tinted viewing disk reveals the watch inside. There is no superfluity. The design includes a grooved card to which the watch is attached (and which doubles as the guarantee card) allowing the box to hold watches either with a flat metal strap or an elasticated metal band in a permanent loop. Its modularity meets the needs of shop display dispensers, packing, and bulk storage.

There are five different types of Irony products, each with its own appropriate color coding representing function and market. We used foil stamping as a hallmark to indicate the aluminum or stainless-steel body of the watches.

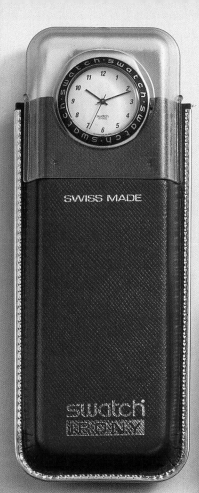

SWISS MADE

swatch
IRONY

SWISS MADE

swatch
IRONY
chrono

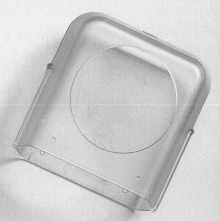

SWISS·MADE

swatch
IRONY
SCUBA

SWISS MADE

swatch
IRONY
LADY LADY

SWISS MADE

Those are the practicalities. The signals indicate a gift, a little mystery, and a sense of expectation – a kind of a cigar box, an irony in a non-smoking world. The box is sophisticated. It has an enduring feel, a tactile quality that might protect a watch designed to last, not to be thrown away. The box is useful in itself; it slips easily into the pocket and can be used to hold a pair of spectacles or pens. It all adds up to imaginative authenticity with a hint of the traditional quality of the Swiss watch that has been a reference point for the Swatch enterprise from the start.

Swatch also asked for designs that would give greater, more appropriate impact, practicality, and security to their shop displays. Packaging design that gives equal billing to practicalities and signals is just as relevant for shop displays and branded shops – which are in a sense large-scale packaging themselves, packaging in which people can walk around.

The shop-in-shop concept was dreamed up for Swatch concessions in department stores as well as in smaller retail outlets such as airport shops. The designs created a series of elements and components that could be orchestrated to suit any particular size and space. They were to be lighter, friendlier, and more interactive for the customers while also being easy to use and secure for staff.

The design creates an animated environment. It has its own curving walls – like the cliffs of a coastline – so that the layout is independent of the containing walls. The system also has its own halogen lighting to create the right illumination high-points and overall effects. There are no cabinets; instead, rotatable display "cones" are set against the concave backgrounds. These displays bring the products closer still to the customer – the watches are either behind or on top of the Perspex and appear to float in space. There is none of the conventional storage space beneath the displays – it is located within the "coastline" contours and can be adapted to fit different environments.

The enjoyment and "Swatchness" of the shop-in-shop-system concepts were expressed on a grander scale in the New York flagship store, the Timeship, which opened in 1996 on Fifty-seventh Street between Fifth and Madison Avenues. Here the approach to developing the Swatch ethos, in progress since the first ideas for Irony packaging, reached a new evolutionary peak.

The coastline concept was first introduced as a prototype in the Geneva store in order to test the architectural components and materials. Plastic laminated over mirrored surfaces was subsequently replaced by aluminum.

Like a Swatch itself the store is planned as a piece of machinery. Distinct functioning parts are stacked one on top of the other and connected by a series of pneumatic glass tubes; the tubes visibly deliver colorful streams of products around the building, evoking the communications tubes used in banks and department stores earlier in the century. Swatch metaphors abound, always reinforcing and giving new expressions to the brand, and the three floors of the store have been designed to represent a watch's three units of time: seconds, minutes, and hours.

The ground floor represents seconds; it is the busiest place. A series of cones draws customers in, and on the blue terrazzo floor long display counters float like ships or clouds. At the rear is the Club Chamber, where customers can become members of the Swatch Club and receive information about upcoming events. The trip to the mezzanine is accompanied by moving watches in their glass tubes. The stairs are used as a projection surface so that changing images can be seen by passers-by on the street.

The mezzanine represents minutes. It is the home of "Doctor Swatch," who provides new batteries, straps, and other accessories. Customers can pass the time watching video monitors.

Among the information displayed is how a Swatch is made. The third floor is about hours; this is where customers are invited to linger a little. Here is the Swatch Gallery, with works by such artists as Keith Haring, Annie Leibovitz, and Yoko Ono. This floor also has the Worldwide Table, where visitors may view clips of current and historical advertising campaigns and other Swatch promotions. There is also the Swatch Runway, a coffee-bar setting where customers can sit and order from a menu of watches.

At the same time, Pentagram was designing new watches. Plastics experts were enlisted to help reinvent the use of materials. New dyes were developed for nylon plastics. Together with new textures and finishes, Swatch's aim has been to enlarge its design vocabulary. The company's constant search for new ideas and styles has given it a greater field of opportunity for the future and maximized its investment in new, cutting-edge processes.

For Swatch, a Darwinian approach to ideas has translated into new forms of the species and new habitats, robust and different enough to win in the commercial battles of natural selection while retaining the continuing references of likeness that define generations of brand families.

In the New York flagship store, the staircase well that connects all floors is followed by diagonal cutouts that incorporate glass tubes with compressed air systems; these display the watches going up and down for delivery to customers.

New designs for wall and engagement calendars, which combine visual eclecticism with informational consistency, give a fresh face and stronger retail appeal to the extensive calendar line of Universe Publishing.

Universe Publishing

Within the paper-thin profit margins of the publishing world, art calendars have perhaps the slimmest. In recent years, with printing and licensing costs rising but consumers remaining tightfisted, pressures on margins have increased. Still, theme-oriented calendars remain a popular consumer item in their own right, as well as an important source for generating bookstore traffic and book sales. Such was the conundrum facing Universe Publishing, a longtime success story in this tough market, when it came to Pentagram in 1995. The company was concerned that the editorial and design treatment of its calendars had become dated, a condition that was dragging down sales and that contravened the image of Universe's parent company, Rizzoli, a leading fine-arts publisher. Pentagram approached the redesign of the Universe calendar collection as a packaging exercise. The objective was to create a highly recognizable Universe

FEBRUARY

A 28 DAY CYCLE

...AY - THE 1ST.... BLAH, VAGUELY ACHY, MILDLY DEPRESSED, LOW ENERGY, NAP IN...

...THE 2ND... HEAVY COFFEE MORNING. SUDDEN BURST OF ENERGY AT 2:30 P.M.

UNTIL 6 PM - TUESDAY THE 3RD. BLAH FEELING ABATES. RENEWED ENERGY, OPT...

INTEREST IN LOCAL AFFAIRS. WEDNESDAY THE 4TH. SLOW MORNING. HUMP DAY

THURSDAY THE 5TH... AMAZING STATE OF WELL-BEING. (EXCELLENT COMPL...

...OD FEELING CONTINUES THRU WEEKEND - SATURDAY THE 7TH. ELATION, HIGH ENE...

...H 8TH - ENERGY SUBSIDES. GENERAL BLAH FEELING PERMEATES - MONDAY THE 9TH DEPRESSION

BLUES!! TUESDAY THE 10TH > MOODY, CRANKY, SLIGHTLY PARANOID, GENERAL OVER-ALL

...TY. WEDNESDAY THE 11TH - INEXPLICABLY ELATED! GOOD HAIR DAY. THURSDAY THE 12TH

...N CONTINUES (POSITIVE - BIORHYTHMIC PERIOD. FRIDAY THE 13TH CONTINUED

...VE FEELINGS OVERWHELM - UNLUCKY #.

LENTINE'S DAY - SATURDAY THE 14TH

...PECTATION, DISSAPOINT - MENT, ACCEPTANCE AND ENNUI.

SUNDAY THE 15TH - BLAH, VAGUELY ACHY, MILDLY

...DEPRESSED, LOW ENERGY. MONDAY THE 16TH

TUESDAY THE 17TH - THE BEGINNING OF THE ● DAY. HEAVY COFFEE...

WEDNESDAY THE 18TH - CAN'T GET OVER THE HUMP DAY. BLOAT

...BLOAT CONTINUES - FRIDAY THE 19TH. FATIGUE

...SATURDAY THE 20TH. BLUE MONDAY

...RAGING - FULL FLEDGED PMS. SUNDAY THE 21ST

...PMS INTENSIFIES, TUESDAY THE 22ND

...MURDER CONTEMPLATED. WEDNESDAY THE 23RD

...PARANOIA. THURSDAY THE 24TH. RAGE

DIAGRAM OF A WEEK

S M T W T F S

...ACHES, FLOW... N 90... TEARS. FRIDAY THE 25TH SATURDAY... SUNDAY THE 28TH...

label, a brand that would carve out and maintain an identifiable presence in booksellers' retail spaces. If the brand became established well enough with consumers and retailers, the only other rules necessary to the makeover would be to let the calendar's subject matter (usually dictated by the franchisee or cultural institution commissioning the calendar) drive the design.

Since Universe wished to retain its existing corporate symbol, Pentagram employed it as an anchor for the collection's overall identity. The atomlike mark was placed within a color box and linked closely to the typography, a condensed typeface known, fortuitously, as Univers. While type treatment could vary within the calendars, the label could not. We standardized the locations for this signature on both wall and engagement calendars, as well as on stationery.

Art calendars embrace an eclectic range of subjects, from beer to ballet to best-selling novels. Each year's collection from Universe, typically ranging from thirty-five to fifty new offerings, begins with a selection process that winnows about seventy-five ideas into the "will-dos," the "want-to-dos," and the "maybe-maybe-nots." The majority are "will-dos," some of which are commissioned by museums and other associations that, along with Universe and Pentagram, have a say in the design treatment. Booksellers and other retailers then pick and choose from the collection, meaning that Universe is in competition not only with other calendar makers but also with itself.

While Pentagram developed a template for the internal calendar data, we recommended design flexibility with the visuals. This was based upon the high degree of subject diversity from year to year. Was it necessary for Pentagram to embellish *Cezanne*, for example? The answer, clearly, was no. *Fly Fishing*, on the other hand, was a wholly different matter. In order to capitalize on the current trendiness of this otherwise obscure sport, it was, in Pentagram's view, necessary to identify it precisely, boldly. Typography had to do the work. Where things could get particularly tricky was in pitting "your" Monet against someone else's. What booksellers could count on with Universe's new line of fine-art calendars, however, was that Pentagram would give each artist a full canvas – no playing around with white space and small images. As for calendars for chocolate lovers, there was no need to editorialize. Just make the subject leap off the page the way dessert chefs make it leap off the plate. In essence, Pentagram's approach to calendar design for Universe was to give the subject matter center ring but to make sure it was clear what stood behind the line – Universe.

A calendar's success is determined as much by visual treatment as by function. From graphic art to fine-art reproductions and photo essays, Pentagram designed Universe calendars with the widest possible latitude for visual impact.

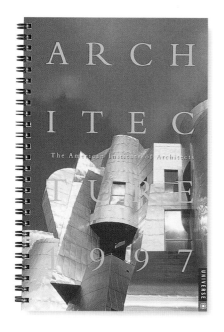

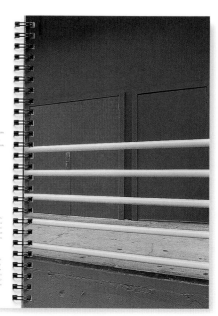

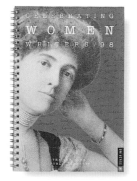

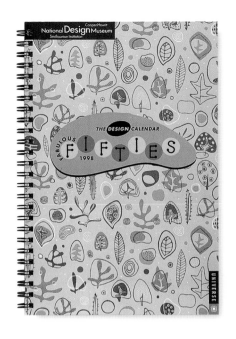

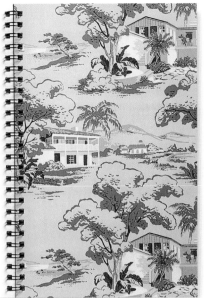

June

Monday 15

Tuesday 16

Wednesday 17

Thursday 18

Friday 19

Saturday 20 Sunday 21

FATHER'S DAY
FIRST DAY OF SUMMER

WALLPAPER WITH
CALIFORNIA VILLAS
NEW CANAAN,
CONNECTICUT, 1954.
MANUFACTURED BY
GRIFFIN SEFTON, INC.
MACHINE PRINTED
GIFT OF SUZANNE
LIPSCHITZ, 1991-69-227

THE CALIFORNIA
LIFESTYLE SYMBOLIZED
THE INFORMALITY AND
INDOOR-OUTDOOR
LIVING THAT APPEALED
TO AMERICANS IN THE
1950s.

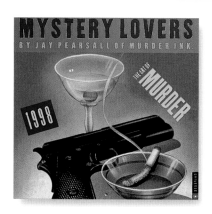

To make an impact in a crowded field with an audience whose native language is not English, a new newspaper adopts a flexible grid, deploys novel typography, and puts the photos first.

Eastern Express

The people of Hong Kong are voracious consumers of news. There are a dozen daily newspapers in Chinese and two in English, dozens of television channels, and ten radio stations all competing for audience share. In this crowded field, the *South China Morning Post* is the better-known English-language newspaper, with a decades-long history marked by respected journalism and a lucrative grip on advertising. An ownership change at the *Post*, however, indicated that the paper would become more pro-China. So the Oriental Press Group, the publisher of Hong Kong's biggest-circulation Chinese daily, decided to launch its own English newspaper. O. P. G. wanted an organ that would take a more independent stance toward the Chinese government than the *Post*. The proprietor recruited a team of talented journalists from the U.K., Australia, New Zealand, and South Africa. From their perspectives on newspapers, Pentagram culled a new broadsheet to stand out in the overly crowded marketplace. It was called the *Eastern Express*.

Some design decisions, such as the eight-column page grid, were mandated by advertising requirements. We also had to make the formats as simple and foolproof as possible, to enable editors and the layout desk to assemble the pages entirely on a computer screen. Still, in several areas, we were able to push the design in directions unfamiliar in the Asian media market.

To differentiate the *Express* from the *Morning Post*, a three-section daily, we organized the new paper into three regular sections – for news, sports, and money – with additional sections devoted to employment, technology, property, and horse racing, which would increase the newspaper's bulk to four sections on some days, five on others.

To make stories in these sections as easy to read as possible, the design team kept the pieces self-contained, without jumps or turns. Cognizant that English was a second language for the majority of the readership, the type size was also made larger than in the typical British newspaper – 8.5 points, compared with 7-point body type in the *Guardian* (which Pentagram had earlier redesigned). For headlines, we chose a condensed font that, to our knowledge, had not previously been used in newspapers: Fenice, whose tall x-height, solid boldface, and distinct lightface allowed us to distinguish easily between news and commentary.

The designers also chose to divide the eight-column pages into thirds and quarters, allowing stories to cover from two to six columns – a far more flexible system than those typically used in newspaper design, and one that eased the process of updating stories in later editions.

The greatest point of difference between the *Express* and its competition, however, was the new journal's bold use of photography. Pictures were not employed merely to fill space but to tell a story, preferably with the briefest of captions. There were no rules on picture size: if a photo merited seven column inches, it was given seven column inches, and the text was designed to fit – rather than the other way around. The photos warmed the pages and had the added advantage of conveying the essence of a story to readers whose first language was Chinese.

One of the greatest challenges was working through nagging technological problems in the newspaper's production. Stories written by journalists on their Atex systems mysteriously grew longer when transferred to designers, who were working in Quark. We solved the mystery when we realized that the Atex fonts were Linotype and the Quark fonts, despite having the same names, were Monotype.

Eastern Express was launched in 1994. Although it ceased publication after four years, it nonetheless left a visual mark on the Hong Kong newspaper business.

Design issues aside, one of the greatest challenges was working through technological problems in newspaper production. Formats had to be simple and foolproof, thus enabling editors and the layout desk to assemble pages on the computer screen.

The first step in building a newspaper page is for section editors to determine priorities and to allocate and position advertising space. Each page is then titled, dated, and assigned a number.

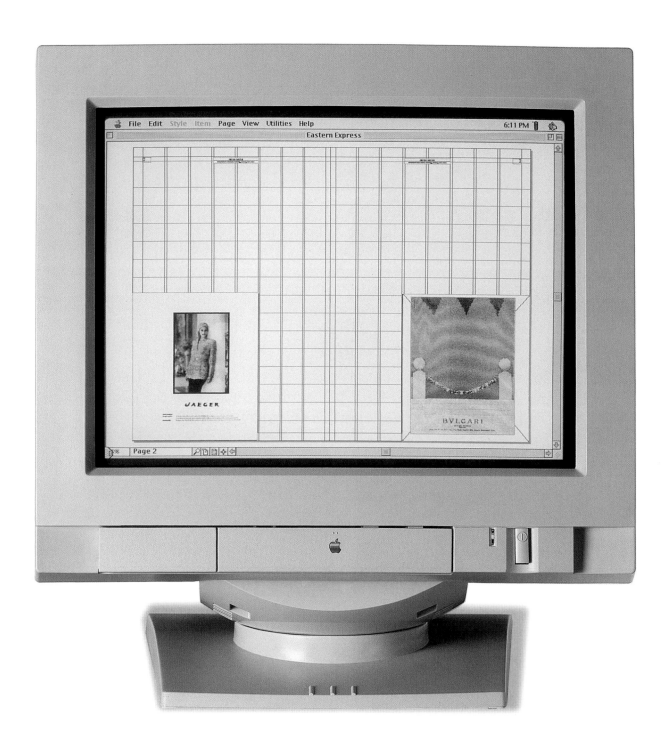

The next step is to position the picture associated with the lead news item. The philosophy is that pictures are not employed merely to fill space but to tell a story. Text is designed to fit the images – rather than the other way around.

Once typed in, headlines and drop caps are viewed in six different sizes by a single keystroke. We chose a condensed font, Fenice, whose tall x-height, solid boldface, and distinct lightface gave us the ability to distinguish easily between news and commentary.

As a page begins to take shape, vertical and horizontal grids become apparent. Both consistency and flexibility within the grids enable facing pages to relate; each page can be assembled by people who never see what the other is doing.

2

IRISH DAILY

China snub in funding for airport

T

Family and friends offering the Sunber development at a Heaven Mews Relate.

Arson toll rise to eight

T

Labour urges China to resume talks

T

JAEGER

Liberals want reforms modified

N

e fur is about to fly

ew Lloyd Webber's blockbuster revival of Cats opens tonight at an invitation-gala of The Lyric
re of The Academy of Performing Arts. The play, which cost $40hn to stage in Hong Kong, wi
arl'Ubby and Behr'tsvhat now been being

Net closes on alleged triad chief

A

AC chief criticises usiness community

Teenager's love 'led her into drug deal"

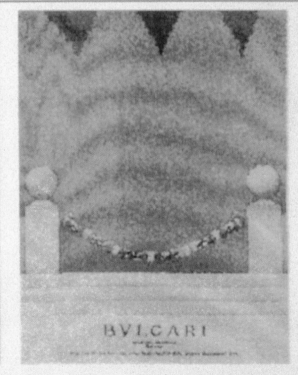

BVLGARI

Gentle curves, cleverly concealed controls, and robust, high-quality features establish an immediate presence for a new form of "entertainment PC" that combines a computer, TV, radio, CD player, answering machine, and phone.

Toshiba

For a consumer electronics company, few challenges were more daunting than the one Toshiba America faced in early 1996. Having established its reputation as a maker of high-quality laptop computers, drives, and other components, Toshiba found itself with no desktop computer line at a time when home-computer sales were exploding. Late to the party, the company had to move quickly, but it could not afford to release a timid or "me too" product. To gain both market share and mind share in the increasingly crowded personal computer market, it needed to make a statement. That statement was the Infinia, the first in what Toshiba and many other consumer-electronics manufacturers thought would be the next big market. Like others, Toshiba believed the convergence of the television and the computer was inevitable. The company gambled that convergence would occur from the personal computer side – specifically, that the computer would serve as the base instrument, with entertainment functions integrated into it. Hence, the concept behind Infinia: a hybrid entertainment-and-information appliance that combines the functions of a television, radio, answering machine, hands-free telephone, and high-end stereo CD player with the power of a Pentium computer. In addition, technical improvements over existing systems, such as a high-speed Universal Serial Bus (or USB), would give it immediate market presence.

In January 1996, Toshiba asked Pentagram to develop a design for the Infinia that would highlight the device's multiple functions but at the same time make it seem a comfortable, familiar product. A fully engineered design was needed by early spring, so that the final product would be ready to ship in the fall – a schedule roughly twice as fast as an average rush on a new product. To finish the project under such a tight deadline, several Toshiba developers camped out in Pentagram's San Francisco office during the design period. Computers linked team members in Southern California, Japan, Taiwan, Seattle, and Palo Alto, allowing them to shuttle sketches, memos, and CAD drawings.

Infinia was an opportunity to examine how real people use their computers at home, to listen to their frustrations, and to improve the surfaces and controls that consumers always complain about. The result would be an appliance with unexpected details and features that would transform it from a chore to a joy – a change we thought crucial if Infinia was to bridge the gap between a work product and a home product.

We commenced a two-week exploratory phase, during which we reviewed potential usages (and usage combinations) and generated sketches. Some of our decisions were constrained by pragmatics. The monitor and the CPU were to be delivered from different sources and assembled in the store or by the user; that meant a minitower-plus-monitor setup. But other decisions were based on our own research and background in technology design.

For example, although users had no trouble using a PC to play games or listen to music while working, the design team knew its audience was reticent about adopting the computer as a television set. We factored that into our recommendations. At the same time, we didn't want to minimize

Infinia includes a freestanding multimedia monitor with high-quality sound, an In-Touch control module, an angle-adjustment foot, and an ergonomic keyboard.

potential entertainment uses. High-quality stereo speakers would have made the monitor overly wide, so we rolled them back to the sides of the monitor and tucked a subwoofer under the display, thereby minimizing the width and creating a soft, friendly appearance more appropriate for a home electronics product.

For screen adjustment, Pentagram redesigned the display foot, giving it an adjustable rear leg with an internal clutch mechanism based on the principle of asymmetric torque. Frequently deployed in laptop computer display hinges, the mechanism moves easily in one direction but offers resistance when moving the opposite way. The unequal resistance allows the mechanism to support a seventy-pound display with ease and allow its height and angle to be adjusted with fingertip pressure. (Toshiba worried about its ability to turn out this unusual support structure on such a tight schedule. To allay its concerns, we worked with Function Engineering, a mechanical engineering consultant, to create the mechanism, design the parts, subcontract the manufacture, and deliver finished assemblies.)

The second critical design feature is on the front of the display. Having experienced a dozen years of screen-based interfaces that confuse nontechnical users, we believe consumers dislike screen-based controls and prefer the immediacy and simplicity of buttons and knobs. So rather than hide Infinia's TV, audio, and telephone controls in drop-down menus on the display screen, Pentagram and Toshiba created an "In-Touch" module beneath the screen that brings up the appliance functions at the push of a button. Resembling a car radio, the module has a large volume knob on the right, a small LCD screen with illuminated icons, and a row of task-specific buttons that turn the various features on and off.

To make the CPU as elegant as the display, soft toroidal surfaces on the top, front, and sides dive inward to create a "belt line" near the base, giving the minitower a pressurized look, like an inflated balloon with an invisible string wrapped around and pulled tight. Because of the accelerated schedule, Pentagram and Toshiba went straight from design reviews – during which we transferred advanced CAD data over the Internet – to final production.

The Infinia's minitower desktop enclosure incorporates a DVD-ROM drive, a floppy disk drive, two expandable media bays, and removable side panels for easy servicing.

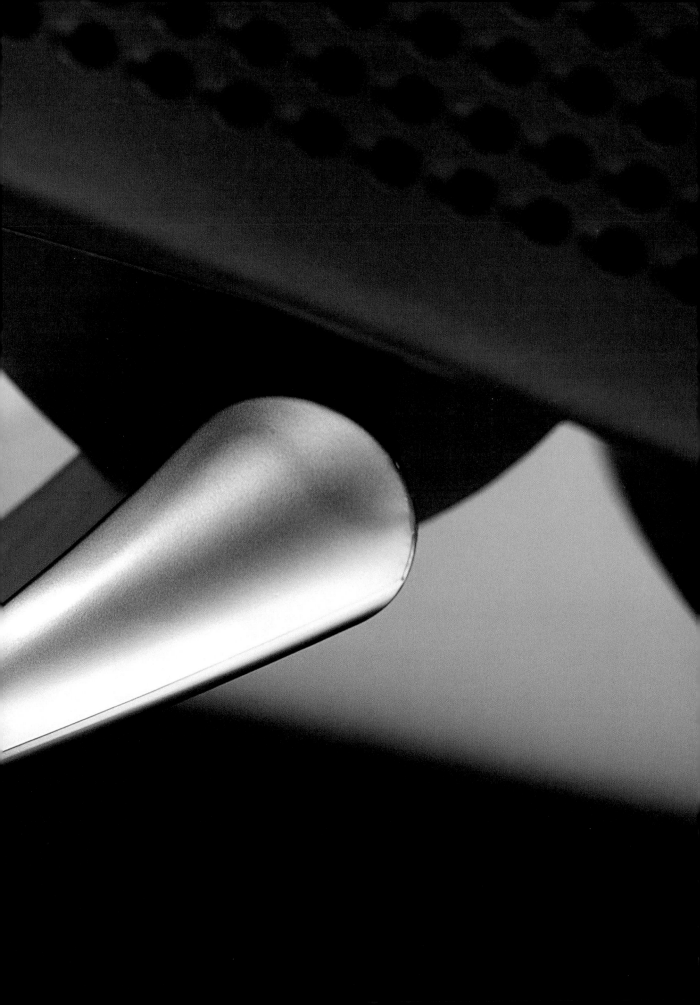

To facilitate sourcing and distribution, the In-Touch module had to be detachable; it was the user who installed it. It snaps into a bracket connected to the structure of the monitor and is strong enough to support the weight of the entire unit.

The system emphasized high-quality sound. Stereo speakers faced front, with a sub-woofer mounted on the bottom of the display. Fabric speaker covers conveyed the message that Infinia wasn't a toy.

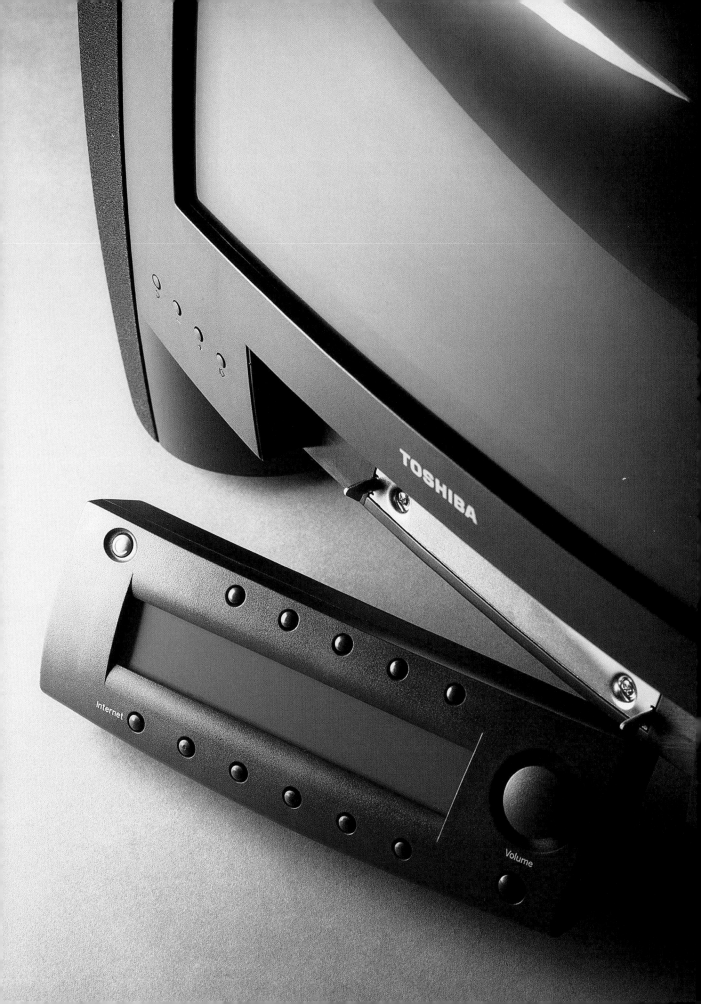

The ventilation details are integrated into a radial teardrop pattern providing visual interest and organizing ventilation.

The design vocabulary of the Infinia system incorporates gentle curves and flowing surfaces that meet in sharp angles to provide visual interest.

A direct-marketing program targets the sensibilities of consumers who are discerning and sophisticated with a soft-sell approach that flatters their intelligence with humor.

Waitrose Wine Direct

The British have a history of wine appreciation dating back at least as far as England's ownership of Bordeaux during the reign of Henry II and Eleanor of Aquitaine. Yet graphically, the country's mail-order wine industry has been a somewhat down-market affair. A chance to repair the problem and expand the market arose in the early 1990s, when the Waitrose supermarket chain acquired the national mail-order wine operations of Findlater Mackie Todd. The latter's approach had been typical of the genre. The mail-order literature sent to customers was characterized by confusing lifestyle pictures, content, and layout, inconsistent formats, and poor branding. Devices such as shaded boxes and underlines abounded. Yet the discerning wine-drinking audience was resolutely up-market and sophisticated. Not only was the disorderly image wrong, but the basic mechanics of ordering wine were made harder by the graphic incoherence.

Waitrose has 117 U.K. stores, mainly clustered in the southeast of England. It saw an opportunity to capitalize on the knowledge of its four Masters of Wine and establish a mail-order wine business across Great Britain. The design team first made some assumptions, based in no small part on a deep love of wine and spirits. We assumed that the target customers were people who led very ordered lives; not only did they like to sit down, read the literature, and fill in the form, but they had to arrange to be at home when the order was delivered. Clearly, these were people who fully enjoyed the process of ordering wine – a very different species from the wine "discoverers" who just browse the supermarket shelves and buy on impulse.

We decided to make the design deliberately procedural and easy to use. We created a new thematic character – a friendly, French-looking van commissioned from illustrator Benoît Jacques – and used it playfully throughout the work. The eccentricity of Jacques' work and the silent challenge of his visual puns made customers feel as if they were part of a friendly, if affluent, family. His wacky van, a pun on the French word *vin*, pops up all over Waitrose Wine Direct's literature. It is especially visible in a regular monthly publication, launched in February 1997, which features the Waitrose Masters of Wine and their selections, showcases monthly special offers, and includes other pieces of interest.

We designed the publication in an A5 format to suggest a magazine rather than a more ephemeral marketing brochure. (Regular customers can even send off for a magazine holder shaped like a hollowed book.) We printed the

Graphic whimsy underlies much of the Waitrose Wine Direct design program. The van on the case of wine not only represents that the wine drove itself to the customer's house – it is also a play on the French word for wine.

magazine on heavy matte newspaper stock in efforts to evoke the earthy quality of a wine cellar rather than the glossy, flimsy feel of a flier. We avoided the standard stock shots of vineyards, focusing instead on unusual items, such as vintage corkscrews, or actual places. Our goal was always to present wine as a gateway to an experience or an activity.

The magazine grid was designed so that a spread is divided into twelve squares, representing the twelve bottles in a case of wine when viewed from above. While the rigidity of the format could be construed as a limitation, in fact it provided a sort of home base to which the reader's eye could return, even as it scanned the case offers that characterize each spread and enjoyed the subtle humor with which they were conveyed. That humor was also evident on the cover of each magazine: an issue showcasing the wines of Australia, to cite one instance, featured the beverage defying gravity, flowing up the page into a glass. By making even slight intellectual demands on the reader, the piece becomes that much more memorable.

We replicated many of these techniques in the direct-response advertisements Pentagram created for Waitrose. Rather than the typically warm and wonderful shot of the oenophile in his or her wine cellar, these ads placed the reader within arm's reach of the fantasy. The wine is given a tactile dimension, for example, by shadowing the bottles on the page. Rubber stamps emphasize the offer and subtly remind readers of the markings outside wine cartons. And, of course, Benoît Jacques' little van is depicted driving toward the coupon – the closest we'd get to a hard sell.

We fashioned a binder in which consumers could stockpile all their Waitrose wine catalogs. Made of bookbinder's cloth with white blocking, it furthers the impression that the monthly mailing is a magazine of value and importance.

Each issue consists of an average of twenty-four A5-size pages and is printed on heavy matte newspaper stock to evoke the earthly quality of a wine cellar rather than the glossy, flimsy feel of a flier.

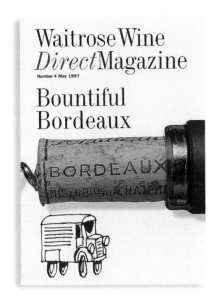

The publication is organized by spreads acting as minichapters – an overview of the issue, a feature story with a geographic or seasonal point of view, and regular selections, as well as wines of the month.

Waitrose Wine
*Direct*Magazine
Number 6 July 1997

The Italian Revolution

The world's oldest wine-maker takes on the New World

The Romans taught wine-making to the French and Germans. An eighth of the world's vineyards are in Italy, and the climate is ideal for wine growing. So why, until recently, has the country been an under-achiever? Master of Wine Julian Brind describes the revolution that has finally made Italy a serious challenger to the New World.

Right: Detail of the Santa Maria Novella façade, Florence

Suddenly, wine critics are full of praise for Italian wines. Tuscan wines are much sought-after – prices for Sangiovese and for top-quality wines from the Chianti and Brunello di Montalcino DOCGs are at record levels. Even wines from less familiar regions like Apulia, Calabria and Sicily are beginning to attract international attention.

And all this from a country that sold most of its wines in bulk well into the 1960s, and even in the early eighties preferred quantity to quality. So what has happened to change the Italian wine industry so dramatically?

Chasing the export market
Italy vies with France as the world's largest wine producer. But Italy's domestic consumption is declining. To survive, the industry needs to look to the export market.

In the 80s, under-flavoured wines from over-cropped vineyards were suddenly no match for the new contenders – fresh, fruity, inexpensive wines from California, Australia and South America.

The DOC (*Denominazione di Origine Controllata*), Italy's equivalent of France's AC, had done little to encourage inspired wine-making. DOC regulations tend to define tradition at the expense of innovation and experimentation. Established in 1963, they froze Italian wines in time, just when the New World was waking up to new styles and possibilities.

To take on the newcomers, young Italian wine-makers began a radical rethink.

Innovation and Inspiration
Italy's vineyards run from the foothills of the Alps to Sicily and Sardinia where they are nearer to Africa than to Rome. No vineyard

Waitrose Wine
*Direct*Magazine
Number 7 August 1997

Full of Eastern European promise

Barriers down and in march the Eastern Europeans

The day the Berlin Wall came down Eastern Europe moved into a new era, both socially and economically. For the wine drinker it means more choice and some excellent wines from areas which have a long history of wine-making. Master of Wine Julian Brind explains how some of these countries have taken advantage of this while others are slower to cotton on.

Our map of Eastern Europe extends from all the countries in the former Soviet Union, the Soviet bloc – Hungary, Romania, Bulgaria, The Czech Republic and Slovakia – and the countries of the former Yugoslavia comprising Macedonia, Slovenia and Croatia, to Greece and its islands.

Although these regions have developed enormously in the last few years, there still remains a certain amount of instability. Countries which have been through considerable upheaval are now adjusting to the freedom of the new marketplace. Change will continue over the next few years and sooner or later we may well be talking about wines from Moldova, a former Soviet state which is a relatively unknown source at present.

A wine fit for the Tsars
Hungary has a history of producing excellent whites. The world renowned Tokaji (or Tokay) dates back hundreds of years and was so popular with Russian Tsars that they had it specially imported. A sweet wine, it owes its flavour to 'noble rot', the botrytis fungus which encourages water to evaporate from the grape, leaving the sugars to concentrate.

Hungary has taken on board a much more commercial approach to wine-making than some of its neighbours. Instead of resting on its laurels and adhering to tradition the Hungarian vignerons have embraced modern technology and ideology in order to produce wines which are commercially viable and can compete in world markets.

A page grid was designed so that a spread is divided into twelve squares, representing the twelve bottles in a case of wine when viewed from above. The format provides a home base for a wide variety of editorial content and visuals.

Waitrose Wine
*Direct*Magazine
Number 8 September 1997

Southern French Renaissance

Regular Mixed Cases

Why not try one of these Regular Mixed Cases, which have been carefully selected by our Masters of Wine? These selections and prices are valid until 30 September 1997.

The new wines for the Regular Mixed Cases this month are shown in red.

Layfish corkscrew by Burchand

French Country
£39.25
Bin FCW/1

2 Domaine de Bose Syrah/Merlot 1996 Vin de Pays d'Oc
2 Domaine Ste Madeleine 1996 Vin de Pays de l'Hérault
2 Merlot/Cabernet Sauvignon 1995/96 Vin de Pays d'Oc
2 Beaulieu Creek 1996 Vin de Pays de Vaucluse
2 Tenet/Chardonnay 1996 Vin de Pays d'Oc, Lurton
2 Domaine de Plantaréus 1996 Vin de Pays des Côtes de Gascogne

Italian
£46.50
Bin ITA/1

2 Montepulciano d'Abruzzo DOC 1995 Umani Ronchi
2 Merlot Alesino IGT 1996 Cortello
2 Negroamaro Del Salento DOC 1996 Le Trulle
2 Chardonnay Delle Venezie 1996 Vallado
2 Pinot Grigio delle Venezie 1996 Fiordaliso
2 Orvieto Classico DOC Secco 1996 Cardeto

New World
£49.50
Bin NW/1

2 Hardy's Southern Creek Shiraz/Cabernet Sauvignon 1996/97 South Eastern Australia
2 Santa Julia Malbec/Cabernet Sauvignon 1995 Argentina
2 Du Toitskloof Cabernet/Shiraz 1996/97 South Africa
2 Diamond Hills Chenin Blanc/Chardonnay 1996/97 South Africa
2 New Zealand Dry White 1996/97 Gisborne
2 Currawong Creek Chardonnay 1996/97 South Eastern Australia

German
£44.50
Bin DER

3 Hock Deutscher Tafelwein
3 Serriger Vogelsang Riesling Kabinett 1990
3 Waltrose Rheinhessen Kabinett 1995
3 St Ursula Devil's Rock Riesling 1995/96 (dry)

Waitrose Wine
*Direct*Magazine
Number 10 November 1997

Sharing the secrets of South Africa

South Africa's best kept secrets

South Africa is, without doubt, one of the most beautiful and magical wine regions in the world. A towering mountainous backdrop contrasts with verdant rolling foothills and coastal plains which stretch far into the horizon. In April, Master of Wine Dee Blackstock spent two weeks in this magical country which has for centuries inspired painters and writers of the magnitude of Tolkien. Basking in idyllic Mediterranean-style summer weather, she set out to discover at first hand what makes South African wine so special.

Since Nelson Mandela took over the reins of South Africa, the wine industry has entered a renaissance. A re-birth which has seen enormous changes, not only in the methods of production, but in how the world perceives it. Suddenly, everyone wants South African wine.

The differences are in the regions
Compare South Africa's total wine growing region with that of Australia and it seems tiny. Yet even within such a small area, there are distinctive climatic differences region by region. These tend to be caused by a combination of factors which include the Atlantic ocean rolling in from the West, the breezes of False Bay, the variable sea currents and the differences in altitude.

The right variety for the right climate
The microclimate of any wine-growing area has a great effect on the end product, so when vines are replanted, their suitability to local conditions is always carefully considered. For example, Pinotage thrives in the warmer areas of Devon Valley and Muldersvlei bowl.

South African Selection
£67.75
Bin WD737
1 bottle of each
Offer closes 30 November 1997
(continued overleaf)

Fairview
Cabernet Franc/Merlot 1995 Paarl
Bin 44974 £6.75 each
One of the most respected of the Cape Winemakers, Charles Black, emphasises the fruit character of his scent-Bordeaux blend with whole-bunch pressing and early transfer into barrels. A supple wine with raspberry and mulberry flavours and attractive spice. Try it with lamb.

Diamond Hills
Pinotage/Cabernet Sauvignon 1995/96 Coastal Region
Bin 82563 £3.99 each
Homebred Pinotage is special to South Africa. Its distinctive banana, black cherry and plum fruit character blends harmoniously with the elegance and finesse of the French Cabernet Sauvignon. A flavoursome, supple wine to enjoy with grills, roasts, pasta and cheese.

Long Mountain
Merlot/Shiraz 1996 Western Cape
Bin 93904 £4.49 each
Robin Day, architect of Australia's Jacobs Creek, has blended wines from different climatic regions to achieve greater complexity. This has a ripe but elegant berry fruit character with beauty oak and a generous finish; try it with roasts, game, cottage pie and cheese.

In addition to the page grid and typographic format, certain design details are consistent from issue to issue. Three-dimensional objects are shadowed to give them depth. Benoît Jacques' illustrations are the only form of art aside from photography.

VILIZATIONS TO FLOUR-
H, TYPOGRAPHY HAS
EEN AN IMPORTANT
OOL IN EVERY CULTURE
ND LANGUAGE. FROM
HE SIMPLEST ATTEMPTS
T COMMUNICATING
FORMATION THROUGH

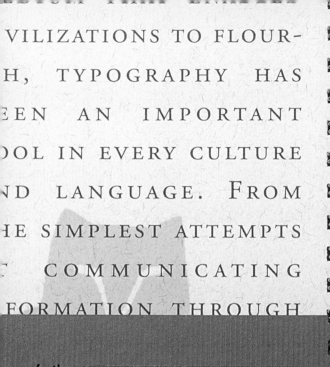

rm of the
Russian (or
as created
ry by two
d Cyril and
hy, rugged
en Chestnut
en Willow
e dramatic
ypography,
ith follow-
olution.

The innovative interpretat
created by Russian Constr
design, far left) and A.
center and right) after
design in the 20th c

KA

OUTH

Paper company promotions have traditionally focused on current design trends and, as such, tend to have a short lifespan. The Tools of the Trade/Artists Series serves as an educational reference tool, thus imparting a longer shelf life.

Fox River Paper Company

In a crowded field of paper producers, Simpson Paper wanted to position itself as the single-source supplier for text and cover printing papers. At the time, its promotional pieces were largely product-focused, aimed at establishing a distinct market identity for each of several grades. The company (which was purchased by Fox River Paper Company in 1996) felt there was a need to link strongly all its well-known brands to the corporate name and to promote the use of its deeply colored and textured papers by demonstrating how to use them to best advantage. Pentagram was asked to develop the format and concept for such a program. As design consultants for Simpson, we were intimately familiar with its product, and the needs of its target market of designers and printers. Indeed, during a fifteen-year relationship, Pentagram had participated in the strategic positioning of many individual brands, including color palette development and the naming, design, and launch of Simpson Paper's very successful EverGreen and Quest grades. To reposition Simpson/Fox River itself, the design team proposed an educational program called Tools of the Trade. A platform for showcasing Fox River's vast selection of colors, textures, finishes, weights, and sizes, this multivolume series gives professionals everything they need to know about printing on text and cover papers. Produced twice a year, these in-depth guides have covered such subjects as paper surfaces, color on color, finishing techniques, watermarks, and printing on a budget. They are a virtual graduate course in print production.

Strong design concepts reinforce the content. The guide to finishing techniques, for example, which details die stamping, embossing, engraving, and the like is told through the metaphor of a tailor finishing a suit or dress. To build anticipation and greater "shelf presence," each volume is numbered and presented in a six-by-nine-inch format with a kraft cover, tip-on image, black banding signatures, and wrapped wire-o binding. Inside, sections are tabbed, with waterfall paper printing comparisons and explanatory captions. Pentagram also designed a convenient box, imprinted with a special Tools of the Trade logo, to encourage customers to display the volumes as a desk set. Logo hats and T-shirts were also created for promotional giveaways.

Paper company promotions traditionally have focused on current design trends and, as such, typically have a short shelf life. By serving as an educational reference tool, Fox River's Tools of the Trade/Artists Series imparted real, useful value and a longer life.

Even as Tools of the Trade was being launched, Fox River recognized the importance of maintaining market awareness of individual paper grades. We were asked to develop a companion series of marketing promotions that would fit under the Tools umbrella. We proposed an Artist Series that would explore the creative tools available to designers. Grade-specific, each nine-by-twelve-inch volume of the Artist Series delves into one creative technique, such as "Photography on Starwhite Vicksburg," "Drawing on EverGreen," or "Collage on Confetti."

As with Tools of the Trade, Pentagram developed the initial design guidelines, including a spine-labeling system and a strong visual cover concept, which would maintain a consistent brand identity even as different designers applied themselves and their ideas to each individual offering. A key objective was to provide enough structure to give a cohesive look to the series while allowing each designer room for creative interpretation. Rolled out over a two-year period, the nine-volume Artist Series and six-volume Tools of the Trade have allowed Fox River to make a strong and memorable impression on the marketplace. Not filed away like "one-off" promotions, the handsome boxed sets are often prominently displayed in design offices, a constant reminder of the Fox River name.

The volumes were timed to be released over a three-to-four-year period, and a special box was designed to hold the entire set. Distributed early on in the program, the boxes built anticipation for future volumes and encouraged recipients to display the collection.

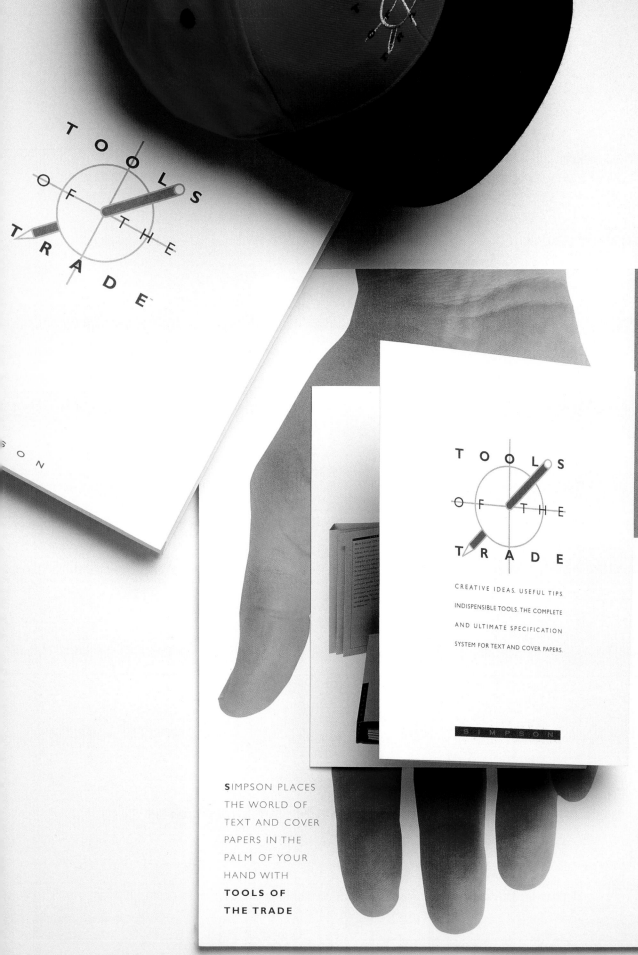

An advertising and promotional campaign was directed at printers, merchants, and designers to announce the launch of the series. Stepped pages were used to contrast and compare paper finishes and textures, using visual metaphors for continuity.

To bring a family look to the Artists Series, covers featured faces rendered in the specific creative tool – drawing, photography, collage. Contemporary illustrations and fine art were used to provide creative inspiration and demonstrate print techniques.

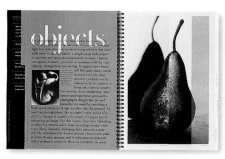

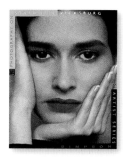

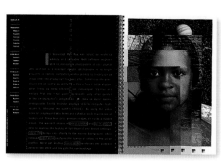

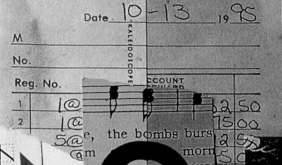

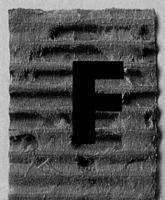

CONFETTI

A vast urban indoor entertainment complex becomes the modern equivalent of a town square – with circles as the transformative device – through a signage and identity program that unifies everything from wall murals to fabrics.

Showcenter Haedo

Showcenter is more than a shopping mall. The seventy-five-thousand-square-meter complex, in the Haedo district of Buenos Aires, Argentina, is closer to a town square with a ceiling. Housing a vast array of indoor-entertainment venues – bowling alleys, cinemas, live-entertainment stages, game arcades, cafés, bars, and shops – Showcenter is a place where local families can go to enjoy a meal or show, watch a movie or play a game, or just socialize with their friends and neighbors. Showcenter is a joint venture between North and South American interests: the Maccarone Emprienditos in Argentina and National Amusements in the United States. Pentagram was retained as part of an ambitious project team that was comprised of mastermind developer Nicholas Maccarone, internationally renowned architect and urban planner Daniel Zylberberg, and Bobbie Oakley of the Boston-based retail architect RMO Associates.

Although the original assignment was to create a logo and signs for the facility, our role grew and we became a full-service design consultant on Showcenter's visual identity. We were involved in setting guidelines for advertising space, store signage, print material, and architectural fixtures, and, more broadly, in expanding the venture's commercial opportunities through design.

Maccarone Emprienditos had conceived of Showcenter as an opportunity to capitalize on the gregarious social habits of the Haedo community, where *estan de fiesta* any time of day or night. Thus, Pentagram's design program is aimed to encapsulate the exuberance of Argentine street life with a set of strong, simple elements.

Photography is used in the graphic program to represent what goes on inside Showcenter. In almost every instance, it was easy to find a defining symbol in the desired circular shape: a bowling ball identifies the bowling alley, a film reel shows the way to the cinema, a wall of plates surrounds the cafés, and a whitewall tire marks the entrance to the parking garage. Black-and-white photos of these iconic round objects were tinted in selected pastel shades, resulting in a nocturnal, almost dreamlike quality appropriate for this indoor world of nighttime play.

The repeated use of circles, photographs, and the Showcenter family of blues, pinks, greens, and yellows retains a sense of visual coherence in the environment but permits flexibility as activities change. Tenants and sponsors may lease sign panels to display their own logos or messages, but the background forms and colors always fit into the overall Showcenter scheme.

Pentagram also brought a playful approach to Showcenter's physical structure. On its facade, the design team created an enormous sweep of billboard-

The identity is centered on an unusual but very effective graphic device: a shape. A simple circle is used in combination with a characteristic pastel color palette and photographic imagery in all institutional communications.

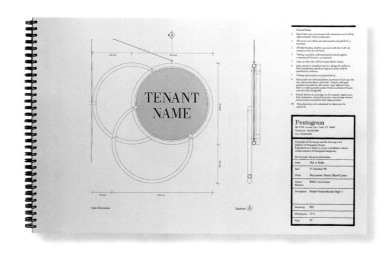

sized panels that not only enhances the architecture but generates revenue as outdoor advertising space. Inside, their plans resulted in a semiordered equivalent of Times Square, with circular signs and fixtures floating, like a flock of iridescent bubbles, in the arcadelike space. The architecture and graphics together thus provide Showcenter with a unified structure and spirit.

In addition to specifying the basic visual elements and a suite of sign structures, Pentagram developed guidelines for institutional print materials and packaging, wall murals and flooring, and directional and identification signs. To help control the high costs of continually producing new items, Pentagram documented design standards for use in Argentina. Fontana Design and other local agents, suppliers, and fabricators can thereby create additional visual information, such as institutional advertising, to coordinate with the original Showcenter image.

The graphic-design program aims to be as much about entertainment as it is about the Showcenter itself. This festive approach is in line with South American middle-class culture, in which relaxing is a group activity, every meal is an occasion, and the public environment is part and parcel of urban life.

The developer's acumen was well rewarded on Showcenter's opening day, when forty thousand people came to see what it was all about. They ended up staying until 5:00 AM. Showcenter has had instant impact on the community, disrupting traffic patterns for miles as locals flock to the site. The project's enormous success has in turn furthered Maccarone's plans to proceed with building similar developments in the Norte area of Buenos Aires, in Brazil, in Chile, and even in the mother of all entertainment centers, Las Vegas.

The choice of a circle made many other design decisions relatively simple; it inspired a floor pattern, stimulated numerous ideas for photographic iconography, and became the form for identification of retail sponsors and for directional signs.

A comprehensive branding campaign for a multinational airline alliance attempts to blend several independent companies across media, cultures, and uses – without sacrificing any single member's identity.

Star Alliance

With the birth of modern aviation in the 1940s, the airline industry evolved as a highly regulated, highly protected activity. National "flag carriers" dominated their own markets; other countries' airlines were relegated to limited services. It was a polite system that, with the internationalization of business and the growth of air travel, allowed air travel to develop into a sector ruled by behemoths. But during the past two decades, the scythe of deregulation – first in North America, more recently in Europe, incrementally but inevitably in Asia – has sliced apart this comfortable oligopoly. With the elimination of trade barriers in the European Union, European airlines can run services wherever they want on the continent, not just to, from, or between airports in their home countries. Although a thicket of regulations still prevents European companies from competing freely in the United States, American and European airlines – and, increasingly,

Asian companies wary of being left behind – have been forming alliances that enable them to link together their route networks, integrate their timetables, and market one another's flights.

Today there are about four hundred such associations. But the most comprehensive is the Star Alliance. The world's largest aviation network, it was formed in 1996 by five of the industry's most powerful players: Air Canada, Lufthansa, SAS, Thai Airways, and United Airlines. In 1997, Brazil's Varig joined the group.

When executives of the newly created, still-nameless group first met, they came to the conclusion that their ability to offer a global web of services and seamless worldwide travel, especially to frequent fliers, was something that should be branded and marketed. "Leading airlines are working together to make global travel more efficient and comfortable for customers," says Jürgen Weber, chairman of the executive board of Deutsche Lufthansa AG. "No one single airline could possibly hope to achieve this on its own."

Never had such large airlines, their combined revenues exceeding $42 billion, each with its own fiercely guarded identity, been assembled as a single group. This was not a merger; the partners still needed to maintain their corporate identity and brand. At the same time, they would eventually share ticket outlets, airport lounges, and check-in areas. Frequent-flyer miles on one would be redeemable on the others, and transfers and baggage handling would be streamlined.

There were no precedents, no pointers, no rules about how to devise a visual identifier for an alliance of this nature. The new mark had to sit unthreateningly alongside each airline's logo – and any others that might subsequently join. It had to work with various

mediums – on stationery, signage, and uniforms. It had to be strong and credible enough to serve as the foundation of a fully-fledged corporate identity, should a new entity eventually be born of the partnership. Immediate worldwide customer comprehension was crucial.

After a competition among three design groups and the submission of various identity programs to consumer testing, Pentagram's naming and branding concept was chosen. The name we devised was Star Alliance. *Star* is an English word, but it registered instantly with customers everywhere. Stars, as symbols and as aids to navigation, resonated positively in all cultures. Star Alliance had the right sound for what was going to become the world's best airline network. For the logotype, we chose Helvetica Thin Extended, an elegant typeface. The graphic mark that crowns the logotype is a star made up of five triangular pyramids, a design with

echoes of other historic symbols, such as the Olympic rings and the twelve stars of the European Union – all of them signs of a commitment to an idea and to quality, and of achievements higher than simply reaching financial targets. The shading of the pyramids gave the star symbol a three-dimensional, metallic quality, and with it, a sense of substance and solidity. Both the star symbol and its colors had to sit comfortably with all the corporate colors of member airlines. We therefore picked neutrals for the Star Alliance color scheme; the star is allowed to appear on black, white, or natural backgrounds, such as glass, wood, or metal.

"The design identity for Star Alliance looks simple at first glance, but it is, in fact, very subtle in its complexity," says Jerry Greenwald, the chairman and chief executive of United Airlines. "That strikes the perfect chord for Star Alliance, because we want customers to

see a smooth, simple, and hassle-free operation. We don't want them to see the incredible complexity that goes into delivering a seamless product, which is our ultimate goal."

If designing the logo for the alliance was relatively straightforward, getting the airlines to agree on how it would be used and where it would be applied was much harder. All had spent decades nurturing their own brands; none were sure what effect this new one would have. Committees with representatives of all the Star Alliance members and Pentagram were formed to discuss and plan the development of the brand. Pentagram drafted design manuals stipulating the mark's correct application to everything from planes, signs, lounges, check-in areas, monitors, timetables, Frequent Flyer cards, and tickets.

The Star Alliance, with its new corporate design scheme, set its launch for May 14, 1997. Launch parties were held at all the major airports around the world serviced by the alliance, but the main event took place in Frankfurt, Germany. On that day, jets from all five founder airlines, each with its chairman on board, flew in formation into Frankfurt Airport, a first in aviation history. With the launch, a $25 million worldwide advertising campaign commenced. A year later, the alliance, a financial success, has proved a model for other such affiliations.

"The Star Alliance identity complements Air Canada's own identity," says R. Lamar Durrett, the airline's president and chief executive. "By evoking the fundamental building blocks of the alliance, it serves as an eloquent reminder of how Star Alliance is unique."

Reporters and news cameras from around the world converged at Frankfurt Airport on May 14, 1997, for the global launch of the Star Alliance. Aircraft flew in formation into the airport, bearing the new logo and the chairmen of each of the five founding airlines.

Sample pages from the design manual showcase the project's distinctiveness. Normally, identity components – symbol, typography, and color – would be considered "untouchable." By contrast, the Star Alliance identity must work in harmony with the other airlines' identities.

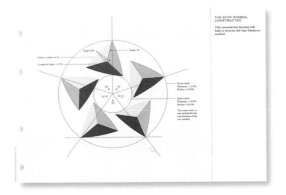

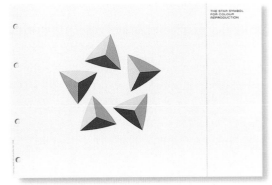

A graphic identity for a New York City business center, appearing on everything from banners to uniforms to garbage cans, takes a dramatic leap into the third dimension to help put an overlooked area on the map.

The Fashion Center

Every part of New York City has its identifying symbol, usually some popular construction that marks a special place in the expanse of the grid and blots out a few blocks on a tourist's cartoon map. Because of the city's size, these orienting features become very important to proud residents and lost visitors alike. Greenwich Villagers stroll past their miniature Arc de Triomphe, Wall Street traders are encouraged by a huge bronze bull, and Brooklynites delight in their bridge. Now the mavens of the Fashion Center – that area in midtown Manhattan more familiarly known as the Garment District, in which the future of American style is perpetually reinvented – have their own icon: a big black button. Propped up by a giant stainless-steel needle, the button caps an information booth that serves as the user-friendly public gateway to the resources of an area that, with its bustle of rolling clothing racks and slender models and suited account

THE FASHION CENTER

THE FASHION CENTER

WELCOMES BUYERS TO MARKET WEEK

 CHASE

executives, until recently labored under an insiders-only reputation.

The Fashion Center Business Improvement District (BID) was facing a difficult problem in creating an identity for its loose domain, which runs from Thirty-fourth Street to Forty-second Street between Eighth Avenue and Broadway. To the south, the busy blocks around Penn Station and Macy's look east to Herald Square and turn a cold shoulder to the Fashion Center that supplies its retail emporia. Just to the north, Times Square celebrates its own rebirth – twenty-four hours a day – with a new generation of outlandish advertising spectacles. Between them, the business of fashion houses and the nation's wholesalers, models, and tailors carries on more modestly, in rows of somewhat forbidding brick towers crowding streets narrowed by double-parked trucks.

As the only BID in Manhattan not based on a known geographic area (others include Lower Manhattan, Columbus Avenue, Grand Central), the Fashion Center felt extra pressure to mark the extent of the district and define its character. This was the impetus behind the original identity program, which Pentagram undertook in the spring of 1993. The initial phase of the identity project involved the creation of a logo: a five-holed black button that forms the letter *F*. The button proved to be a potent symbol for the district – so basic it would never go out of style – and it was used in all Fashion Center advertising and publications and on trash cans and streetlight banners that locate and publicize the district.

The kiosk, part of the larger graphic program, evolved out of the need to provide a functional focus for

The Fashion Center's button logo has been used effectively to reveal the hidden spirit of the area, on the streets and in advertising (below). Banners on Broadway greet business travelers and define one edge of the center's amorphous terrain (left).

the fashion industry, primarily as a central place to greet and orient visiting businesspeople. The kiosk's whimsical appearance belies the difficulty of its design and construction. The project required the reuse of the existing kiosk on the corner of Thirty-ninth Street and Broadway. Built in the 1970s as a temporary structure, the booth had lasted long past its time, then fallen into disrepair after its last tenant, a florist, left it vacant. Still, intricate building-code and zoning technicalities meant that it could not be razed. To add to the complexity, the site straddled public sidewalks and a private plaza, each of which had its own limitations on construction.

The button itself is composed of foam-injected fiberglass around an armature of steel. Its substantial weight, and the need to resist strong winds, demanded a very solid base. Because the aging kiosk could not support the necessary loads, its structure was beefed up, and the needle itself was used as a functional structural support. Far from being merely a symbol, the needle forms one point of a concealed tripod that supports the big button. Because this solution depends on the perfect rigidity of the joint between the needle and the button, additional creative engineering was needed to maintain the illusion that the needle passes lightly through the hole in the button. At the point the stainless-steel spar meets the sidewalk, the design team added a swatch of oversized steel mesh to hide the substantial bolted fittings – an addition that also continues the lighthearted play on fashion iconography.

Kiosk attendants field inquiries from behind a round desk designed in the shape of a giant spool of thread. Here, visitors can browse the Fashion Center web site, making the kiosk the physical point of presence for the substantial on-line offerings.

The principles of modernism shape a home-appliance maker's fortunes and an entire industry's sense of purpose, reassuring consumers amid the ravages of fads and fashions.

Kenwood Appliances

The more things remain the same, the more they change: that is the moral underlying Pentagram's relationship with one of its oldest clients, Kenwood. The appliance maker has undergone several changes of ownership and grappled with a transformation in consumer expectations. Yet its design aesthetic has endured, a testament to the solidity of the principles that underlaid its creation more than three decades ago. That aesthetic is solidly modernist – the language of the Machine Age for much of this century, and still relevant, at least in the home-appliance marketplace, despite a broader cultural passage through eclecticism to postmodernism and whatever lies beyond. While the field has not been immune to fashion (who out there does not like a Dualit chromed toaster), Kenwood's continuing success testifies to the power of adaptation within an unwavering design framework. It is important to recall just what home appliances meant to Europeans in the late 1950s and early 1960s. World War II was little more than a decade past. Families had endured years of privation, when even a tomato – let alone a refrigerator in which to store it – was a luxury. The arrival in the consumer marketplace of companies like Kenwood and Germany's Braun heralded, finally, an emergence from hardship. They and their products – washing machines, hair driers, stoves, mixers – represented the promise of a limitless future.

Kenneth Wood manifested that promise in the moral obligation he felt toward his consumers. He made his products to last, and last they did. He built enough profit into his machines that the most trifling complaint would be attended to by a Kenwood employee driving a little Kenwood van with Kenwood's Chef symbol bolted to the roof, who charged nothing for servicing a product. Parents would, as by right, expect to see a Kenwood Chef in due course in the kitchens of their children.

That sense of promise needed a physical shape, however. We found it in the geometry of modernism, which we took quite directly from the Bauhaus architectural style of the 1930s. While some European manufacturers, particularly in Scandinavia, had experimented with the rectilinear shapes of a Le Corbusier or a Mies van der Rohe in designing first-generation postwar home appliances, in much of the Continent, and certainly in the U.K., the look was radically new. Indeed, some firms were still showcasing as novel washing machines that were little more than ironbound wooden tubs with electric motors strapped to the top.

Kenwood and Pentagram have evolved the look of the company's appliances since then to reflect significant changes in cultural temperament. When we started out together, formality was considered a merit; today, the emphasis is on friendliness and accessibility. Thus, the mixer we designed in 1980 is austere, with unyielding geometry; a decade later, the style is more relaxed, with the controls more evident. A contemporary clothes iron is open, airy, and buoyant, in stark contrast to the heavy, foreboding irons of yore. Shapes are rounder; the plastic is lighter. The machine is no longer the controlling structure in the kitchen or laundry room – today, it is all about the person in charge.

But what is more striking is the strength of the design foundation. That is because, thanks to Kenwood, modernism became the accent by which home appliances as a category could be recognized. Even as prices plummeted and devices once considered luxuries became disposable, the Bauhaus contours still signal that the purpose and the promise remain the same. And so does our relationship with Kenwood – thirty years after Kenneth Wood sold the company.

A visual overview of products (right) spanning more than thirty years demonstrates Kenwood's commitment to product personality through design consistency as a means to maintain their valuable presence in the marketplace.

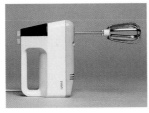

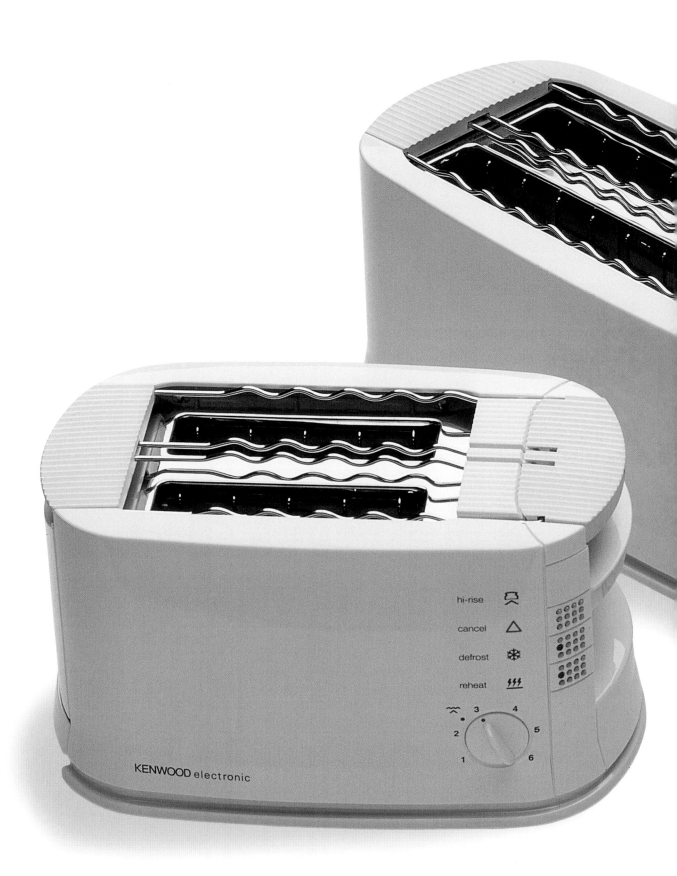

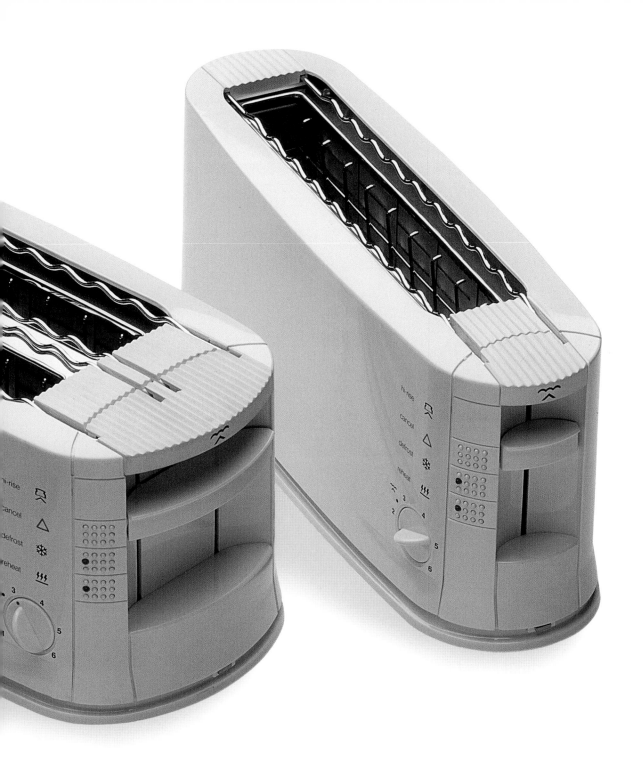

Nineteenth-century theatrical advertising traditions create a streetwise visual language for a venerable performing-arts organization and its new leadership, branding them as aggressive and culturally open.

The Public Theater

Long before "diversity" became a cause and a cliché, the legendary producer Joseph Papp promoted cultural integration through the New York Shakespeare Festival. Over thirty-seven years, Papp built the summer festival and its year-round offspring, The Public Theater, on the belief that performing arts of the highest quality should be available to all people, regardless of their background or income. In his choice of productions and his casting, his work would reflect New York's polyglot cultures. Beginning in 1954 with a program that took free productions of Shakespeare's plays to city parks and playgrounds, Papp built a formidable institution. In 1962, his Shakespeare Festival found a summer home at the Delacorte Theater, an open-air performance space in Central Park. Five years later, Papp rescued from demolition the Astor Library, which is in a historic but rough neighborhood in the city's East Village. In it, with the world premiere of

Hair, he opened The Public Theater. From its year-round address on Lafayette Street, with plays like *A Chorus Line* and *The Normal Heart*, featuring talented actors like Meryl Streep, Morgan Freeman, and Sam Shepard, the theater earned popular and critical acclaim, raking in Tonys, Obies, Pulitzer Prizes, and Drama Desk Awards. But by the time of Papp's death in 1991, The Public was also facing a crisis, brought on by its own prominence. Despite its commitment to multiculturalism, its audience was becoming smaller, wealthier, whiter and older.

Visual cues compounded the problem. The opulent, salmon-colored lobby of the Lafayette Street theater was reminiscent of the luxury apartment building lobbies of the Upper West Side, bastion of the city's well-heeled liberals. Focus groups showed that audiences tended to conflate The Public Theater with the famous PBS television series "Masterpiece Theatre." That association had led too many people among The Public's potential audience to think of it as an "educational" institution for the city's elites.

It fell to George C. Wolfe, who was named its new producer in 1993, to find a new audience by driving The Public Theater and the New York Shakespeare Festival back to their roots. He wanted to fill The Public Theater's seats with a mix of people who would truly represent the cultural variety of New York City.

"I'm trying to create a truly American theater," said Wolfe, who as writer and director had been associated with such groundbreaking work as *The Colored Museum* (which Papp had produced at The Public) and Tony Kushner's Pulitzer Prize-winning AIDS drama *Angels in America*. "I'm interested in breaking boundaries, telling a story, defying a truth that has been accepted."

Executing Wolfe's strategy was complex, in part because of his organization's structure. Although the New York Shakespeare Festival was a production of The Public Theater, the festival, as one of the city's most enduring annual events, had a higher profile than The Public. Not only that, but the Lafayette Street building housed a collection of smaller theaters. While each of them needed individual identification, Wolfe wanted the parent organization to be the dominant force. The Public thus had a classic corporate identity problem: it needed an overall image as well as sub-branding.

In the spring of 1994, Wolfe retained Pentagram as design consultant to clarify the relationship between the "corporate" and "brand" activities. His directive was this: create an image of the future in the context of present needs; shape that image to be street-

For inspiration, our team turned to the typographic traditions of nineteenth-century posters. Resurrecting Victorian wood display type, we sought to draw playgoers' attention to the name of the play, the time and place of the production, and the price of the tickets.

wise and inclusive; and give it an enduring, unifying language. He wanted style with grit and a voice with an edge.

Pentagram's first urgent project was promoting that summer's upcoming New York Shakespeare Festival. The design team made two immediate decisions. We eliminated illustration from the campaign. We also recoiled from the conventions of modern theatrical advertising, which relied too strongly on banal logos and cute headlines that tended to blend all theatrical promotion into an indistinguishable wash. The designers decided instead to let the news and words drive the advertising.

Individual words, rather than whole sentences, were emphasized, and key messages were communicated through a kind of shorthand. *Kiss Me, Kate* became an in-your-face "KATE," while *The Merry Wives of Windsor* went on the streets by "WIVES." Because New York – despite more than seventy television channels, three daily newspapers, and innumerable high-rises and skyscrapers – is still a pedestrian city, the street is the one medium that can unify its disparate population. So it was logical to make the street the main vehicle to carry an identity campaign that was, in fact, its inspiration. Posters were put up everywhere they were allowed. Buses, water towers, outdoor walls, and building lobbies also carried The Public's new visual message and news about its productions. Buttressed by more traditional media such as newspaper advertising, the effect of the campaign was to shout "Hey, you!" – a very New York form of address.

Pentagram has continued to evolve the "shouting type" into a complex visual language. While the typographic umbrella has remained consistent (the entire range can be read within the word "Public," which runs from a thick *P* to a thin *C*), the vocabulary has been stretched and remolded extensively to accommodate new plays and venues, to remain fresh and surprising from season to season.

The work has been honored widely. Among the multitude of national and international design competitions and exhibitions in which it has been recognized is the American Center for Design's 1995 Beacon Award for integrated corporate design strategy. The Public Theater posters are housed in the permanent collection of the Cooper-Hewitt National Design Museum in New York City.

"We were trying to cleanse the visual palate, and also have a very contemporary, very nineties edge," George Wolfe has said of the program. "I was looking for something that had a certain attitude, that said 'Yeah, I'm here. Deal with this. Hop on board.'"

To circumvent any nostalgic associations, the all-copy design was updated, with scales, proportions, and colors aligned to contemporary tastes. Individual words were emphasized and key messages were communicated through a kind of shorthand.

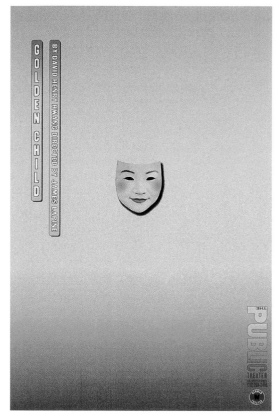

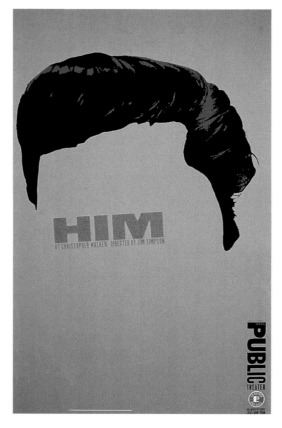

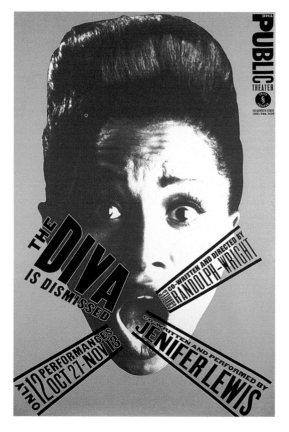

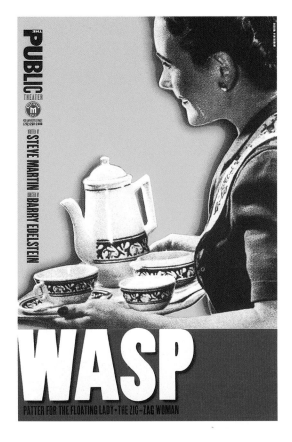

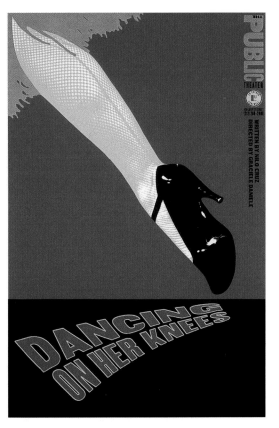

In the beginning of our relationship, we learned each
other's language Like over-eager babies
Mouthing unintelligible gaggles and sounds
Unable to articulate
Clumsily tripping on words
Falling into abject frustration
But once we found the common language –
Each action and deed, every word and sentence was a
joy, and an excitement A tingling of senses
A radiant discovery
Then, as through osmosis, we used each other's words
and expressions Borrowing shamelessly and
indeliberately Incorporating them into our language
Speaking as one
Thinking as one
Feeling as one
And in the course, we invented new words
Gave existing words new meaning
Redefined and polished our language
Making it a special one of our own
One that we selfishly shared
One that no one could decipher or understand
One that we used in the comfort of each
other's arms in quiet evenings Then, slowly
but surely, we tired of it We lost interest
Got lazy Became indifferent
Words gradually lost their meaning
and significance
Phrases forever locked in an impenetrable
vocabulary vault with its key thrown away Like drunken
dancers, we emphasized the wrong accents in words
Sentences led to misinterpretations
Misinterpretations led to misunderstandings
Misunderstandings led to inevitable silence
In the end, we spoke different languages
Even though, we wanted the same thing

LANGUAGE OF THEIR OWN

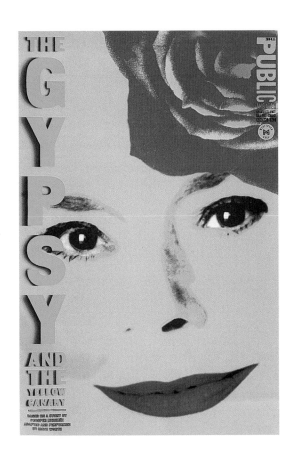

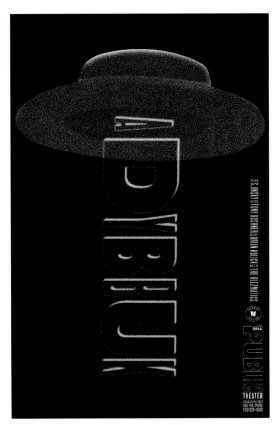

A new range of the finest food, endorsed by leading chefs, employs packaging and presentation that communicate all the right design signals to an untried target market.

Tesco's Finest

Tesco is the U.K.'s largest supermarket chain. For some time they had been aware of a growing demand from customers for delicious foods that combined convenience with taste, a demand that represented a completely new market opportunity. Early in 1998 they launched a new range – Tesco's Finest – targeting this new market. The aim is to offer products that reflect the quality and choice of dishes that people currently enjoy in good restaurants. So Tesco enlisted the help of leading chefs from famous restaurants to develop and endorse the dishes and produce that form the comprehensive premium range. Because Tesco's Finest is a totally new concept, it has to carry a new and different identity in its packaging – quite different from anything else in the store. With such a high demand already in place, the packaging could afford to be quiet and refined. Photography, color, and typography were used in a way that had never before been contemplated by Tesco.

There are about 150 items in the Tesco's Finest range. They include a number of prepared dishes in the style of contemporary and Mediterranean cuisine, reflecting the qualities one might expect in a smart restaurant.

There are also "raw materials" such as fine cuts of meat and luxury seafood. And there are many other products, from ice cream, cookies and biscuits, and chocolate truffles to balsamic vinegar and special blends of teas and coffees. The range is sold from its own chiller cabinets, separate from the other product lines in the stores.

The design task was to create a two-dimensional and three-dimensional language for the range that would be distinctive and different, reflecting the market positioning of the range. Tesco already has a luxury product line so the differentiation from this had to be particularly clear and effective.

Design principles were established based on a geometric theme of rectangles, squares, and circles. Thus the face graphics for the packaging are organized into quadrants of one third, one quarter, and one sixth. Photography takes up a maximum of one quarter of the printed surface and is always confined to the top left-hand corner. This is in radical contrast to most supermarket packaging, where the photography dominates and covers the total print area as both foreground and background. The style of the photogra-phy deliberately emulates the high-class food photography featured in such magazines as *Vogue* or *Marie Claire*. Two leading photographers, James Murphy and Roger Stowell, were commissioned to give the project the intended editorial quality and to ensure a consistency of approach.

Only two colors – silver and black – are used. This gives the range strong unified branding with a classic look. The silver is used uniformly for the background of all printed surfaces; the black is a subsidiary counterpoint, used for the lids of metal tea containers and caps of bottles.

The typography is restrained and tightly disciplined, employing only one typeface – Baskerville. The brand name "Finest" is differentiated and given impact since it is set in italics and carries an asterisk. This asterisk adds further distinction to the signature and also indicates the endorsement aspect of the "Finest" proposition; it refers shoppers to the well-known chef whose name appears on the packaging – with different chefs endorsing different products. This device receives an interesting twist on Christmas produce, where the asterisk is replaced by a little holly leaf and red berry. The name of the product itself appears under the branding signatures, supported by well-written copy that describes the product and how best to prepare and present it.

Package engineering follows geometric design principles. For example, where windows are used, they fit into the quadrants, and where special container bodies are required, they have been sourced to complement the geometric theme (right).

TESCO

*Finest**
Darjeeling
& Assam
Blend·Leaf
Tea

Chef Anne Edition
seasonal
The elegant
refreshing tea which
harmonises the finest
blends and leaves
sourced distinctive
Darjeeling with an
full-bodied
aromatic Assam

125g ℮

The editorial style of the food photography by James Murphy and Roger Stowell rein-forces the contemporary restaurant positioning of the range and deliberately emulates the look of fine-food photography featured in such publications as *Vogue* and *Marie Claire*.

Special considerations were taken into account when designing packaging for the line. Ice-cream containers incorporate an internal round base so that an ice-cream scoop can be easily used.

All food packed under the
Finest brand name is guaranteed
to be of the finest quality

Finest ★

£1.69   £1.69

£1.19   £1.19   £1.19   £1.35

£1.69   £1.69

£3.99

An apartment interior encompasses the detailed professional requirements and 1940s- and 1950s-era cultural interests of a dual-career, work-at-home family whose lives and labors revolve around creativity.

New York Loft Residence

He is a film editor and music enthusiast. She is a writer. Each had professional and personal design requirements. This New York couple's needs combined with their – and their designers' – affection for post-World War II styles in a fusion of living and working space quite appropriate to the bustling 1990s. The loftlike apartment occupies the entire floor of a long, narrow building in Greenwich Village and has large windows on three sides. Starting with a blank-slate floor plan, the designers wanted to enhance the expansive aspect but retain a homey feel. Careful framing of spaces and the juxtaposition of highly finished furnishings with industrial elements, such as exposed ductwork and lighting, achieve the desired effect: loft-cum-apartment. Custom furniture, a critical aspect of the design, bridges the scale from large architectural pieces to small individualized details. The inspirations for most of the custom pieces were usually modern precedents, and the treatment of surfaces and elements as furniture rather than architecture reflects a modern(e) design attitude.

A cohesive collection of furniture is the project within the project. It creates a set of references, opportunities, and spatial complements that both reinforce the architecture and allow the apartment to serve as a growing collection of lovingly selected pieces, rather than a completed work of art.

In the kitchen area, the designs were derived from a traditional, compartmented armoire and the magical American kitchen of the 1950s. The complex and tight composition recalls an old-fashioned steamer trunk, with a space for everything packed into a neat shape. In the sink alcove, the designers created a little "chapel for dishwashing" (one of the husband's meditative pleasures) incorporating a restaurant-supply spray faucet and teak-lined drying racks. The central work surface is treated as a table, not a solid built-in, to reinforce the idea of the kitchen as a collection of furniture pieces.

The need to conceal the bedroom – to understate the apartment, deter over-night guests, and insulate her writing from his music – was expressed as a reinterpretation of a padded privacy door (like the door to M's office in James Bond movies).

The bathroom poses an abstract wall of lights, mirrors, and shelving against a very traditional white-tile New York City washroom. The long sloping bathroom sink expresses the idea of washing at a mountain stream and sharing a single grand-scale sink. It is also a nod to the traditional terrazzo kitchen sink common in Italy and the famous table by Le Corbusier (in the Maison La Roche-Jeanneret) made from a mortuary slab.

The apartment attempts to speak less in architectural language than in an accessible and explicit language of furniture and common objects and simple references. Wit counts more than ponderous ideology. Fun counts more than perfection. Interesting arguments count more than bland concurrence. The redesign reflects the notion that nothing in design is really new, just reinterpreted and given new meaning and context.

A Jean Prouvé cabinet and new shelving inspired by Prouvé and Charlotte Perriand define the space in and around the living room (right). The passage from the public world to a private realm is marked by three steel doors at the entrance (below).

Shelving is expressive of the stacks of stuff it is meant to hide. While "books" hold up the living-room bookshelves, "boxes" support the owners' considerable audiovisual equipment (below).

Robsjohn-Gibbings dining-room table and chairs are part of the collection created by the owners and were among the inspirations reflected in a new series of furniture designs Pentagram created for the loft.

Perforated metal-faced kitchen storage cabinets fuse American pie safe and French *garde-manger* (below left). The prep table's legs – inspired by a Jean-Michel Frank sanded oak table – hide a network of water, drainage, gas, and electrical lines (below right).

The leather-covered bedroom wall/door was borrowed from Jean-Michel Frank's 1930s decorating, but the orange color is pure 1960s Naugahyde and visually complements brick buildings visible outside (below).

In the master bathroom's cast terrazzo sink (opposite), water flows gently down the basin to a single concealed drain at the end. Rear lighting and adjustable oval mirrors reflect the tile shelves opposite, merging the traditional city bathroom with an inventive alternative.

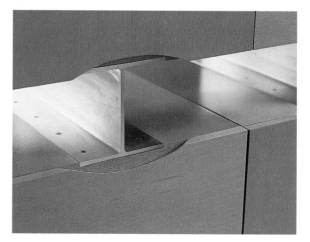

The study storage unit and the shelving (both with aluminum structural elements) restate the loft/apartment polarity (above and below). Combining a base metal with precious woods creates an interesting visual argument rather than pleasant agreement.

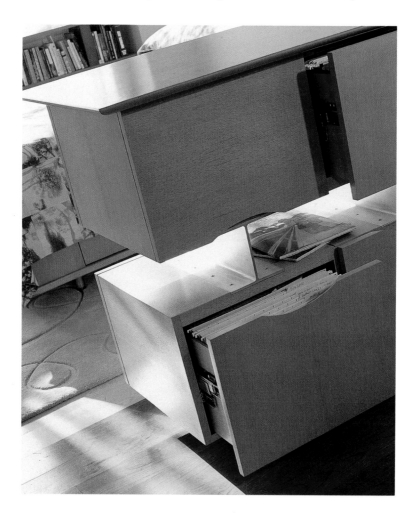

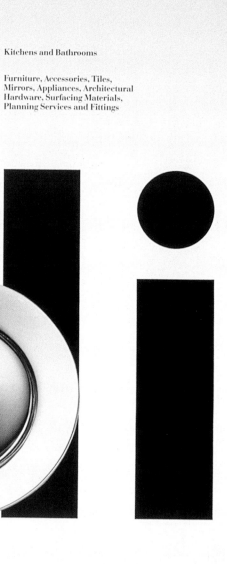

Kitchens and Bathrooms

Furniture, Accessories, Tiles,
Mirrors, Appliances, Architectural
Hardware, Surfacing Materials,
Planning Services and Fittings

You'll find it all at IDI 93
The Interiors Show
Earls Court, London
6-10 June 1993

Interior Design International

IDI 11 Manchester Square London W1M 5AB Tel 071 486 1951

Designs by Pentagram

The new corporate design for London's annual interior-design show helps create stronger and more focused promotional material – both to attract visitors and to communicate effectively with exhibitors.

Interior Design International

Interior Design International ran a highly successful annual interior-design show at London's Earl's Court exhibition center. Exhibitors included a wide range of specialists, from lighting companies and ceramicists to indoor and outdoor furniture designers. The organizers initially commissioned a new corporate design to help them promote the show to interior designers and specifiers. After consideration of the use that would be made of the new design, it was decided that no single image could convey the variety of the products and materials on show. So the project was redefined and the identity established through a series of promotional posters. These had Interior Design International's initials in lower case, with the bowl of the *d* substituted by an appropriate object or architectural detail. Ten posters were produced featuring objects such as a spiral staircase, a Tiffany lamp, a bath plug, a roll of carpet, a clock, and the bolster cushion of a chair.

Floors

Carpeting, Hardwood, Raised,
Stone, Mosaic, Vinyl Flooring,
Matting, Rugs, Tiles, Ancillary
Products

You'll find it all at IDI 93
The Interiors Show
Earls Court, London
6-10 June 1993

Interior Design International

IDI 11 Manchester Square London W1M 5AB Tel 071 486 1951

Design by Pentagram

Furniture

Bedroom, Reproduction, Antique,
Fitted, Upholstered, Cane, Bespoke,
Cafe/Canteen, Bar and Hotel/
Restaurant, Seating

You'll find it all at IDI 93
The Interiors Show
Earls Court, London
6-10 June 1993

Interior Design International

IDI 11 Manchester Square London W1M 5AB Tel 071 486 1951

Designs by Pentagram

Outdoor

Plants and Planters, Exterior
Lighting, Garden/Patio Furniture,
Conservatories, Fountains, Pools,
Balustrades, Gates, Statues and
Ornaments

You'll find it all at IDI 93
The Interiors Show
Earls Court, London
6-10 June 1993

Interior Design International

IDI 11 Manchester Square London W1M 5AB Tel 071 486 1951

Design by Pentagram

Lighting

Lamps, Fittings, Accessories, Low
Voltage, Shades, Systems, Exterior,
Security, Track, Period and
Traditional

You'll find it all at IDI 93
The Interiors Show
Earls Court, London
6-10 June 1993

Interior Design International

IDI 11 Manchester Square London W1M 5AB Tel 071 486 1951

Designs by Pentagram

Architectural

Cladding, Ceilings, Partitions,
Staircases, Ironmongery, Doors,
Windows, Specialist Joinery,
Heating and Air Conditioning,
Fireplaces

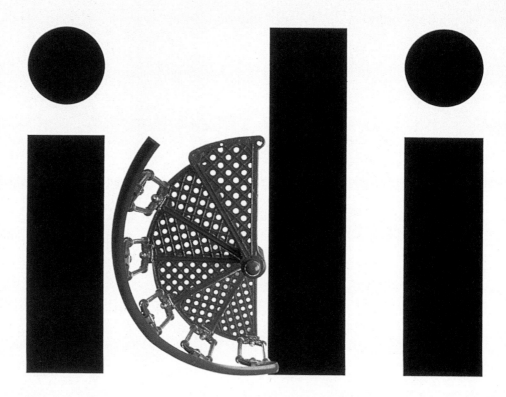

You'll find it all at IDI 93
The Interiors Show
Earls Court, London
6-10 June 1993

Interior Design International

IDI 11 Manchester Square London W1M 5AB Tel 071 486 1951

Finishing Touches

Blinds, Sound Systems, Art, Plants
& Planters, Sculpture, Music
Systems, Tableware, Mirrors,
Bedding, Signage, Services, Murals,
Antiques, Accessories

You'll find it all at IDI 93
The Interiors Show
Earls Court, London
6-10 June 1993

Interior Design International

IDI 11 Manchester Square London W1M 5AB Tel 071 486 1951

An original design language and fresh metaphors help a new family of infor-mation-based consumer-electronics products prove their value – months, even years, before the products themselves exist.

Diba

For years, information appliances have been touted as the next breakthrough in personal technology – inexpensive, simple, task-specific machines that will transform the way we live to a degree not even approached by the television, stereo, or PC. But IAs remained very much a dream and a research project – until 1995, when a former Oracle vice president, Farzad Dibachi, and his brother, Farid, founded Diba, a Silicon Valley company with a piece of software that could render the concept practical and economical. Instead of building IAs itself, Diba's business plan called for it to license its software and hardware architecture to consumer-electronics firms and service providers. Illustrating the huge market potential to licensees required Diba to show how such products might look and perform. In January 1996, Diba invited Pentagram to develop seven task-specific concepts to showcase the range of prod-ucts and services that were possible with its architecture and could be translated into real-world products. One of our first duties was to brainstorm with Diba executives to determine exactly what each device would do. The technology, after all, allowed for an almost unlimited set of applications; an E-mail retriever, for example, could incorporate other functions, from CD player to television set. But it became very apparent that the power of IA applications had to lie in their simplicity. That, in turn, led us to the central metaphor of the design language we developed for Diba: elegance. A combination of clarity and expressiveness would be recognizable and convey distinctive object value across the range of unique devices.

Drawings and foam sketches led to finished hard models that have subtle shapes, gently curved surfaces that attract the hand and the eye, and a familiar relationship that translates well in photographs – a critical factor when seeking media attention. All the devices projected a sense of authority. And to make even computer-illiterate consumers comfortable, they used simple iconic shapes on strategically placed hard buttons rather than screen-based controls. "We wanted to build functionality right into the plastic," says J. Stewart Reed, Diba's vice president of market development.

The most important aspect of the design vernacular is that it floated atop each individual product, clarifying a device's purpose from first sight and first use. Our intention was to get the user as close as possible to the desired outcome, usually with one or two button clicks. Diba Mail, for example, is a

Diba Tour Director (previous page). Diba Internet (below) has an elegant handheld remote control with task-specific buttons set to finger-shaped depressions, a trackball for easy thumb access, and a lid that reveals a small Qwerty keyboard (opposite).

low-cost communications appliance with hard-button controls that let E-mail and fax users create, send, reply to, forward, and delete messages without forcing them to navigate a screen-based interface. Conceiving it meant wiping away the preconceptions inculcated by Macintosh and Windows interfaces to cut to the core of the products' intended use: to contend with messages, not with desktops, folders, and the like.

Diba Internet, a TV-set-top box that offers E-mail and web access, is playful, a quality that mass-market products often lack. Unlike the cool, competent shapes employed on our executive concepts, Diba Internet features an off-beat "melon slice" unit with a wedge-shaped case, concave top surface, and amusing conical vents that resemble watermelon seeds. The tactic was aimed specifically at differentiating the device from the numbingly similar matte-black mass that defines the consumer-electronics marketplace.

Unveiled in April 1997, the concepts resulted in a significant chain of events. They landed Diba in the pages of the *Wall Street Journal* and several other national publications at a pivotal moment in the company's history; secured partnerships with such highly held industry leaders as Motorola, Panasonic, and Mitsubishi; and led, in turn, to Diba's acquisition by Sun Microsystems in July 1997. Pentagram's designs received a Silver Award from the Industrial Designers Society of America in its 1997 Industrial Design Excellence Awards and the Red Dot for High Design Quality from the Design Zentrum Westfalen.

While fingers are typing, data travels from the keyboard/controller via infrared to the main unit (overleaf), whose "melon slice" design and seedlike vents attracted the attention of both mainstream publications and influential industry journals.

power

Diba Mail combines telephone and Internet capability in a smart all-in-one case with, on the outside, a traditional handset, keypad, LCD, and buttons for sending and receiving E-mail and faxes and, on the inside, a keyboard that flips down to reveal a flat panel display.

Diba Silent Partner is a financial assistant that integrates on-line banking, credit accounts, and analysis functions into a familiar, leatherbound ledger format. Diba Yellow Pages (overleaf) is a simple terminal for access to Internet-based telephone directories.

A multifaceted graphic identity and signage program for a mecca for children in downtown St. Paul provide a visual dramatization of the institution's participatory credo that is understandable by all ages.

Minnesota Children's Museum

There is not a designer at work today who hasn't bluffed his or her way through a project presentation inventing a grandiose rationale for what is, in truth, an elemental or intuitive decision. Not so with Pentagram's identity program for the Minnesota Children's Museum: we embraced the obvious and ran with it. Simply put, the museum wanted to be known as a center for hands-on learning; the design team enlisted all hands on deck, developing a graphic program based on children's hands photographed in gestures of active exploration. The museum director, Ann Bitter, has defined the museum's twin objectives as making kids feel happy and giving them power. When Pentagram took on the design of the museum's signage and identity in September 1994, we grown-ups approached the problem directly, trying to reach both goals. Several of the signs are complex visual jokes designed to recognize a child's appreciation of irony.

The girls bathroom sign, for example, consists of a photograph of a hand holding a conventional girls bathroom sign – the silhouetted icon familiar to anyone over the age of four. Such images suffuse the building with humor at a scale that children can understand and set the museum apart as a place where the usual rules may not always apply.

A second major feature of the graphic program – the red ball – was cleverly derived from the architecture of the museum itself, which, designed by James/Snow Architects in 1995, includes circular windows, doors, and other elements. The balls act as the subject of the hand's exploration – they are grasped and spun and sometimes miraculously balanced in photographic signs throughout the museum.

The most notable use of this motif was in a spectacular photomural that hung temporarily on the main facade of the museum: a series of monumental, forty-five-foot-high children's hands catching, balancing, and gripping the red ball. In the final frame, Pentagram replaced the ball with one of the museum's porthole windows, reinforcing the strong connection between the graphic program and the architecture of the museum. In addition to trumpeting the museum's mission to become a place where children could continually profit from direct, experiential learning, the hand-and-ball motif also helped to create seamless links between the museum and its building, and, perhaps most importantly, between that building and the children themselves.

Pentagram's graphics for the Minnesota Children's Museum appeal to children while avoiding condescending design clichés – like basic geometry and crayons – that are common in children's museums.

The hand-and-ball motif was reinterpreted functionally in the oversized "hand-held" directory and clock in the museum lobby. The red ball reappears in three dimensions as the mounting hardware for every kind of sign.

The hand theme extended very naturally to the museum's floor indicators and room number signs. The floors are marked by raised fingers, counting from one to five. Everyone on the project was happy that the museum had only five floors.

Cocktails
The Present
From The Past

A new graphic program for the Savoy Group, owner of some of the world's most famous hotels, develops its own identity without submerging the strong and individual identities of its constituent parts.

Savoy Group

The Savoy Group of hotels and restaurants includes The Berkeley, Claridge's, The Connaught, and The Savoy in London. All are among the most prestigious hotel names in the world, with huge reputations for luxury and individuality. The Lygon Arms, a sixteenth-century coaching inn in the Cotswolds, is also a part of the group, as are The Savoy Theatre and the unique British restaurant Simpson's-in-the-Strand close by. The project required us to advise on and develop the identity of the group, producing publications, promotions, and other print both for the individual establishments and the group itself. The answer was not to impose a standard group design on all the establishments, as each had its own strong and important identity. The solution was to concentrate on defining and expressing these different identities. The group's own identity would in turn be represented by the quality of each of its constituents.

The Savoy Group had been through a period of some difficulty when it appointed a new general manager, Ramón Pajares, in 1995. He came as one of the world's leading hoteliers with a mission to revive the fortunes of the group. Although the hotels were managing to maintain their appeal in the marketplace, many were living on borrowed time and relying too heavily on past glory in the image they presented to the world.

Pajares understood that the assets of the group lay in the individual reputations of the hotels. He also realized that the group's overall image needed to be given a considerable boost, which was possible only by improving the performances of its constituent parts. Plans were drawn up for a heavy investment program to restore the famous fabric and furnishings of the hotels. The goal was to revive not only their physical attributes but also their spirit, thereby bringing the group into a new era of achievement. Marketing was rationalized, some of the group's properties were divested, and an analysis and development program for the group's visual identity was commissioned.

The main design effort was concentrated on expressing the individuality of the hotels and other parts of The Savoy Group by producing a clear, high-quality, and different identity for each. This attitude was crystallized by coining the tag line, "England's most distinguished and individual hotels and restaurants," which was adopted to accompany all instances where the Savoy Group name appeared.

A rule was established that, wherever the hotels were being promoted to the consumer, from in-flight magazines to carrier bags, it should always be with their own design identity, not a group identity. Thus group publications promoting aspects of each establishment also had to retain the individual identities within them. The group does have its own house style, which is used only in business-to-business communications, such as with travel agents and corporate buyers.

The Berkeley was built in the 1970s near Hyde Park in Knightsbridge after it was moved from its original site in Piccadilly. The hotel has the air of an undiscovered secret, unassuming on the outside, discreet and unashamedly luxurious inside. The elements of the identity were chosen to express the anonymity and intimacy of the hotel. The design palette therefore includes detailed black-and-white photography and a neutral color scheme of black,

Corporate-wide publications like *The Savoy Cocktail Book* celebrate not only the rejuvenation and restructuring of the hotels but also symbolize a whole new attitude toward identity.

white, silver, brown, and warm gray. The logotype is based on the subtle lettering that is cut into the stone on the front of the building.

Claridge's in Mayfair has long been associated with the patronage of leaders, royalty, and distinguished families from around the world. The property was built in the 1890s and added to in the 1930s. This gives it a unique juxtaposition of styles within – Victorian traditional splendor on one side and some remarkable examples of fine Art Deco interiors and ornament on the other. A graphic palette was developed with photography that highlights the provenance of Claridge's interiors,

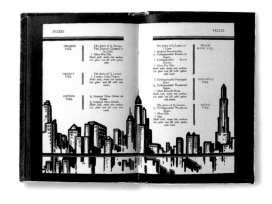

such as details of the original Lalique glass, the 1930s bronze metalwork, and furniture from the famous cruise liner the SS *Normandie*. The color references are elegant pastel and metallic tones, a repeat pattern has been introduced, and the logotype was redrawn in copperplate to complement the original version of the coat of arms.

Since the days of César Ritz and Auguste Escoffier in the last century, The Savoy has been a focus for London high society and one of the most distinguished hotels in the world. Close to the theater district, it has always attracted artists and writers as well as politicians, lawyers, and City financiers who meet in its restaurants and bars. This particularly cosmopolitan air is expressed in the new design. In contrast to The Berkeley, the design palette reflects theatricality: colors include red, gold, silver, and black. The photography of hotel details is vibrant and documentary in style. The logotype and the overall typography are derived from the famous neon lettering on the canopy over the front entrance, with numerous references to Art Deco motifs.

A major Savoy Group event requiring printed publicity was the announcement and promotion of the completion of the investment program. A silver book – *Cocktails – The Present From The Past* – was a gift made to mark the "new era"; it contained a reprint of the original classic *Savoy Cocktail Book* from the 1930s, opening with a new cocktail from each establishment.

The Savoy Group and its constituent hotels and restaurants now have their own identities, which reinforce one another in an overall and consistent manner, projecting quality and distinction for themselves and for the group as a whole. Reputations have been reestablished based on present excellence as well as past greatness.

The Art Deco motifs of The Savoy, the quiet sophistication of The Berkeley, and the heritage of Claridge's are all visual themes expressed in a wide range of applications distinctive for themselves and for the group as a whole.

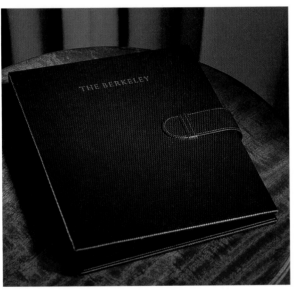

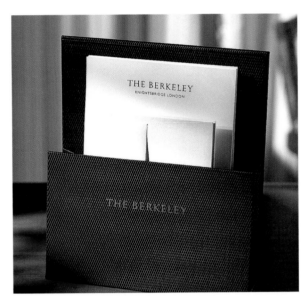

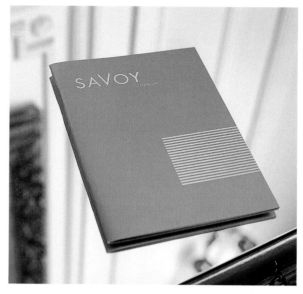

A visual vocabulary of colors, shapes, and patterns that can be mixed and matched to reflect the specific personality of togs or toys, tags or interiors, underpins a new branding system for a beloved children's manufacturer and retailer.

Gymboree

As Gymboree neared its twentieth year in business, the child-focused company decided it was time to develop a new branding system. Its original identity, created when its first parent-child play program was launched at a neighborhood community center, looked dated and provincial. It didn't reflect a multimillion dollar company that manufactured a full line of children's clothing and developmental toys and operated more than 200 franchised play programs and 280 retail stores. In asking Pentagram to design a new brand identity, Gymboree sought a graphic image that communicated the premium quality of its products and its warm, playful, and contemporary personality. At the same time, it wanted to preserve the equity it had established with the existing program (bright colors, bouncing letters, and Gymbo, the clown mascot). But given its rapid expansion, the company also needed a system that would be flexible enough to translate across all media, from storefronts and products to packaging.

Rather than design a fixed identity system that would have to be executed with cookie-cutter sameness, we chose to create a visual vocabulary that could be developed into a "branding language" for Gymboree. Made up of core graphic elements including a logotype, color palette, and distinctive geometric patterns, this vocabulary provides Gymboree with the ability to apply elements individually, in combination, or in total, as appropriate to the situation and need.

For example, Gymboree's branding may be suggested on clothing and toy products through the use of the color palette. Or it can be applied to the concrete facade of an urban storefront by means of its familiar checkerboard pattern. The freedom to draw from this visual vocabulary not only allows the brand to stay fresh and relevant over time but also lets others adapt the identity system seamlessly to the multiple fast-changing needs of the company.

The branding changeover was designed to be more evolutionary than revolutionary, so that consumers would find comfort in familiarity. The design team made the original color palette brighter, warmer, and more sophisticated. They chose a more contemporary styling of the typeface for the logo, adding patterns that have always been an integral part of Gymboree products. To address the ongoing need for signage, stickers, and labels, they also condensed the core identity elements into a new *G* symbol.

Pentagram drew upon this basic visual vocabulary in the design of Gymboree printed materials, including products, hang tags, labels, packaging, signage, store aprons, and retail interiors and exteriors. During the first three years of the program, we handled the branding and redesign of more than seventy-five items. In collaboration with the Gymboree staff and BAT, a retail architectural firm, we developed visual guidelines for the prototype of Gymboree's next generation of retail stores.

Introduced in phases, the new branding system helped Gymboree to realize its largest increase in same-store sales by the end of its first full year. Repackaging also helped to revitalize existing products, and actually helped some to sell out. With a brand identity designed to look current and interesting over time, the company has continued to expand its business beyond the stroller set by proving its relevance to a broader base of customers.

Gymboree's visual vocabulary is well demonstrated in its application to the stationery system. The letterhead and envelope carry the logo and color palette. Business cards (left), with their colorful, multipatterned backs, telegraph the company's playful approach.

 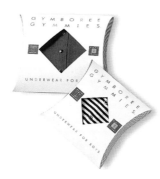 

A major goal of the packaging program was the transformation of store box to gift box. A more upscale, full-color box with a special closure was created from recycled materials (above right), adding perceived value to the contents and the brand.

The program of stripes, polka dots, and checkers provides flexibility in creating package tags and products, allowing wide ranges of shapes, sizes, colors, and production values (above and below).

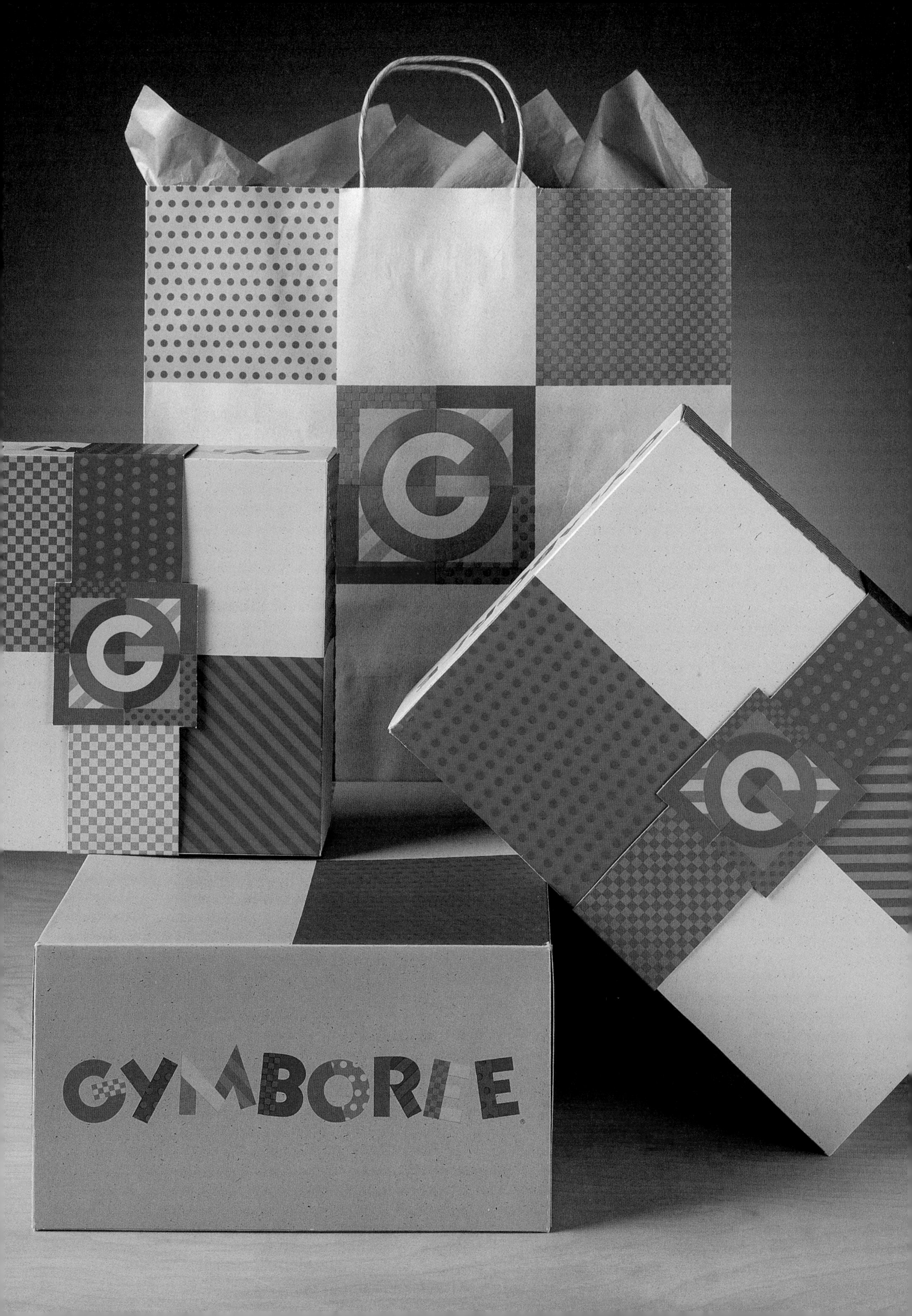
GYMBOREE

Gymbo, the clown mascot, was originally created for the company's play program. The character proved so popular that a line of products was created around it. Gymbo is now proudly displayed on a broad spectrum of clothing and retail products.

How and when to use Gymbo, and other logo products and new product packaging as well, was all codified in a graphics-standards guide that specified colors, typographic rules, pattern scale, and color combinations.

A prototype store in San Jose, California (above), gave Gymboree the opportunity to test experimental architectural systems, interior signage, new products, and a newborn department called CradleGym.

The brand is in the details (below): from three-dimensional signs to six-color embroidered aprons and stroller-wide aisles, everything communicates and enhances the shopping experience.

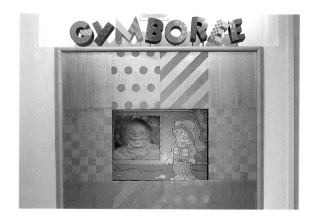

Adapting the geometry and transferring the cultural familiarity of gable-top cartons gives a footwear manufacturer a cost-effective means of endorsing brand values.

Superga

Let's face it: shoe boxes just aren't convenient anymore. Many of us like to keep them around to store photographs, letters, and mementos once the shoes have been removed, only to discover that their shelf life is short and their protective abilities compromised by the low quality of the flimsy materials used to make them. The liabilities of the shoe box offered an opportunity to Superga of Turin, Italy. A company steeped in tradition, Superga in its earliest days made bicycle and car tires for Fiat before moving into the business for which it is known today – the manufacture of rubber-soled sport shoes and rubber fishing and hunting boots. But in the increasingly competitive shoe business, tradition and heritage were not enough to maintain market share. Superga's new management wanted to revitalize its brand by expanding beyond its signature sport shoes into casual leisure shoes. New packaging could emphasize to consumers that the new shoes were made of natural materials (thus keeping to its manufacturing tradition) and help them distinguish between spring-summer and autumn-winter collections.

The design team decided to create a box that would be more than a mere branding device and would actually have inherent worth. In the past, shoe boxes were tough and could be used again and again; it was cost-consciousness that, in recent years, made them cheaper and flimsier, encouraging consumers to leave them in the shop. We proposed something stronger, which would also be attractive enough for consumers to want to take home and reuse – reminding them of the brand and its personality every time they opened their closet doors. This reconceived box also had to be collapsible, so that it could be folded flat for easy storage when it was not being used. Of equal importance, it had to be retailer-friendly, a container that would reduce the time and effort it takes a salesperson to remove the conventional box from the shelf and lift its lid to display the shoes inside.

Pentagram's first insight was to change the shape of the packaging. Instead of the ubiquitous coffin-shaped box, we echoed the contours of milk and orange juice cartons, a gentle suggestion to the busy consumer that the contents inside this container are natural. By entering this "fluid" cultural territory,

we not only fashioned a box that was stronger and more durable, but one that can be collapsed and reerected for use as many times as needed, allowing for a variety of secondary uses in the home.

To reinforce its utility, we imported a device from a different cultural terrain. The team added to the box a fastening clasp modeled on those used on doctors' bags. A rubber tab opens and closes the package with a satisfying snap. This snap fastener not only insures that the contents do not fall out, it also reflects the rubber content of Superga's products.

The packaging is made of durable paperboard, uncoated on the outside, which, when printed on, communicates the naturalness of the brand in rich color that seems integral to the board. The boxes cost no more to produce than conventional ones, and the shape and collapsibility allow for personal reuse, not just recycling. In the shop, Superga cartons lie on their sides, stacked, so that their contents can be pulled out, displayed, and replaced quickly and easily. Boxes can also stand upright, for display or for home storage.

Pentagram used this same basic geometry to produce a larger container for Superga's range of hunting and fishing boots. It, too, opens like a doctor's bag, and can be used to safeguard a sportsperson's car from the mud and grime collected on shoes after a morning in the fields – to protect the boot from the boot, as it were.

The solution for color coding was created to follow seasons and reasons: brown and blue for autumn-winter; red and silver for spring-summer; moss green for hunting and fishing boots.

Superga's shoe box is opened by simultaneously pulling the two rubber tabs to pop the top, an action possible thanks to the geometry of the gable top (below). The box can be collapsed by pushing on its underside.

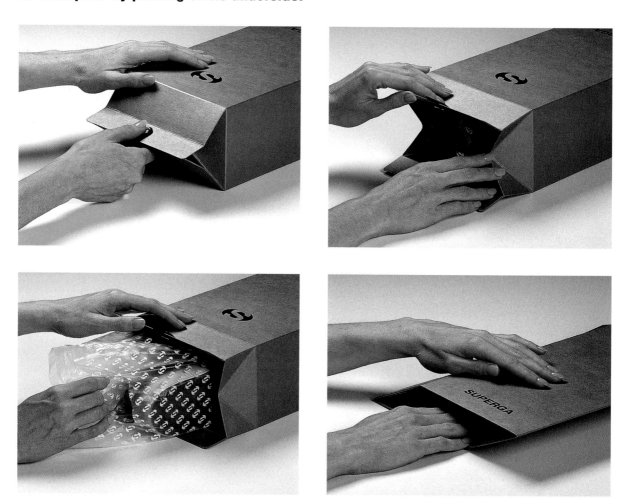

By using a micro-perforated open-ended sleeve (below), shoes can be inserted at each end. The sleeve can then be folded and brought together with handles at either end – a bag with two openings.

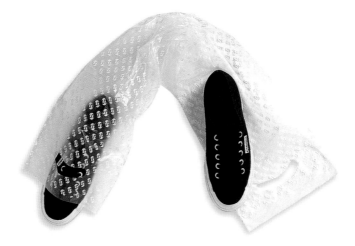

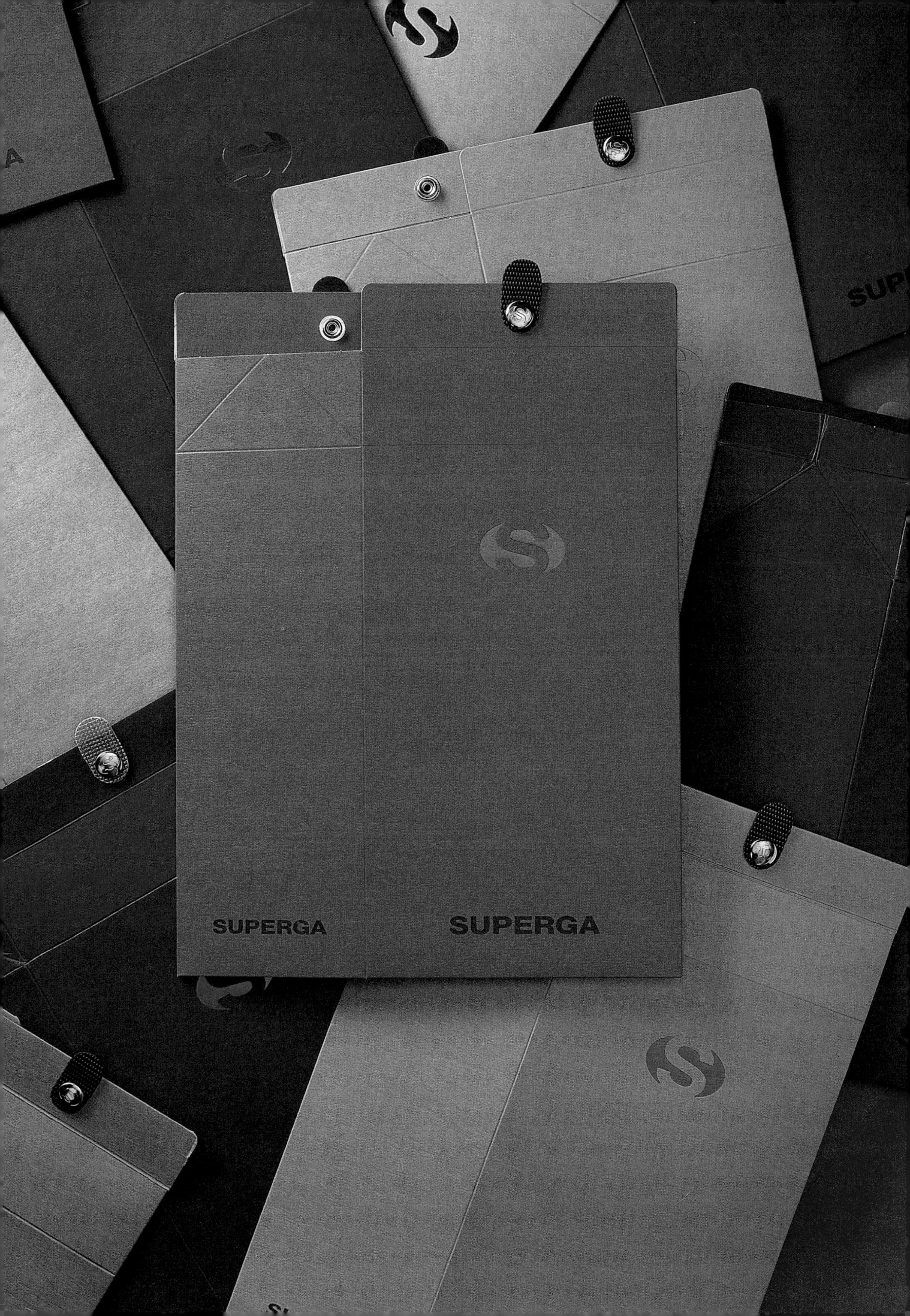
SUPERGA
SUPERGA

A 1990s restaurant interior evokes a 1920s Automat, serving a practical purpose – fulfilling a changing neighborhood's day-long dining needs – and a democratic vision – appealing to the hip without turning off the proletariat.

The Globe Restaurant

Restaurant design in New York City is a search for an enduring balance between the functional and the fantastic. Too much of one without the other, and a new establishment is doomed to be a flash in the pan. With literally hundreds of choices in any given square mile, a hungry customer can afford to pass by a place that doesn't perfectly suit the mood of the moment. The restaurant designer's task, then, is to examine the collective psychology and explore, in a cultural as well as in a culinary sense, neighborhoods, spaces, and people, using the discoveries in each area to drive interior and exterior design. That, indeed, was how The Globe was born. The site that became The Globe Restaurant is located in a fast-changing New York City neighborhood. Within a five-minute walk of its Park Avenue South address are two major hospitals, the townhouse-lined gates of Gramercy Park, several educational institutions, the edge of the new computer

PIZZA

Classic Plum Tom...

Roasted Vegetables...

Wild Mushroom, Roas...
O... Smoked Mo...

...ued R...

ENTRE...

Tuna Frites, with a C...

Grilled Wild Striped Bass... samic...
Wild Mushroom Risotto Cake

Grilled Sirloin with Huge C...
Potatoes and Cara...

Rotisseri...

SIDES

French Fries
Creamy Polenta
SautÈed Spinach
Onion Rings
Mashed Potatoes
Steamed Vegetabl...

communications district called Silicon Alley, and countless corporate offices, including Pentagram's. Two Art Deco landmarks – the Metropolitan Life Insurance building and the gold-capped New York Life Insurance building – anchor the street. In 1997, CS First Boston Corporation, a fast-moving financial services firm, relocated three thousand of its employees to the Met Life building, adding to an already diverse core population of service industry workers, students, and well-heeled residents. The Globe's owners wanted to provide these potential customers with a different kind of service. The model that seemed to represent the scale and atmosphere of the dining experience they sought was the early-twentieth-century New York City cafeteria.

At the turn of the century, restaurants were only for the rich and the rugged. In the 1910s and 1920s, the evolution of American society created a strong new demand for decent, affordable places to eat. During this period, urban populations swelled and a new middle class moved to the suburbs. Commuting left less time to prepare meals at home, and dining out became more and more common. Moreover, business organizations were beginning to function twenty-four hours a day; workers between shifts needed a place to get a hot meal quickly. Advances in science, and the deadly influenza epidemic of 1918, raised public standards of hygiene. People wanted wide open, well-lit interiors where they could assure themselves that food and utensils were clean and properly handled. Cafeterias and Automats, such as the legendary Horn & Hardart and Childs, served these new social expectations.

New York City in the 1990s is experiencing a similar social evolution. New industries are flourishing; the popular culture is health-conscious. The 1980s lust for exclusivity has given way to a yearning for shared experience – witness the rise of public readings at book superstores, or the appearance of Parisian-style cafés. The time was right to revisit the cafeteria concept and update it for modern sensibilities.

As its name suggests, The Globe is large and diverse. Within its six-thousand-square-foot space, take-out and sit-down options are available throughout the day, and the menu covers everything from custom pizzas to oysters on the half shell. Pentagram's design for the new restaurant plays with the referential aspect of The Globe's ethic: it is a new place you have been to before. All the building materials – stainless steel, terrazzo, porcelain enamel, linoleum, brick, vinyl, and aluminum – are time-tested classics, but the installations and

Graphics combining images of the materials used in the restaurant along with photographic cityscapes and a fitting logo of redrawn period typography set an appropriate mood at the Globe.

forms are new. The interior design for the L-shaped space begins with a very active area in front, progresses into a wide-open cafeteria-like dining room in the center, and ends in a softly lit lounge in the ell. Two entrances, one on Park Avenue South and the other on Twenty-sixth Street, set different paces and moods as the customer enters.

The Globe's Park Avenue South facade is clad in a smooth sheath of brushed bronze. The glass front doors and windows reveal the huge, round, stainless-steel counter. In the morning, this rotunda is a beehive of activity as people fetch bagels and coffee to go and tuck into enjoy hot breakfasts at the counter. In the evening the pace slows and the versatile area becomes a bar.

The streetside rotunda is the first of three circular events that not only define the restaurant's offerings but are the only explicit symbols of The Globe name. A host's station is a subtle divider between the counter area and a sea of loose tables bracketed by the widest variety of shaped booths imaginable: round Hollywoods, square eight-seaters, and a line of four-seaters stretching the length of the central space. The next round element is the wood-burning pizza oven at the heel of the L-shaped space, a tower of glazed brick and stone visible from all points. It completes an open kitchen area that positions the food-service style as more diner than fine dining, more theater than theme restaurant. In its massiveness, the oven is also a visual counterbalance to the final round element, the bar, which wraps around the elbow of the ell and takes full advantage of its unique pivotal location. Its three-quarter-round top is white glass, lit from below and offset by a towering, fully stocked backbar.

The bar and its crescent of Hollywood banquettes link the dining area to the lounge around the corner. Here, the tones are darker, the lighting more moody and eccentric, and the walls lined with plush green mohair instead of the shiny white porcelain enamel of the main hall. Multicolored club chairs and a large-scale banquette are lower to the ground and fit precisely the room's cool, reclining atmosphere.

Connecting the multitude of choices in The Globe is a large, multicolored terrazzo floor. The floor is lined in a striped and spotted pattern of red, black, gold, and green, all traditional terrazzo colors with a sense of exuberance. Constellations of eclectic light fixtures create a bright firmament overhead. Big, open, and friendly, new yet comfortably familiar, The Globe is a reinvention of the cafeteria that made New York a home for the world.

Round Hollywood booths circle the bar while the pizza oven terminates the long visual axis from the entrance to the rear of the daytime room. Custom-designed light fixtures include separately adjustable up- and downlighting, allowing the mood to be almost infinitely fine-tuned.

Borrowing elements from the traditional New York cafeteria, the seating ranges from the round front bar/counter to clubby booths surrounding a sea of tables. The corner bar connects the daytime front spaces to the late-night rear lounge around the corner of the ell (below).

The lounge style shifts to soft mohair walls, low club chair seating, colorful Venini glass lighting, and black terrazzo flooring. Although it is open to the main dining space, its location creates a restaurant within a restaurant.

A comprehensive design-management program helps a major retailer project a coherent brand identity across packaging, promotions, point-of-purchase displays, interior architecture, and exterior frontage.

Boots

Boots is one of the best-known names on the British High Street, a traditional chemist, or pharmacist, that also successfully sells beauty products and some time ago branched out into other items such as food, children's clothes, leisure products, and kitchenware. But for all its presence, Boots faced some familiar problems: a lack of coherence in its brand packaging; no clear policy in promoting the values of the brand; no common ground between the graphic and three-dimensional identity elements and, perhaps most significantly, several buying divisions that behaved like separate domains in the way they commissioned and managed design. Pentagram's work with Boots, which began in the 1980s, has sought to address these problems, but not via a conventional relationship between designer and client. We have actually designed very little for Boots – and no packaging whatsoever. Our role has been strictly advisory over a long

period at a very senior level within the company. Our goal has been to make the process of design management work more smoothly for a large retailer.

The struggle at Boots to project a coherent brand identity through its own-label packaging reflected, in our analysis, a complex management problem, not a straightforward design issue. So we looked for a solution not in a short-term quick fix of design guidelines, but in the development of a long-term management strategy that would shape the way design services are procured and design suppliers are treated at Boots. This context set Pentagram in a new consulting role, as the senior design manager working closely with Boots' executives at the board level.

There was a visual incoherence to Boots' packaging that reflected widespread ambivalence about the Boots brand within the company. When products were perceived internally to be poor in quality, Boots' famous lozenge-shaped logo was enlarged to help sell the merchandise. On goods regarded as of high quality, however, the Boots logo was seen as a hindrance and reduced in size. Boots got the packaging it did because of the way it acquired design. There were nine or ten different product fiefdoms, in which junior product managers, most of them a year or two out of university, were commissioning designers. These buyers – inexperienced, open to peer pressure, right at the bottom of the management pyramid – disgorged different interpretations of what the brand stood for.

We suggested that Boots introduce a new system of design purchasing in which different designers would be commissioned, key decisions would be made at a much higher level within the company, and core principles would be established about what the Boots brand represented. Importantly, it had to be done in a way that didn't diminish the junior buyers' motivation. We worked with senior Boots managers to put a new system in place with two central elements. First, a Design Policy Group, operating just below board level, was set up to vet all the briefs and concept solutions agreed upon by product managers and their external design suppliers. Design decision making went straight from the foothills of the company to the top, instead of working up and down through a tortuous line of middle management, which had often blunted objectives.

Pentagram selected a roster of quality packaging-design firms to be briefed on what the core values of the Boots brand were. Initially, only a handful of firms were involved; today, as the program has expanded, there are about twenty. Product managers retained some measure of autonomy, provided they

Pentagram designed a new shopping basket for Boots that reflects the values of the brand in the care it shows for consumers. Its single handle is padded; the basket is rounded, with no sharp corners; and it contains a tray for small items.

sourced their design from this approved roster. We organized workshops for design suppliers, held meetings with product buyers, and hosted exhibitions and parties to build up a team spirit in which everyone involved could pull in the same design direction while interpreting the Boots brand values in their own individual, creative way.

To make this system work more effectively, we needed to define a view of the Boots brand that would be easy to communicate. We went back to the company's roots and described the idea of "the man in the white coat – the nation's chemist." Despite the diversity of Boots' products, we argued that customers could find reassurance, confidence, and security in own-brand goods that visually reflected "the man in the white coat." We believed this concept encapsulated the properties of the brand in the qualities of the pharmacist: trustworthiness, integrity, intelligence, straightforwardness, and professionalism. The only design rules we set focused on the use of the Boots lozenge and the preferred Boots shade of blue.

Yet we accepted that even this amount of change could take Boots' brand image only so far. Many of the three-dimensional design elements that contribute to retail identity – window displays, shopfittings, fixtures, finishes,

fascias, and lighting, for example – remained outside the orbit of the new design management system. And there was no communication whatsoever between the large in-house architectural department, which was responsible for implementing capital projects, and the graphic-design department, although both shared responsibility for managing the brand. We believed that the two should mesh – that the store interior, a box one stands inside, should complement the boxes one views outside.

So five years after the first wave of change, we recommended another innovation. A design executive position was established to oversee design decision making in the three-dimensional and architectural areas of retail identity. New mechanisms were put in place to try to ensure that the graphics and architecture teams within Boots talked to each other more and cooperated more fully in focusing on the brand.

We believe that these three-dimensional design developments support the brand building that has now gone on at Boots for more than a decade. We think they make an added contribution to the constant evolution of a policy that has revealed to Boots the need to manage design consciously, as a corporate asset at the highest levels of the company, in the same way as computing or finance.

The Boots shopping basket shown here is filled with items whose package design, supervised by us, was provided by outside suppliers. Among them: Maddy Bennett, Howard Brown, Chrissie Charlton, Haines McGregor, Lewis Moberly, Lippa Pearce, Ian Logan Design, Newell & Sorrell, Roundel Design, Silk Pearce, Smith & Milton, Trickett & Webb, Tussels Limited, Michael Nash Associates, Point Design, Ali Nash, Frost Design, Bev Whitehead, Workhouse Design, AM Associates, Ruth Tyson, Flo Bayley, and Blast Design.

A new brand of luxury products for the world's largest duty-free retailer is created through retail environments and printed materials that fuse Renaissance paintings with a touch of late-twentieth-century irreverence.

Gianfranco Lotti

DFS Group Limited practically invented the modern duty-free shopping business. Started by Charles Feeney and Robert Miller in 1961 as a single concession in Hong Kong's Kai Tak Airport, the company now operates 180 stores – many of them as large as major department stores – in twelve countries, mostly in the Pacific Rim. In 1996, DFS stores sold about $3 billion worth of merchandise, roughly 15 percent of the industry's $20 billion annual sales. Expansion of duty-free shopping into a global industry has been good for DFS, but with this growth has come increased competition. Travelers who once looked to airport shops for little more than liquor and cigarettes now browse for the latest electronics, perfumes, jewelry, specialty foods, designer apparel, accessories, and much more. Airports themselves are becoming indistinguishable from shopping malls, with brand-name retailers constantly jostling for preflight attention.

DFS determined that one way to compete was to develop its own private-label designer goods, a line with the feel and cachet of established labels.

To provide a foundation for its own-brand effort, DFS in the mid-1990s signed a licensing agreement with a Florentine craftsman named Gianfranco Lotti to develop high-end leather goods to be sold exclusively in DFS stores. But product quality alone wouldn't be enough to set the line apart. The competition for consumer attention included some of the fashion world's most venerable names – Gucci, Cartier, Aquascutum, Giorgio Armani, Gianni Versace, and Louis Vuitton among them. Against this array, Peter Allen, vice president and executive creative director for DFS, knew his new product line required more than pretty packaging. "We needed the look of history – instantly," Allen recalls. "It would have to be finessed."

Allen gave Pentagram the brand-development task, which included designing retail environments in sizes ranging from five-hundred to two-thousand square feet, as well as a full range of product packaging and retail display signage. Our design team relied on a few primary elements. We used a classic typeface – Bodoni, which dates to eighteenth-century Italy – and a muted color palette that mimicked the appearance of fine stones and jewelry by stamping the brand name (Gianfranco Lotti, what else?) in glossy gold on a limestone background. To add true luster and historical depth to the work, we excerpted images painted by the great masters of the Renaissance, among them Bronzino, Ghirlandaio, Gozzoli, Mantegna, Carpaccio, Melozzo da Forli, Botticelli, and Raphael.

To add a personal signature – and a bit of whimsy – to this elegant expression, we incorporated the products themselves into the images, making them appear a part of the paintings, albeit naturally and unobtrusively. Our approach was to play it straight on the primary panels of the packages, but to use the gusset of the bag or the bottom of the box for the visual punchline. It was this slight touch of irreverence that gave the label not only a personality but a sense of confidence, a kind of quiet bravado a consumer would expect only in a product with lineage behind it. These images were used sparingly but effectively throughout the program.

Some identity elements found their way onto the products themselves. A keyhole icon migrated from the storefront awning to a men's necktie, and the color palette was used on numerous products. Gianfranco Lotti proved to be successful in its own right and beneficial to store traffic. But the line was short-lived. Soon after the launch, DFS was acquired by LVMH Moet Hennessy Louis Vuitton, and the new parent elected to pull the product off the market and concentrate its efforts on established labels.

The Gianfranco Lotti brand identity is a study in contrast. Retail environments and core identity components are classic and elegant, offset by a bit of whimsy – achieved by incorporating products themselves into paintings by great masters.

GIANFRANCO LOTTI

FIRENZE

GIANFRANCO LOTTI
FIRENZE

Seating and tables imbued with modernist references provide a new Italian furniture manufacturer with products whose comfort matches their contemporaneity, giving the company the rapid market impact it needs.

Mastrangelo

The opportunity was unusual: to create a range of furniture that would have the express effect of drawing the attention of both the market and the trade to a relatively unknown Italian furniture company. The timing was tight. We had only three months to develop the entire line before we could put it into production to meet the deadline for the 1997 Milan Trade Furniture Show – where Milan-based Mastrangelo was determined to make its presence felt. Mastrangelo appreciated the merits of design driven by genuine conceptual thinking and architectural disciplines. This gave Pentagram's designers a starting point. The Mastrangelo pieces – we created an armchair and two- and three-seater divans, plus a complementary range of occasional tables – would temper eye-catching originality with classic resonances; they would have intriguing structural values, special qualities of comfort, and construction simple enough for cost-effective manufacturing and assembly.

The structure is designed so that the upholstered components of the armchairs and divans can be removed easily for cleaning. This approach also aids the modularity of construction and versatility of finishes.

The armchairs and divans were carefully designed as a meeting of architecture and soft furniture, infused with classic cultural references – notably, the spirit of Le Corbusier and the rigor of Mies van der Rohe. Although these influences are deliberately recognizable, they were employed not to lend nostalgic appeal but because their admirable qualities of structure, form, and design philosophy remain highly relevant. Bridging Le Corbusier and Mies van der Rohe in this way while creating something entirely new inspired the name of the seating products: Link.

We conceived the Link seating for both domestic and office use. Its form is based on the basic geometry of squares. A flat platform for the chair rest and interlocking pad components provide an easily dismantled structure. Although the pads are modular blocks, when assembled they form a continuous volume. The simple construction features a steel base frame with vertical elements that hold these interlocking cushion pads. Made of spring steel, these ele-ments flex very comfortably under the weight of a relaxing body, while sup-porting the back and sides. The cushion pads can be finished in various fabrics or colored leather, to promote further the furniture's unique suitability in a variety of settings.

The design included several visual tricks. Looking from the side, the viewer sees only one leg; the volumes seem to float magically. A walk behind the divan reveals the secret: the feet are actually set off from the four corners of the base frame. The rear, however, is not meant to be hidden. Unlike so much seating, contemporary or traditional, Link does not have a best angle; the back is as aes-thetically appealing as the front.

The tables were designed to com-pliment Link. They were given the name Chase because the legs are set away from the four corners – sequenced, or chasing each other around the table. Available in three sizes, the tabletops come in etched glass or a distinctive glass laminated with mirrored material in blue, yellow, or silver.

The geography of the varisized units was conceived with a clear modulation, which expands from the single-seater to the three-seater. The tables were designed to complement each configuration.

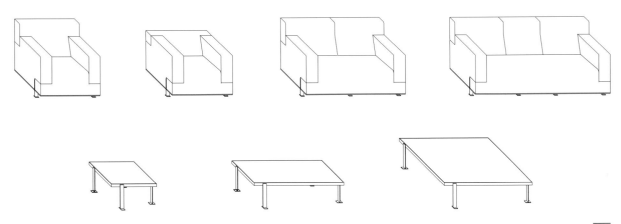

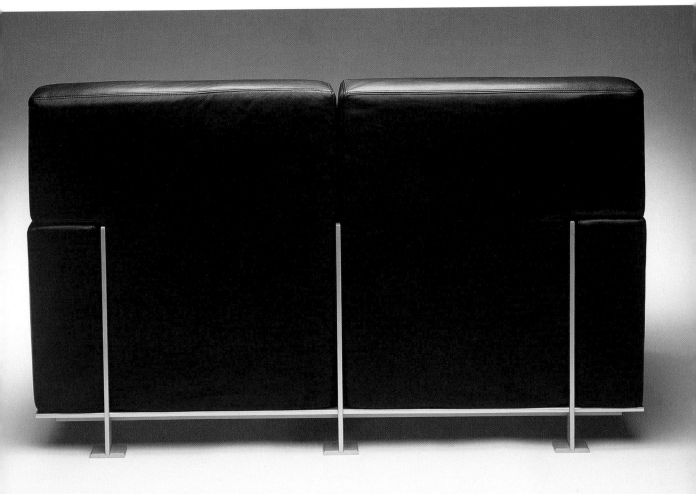

Graphics for a new craft-beer maker celebrate the independent spirit of this revived American profession without resorting to the nostalgia that infuses so much of the microbrew movement.

Flying Fish Brewery

In the 1970s the first wave of microbreweries, small-quantity beer producers, began bubbling up in the western United States. While some considered the craft-beer movement a pleasant but passing fad, beer enthusiasts warmed to a variety of new flavors and forgotten styles. Within the last decade, a veritable industry has gathered steam. Gene Muller ditched his corporate job and joined its ranks in the spring of 1994, bringing only his resourcefulness – and Pentagram – along with him. Muller had first come in contact with us two years earlier when, as the creative director at Albert Einstein Healthcare Network in Philadelphia, he hired us to redesign its institutional identity. Later, on vacation out West, he and a friend noted the successes of several new microbreweries. Somewhere in Arkansas, they conspired to quit their day jobs and bring the idea home to Philadelphia, the fifth-largest beer market in America.

Muller had spent ten years in the advertising business; the right brand identity, he knew, would be critical in making the connection between his product and his target market, and in distinguishing his package at the point of purchase. "When you're a startup, all you have is your story and your business plan," says Muller. "Anything else you can bring in terms of credibility and credence is really important."

He incorporated Flying Fish Brewing Company in Cherry Hill, New Jersey, where a hundred beer makers – all now vanished – had operated at the turn of the century. Flying Fish could have exploited its fortuitous local tradition. But Muller rejected nostalgia. "There were already enough clipper ships and revolutionary war heroes on the store shelves, and besides," says Muller, "the world wasn't waiting for New Jersey beer. This was a new venture for new times. The Flying Fish brand called for something smart and contemporary, a visual identity that had the handmade quality and seat-of-the-pants appeal of the microbrew phenomenon itself."

The graphic design program is based on a speedy little drawing of propellored fish bones surrounded by a red border. Printed white against a black background, the Flying Fish symbol has the dashing antiestablishment aspect of a pirate flag. Barware, six-packs, and shipping cases feature wry applications of the emblem, the chosen Matrix typeface, and eye-catching patches of multicolored sky. The sketchy skeleton captured Muller's swashbuckler-meets-bootlegger marketing concept, and the professionally produced graphics sent a firm message to investors, vendors, and potential customers that he was serious about the brewing business.

"A well thought-out and comprehensive identity made all the difference," Muller says. "It really showed investors we could market something that didn't exist yet. Without it, I don't think I ever would have gotten the financing I needed."

Labels and cartons incorporate the Flying Fish symbol and combine it with several color variations of a cloudy sky pattern. The wraparound type allows for a posterlike reading at the point of purchase.

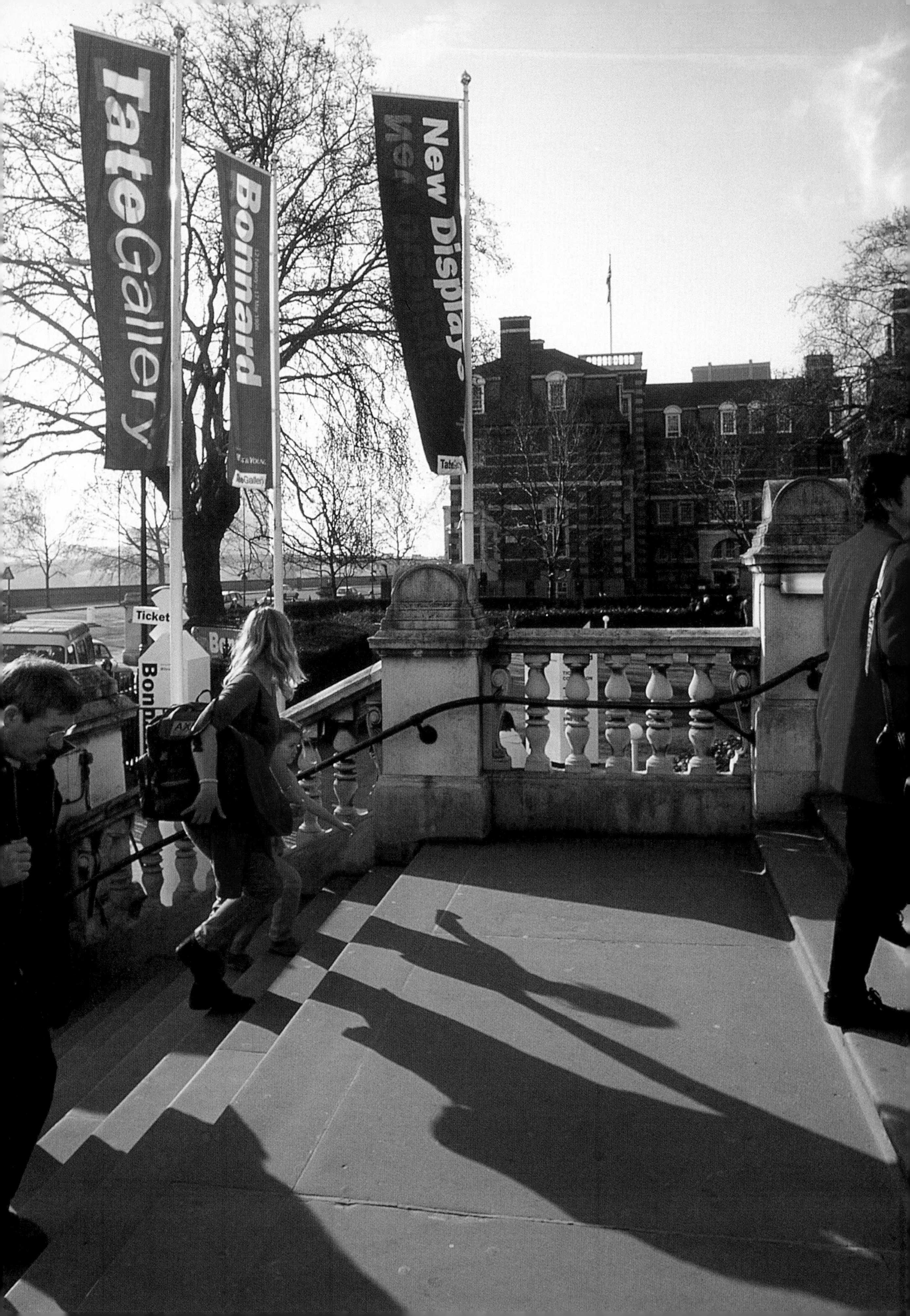
TateGallery
Bonnard
New Displays
Ticket

Several museums are unified under a common brand umbrella, which – through the clever use of color and typography – allows each to retain its own identity and paves the way for future expansion.

The Tate

The Tate has grown from one gallery to three, with plans to open a fourth at London's Bankside by the year 2000. Each has its own individual identity but also has to emphasize its place within the Tate organization. The Tate galleries in London, Liverpool, and St. Ives have common ownership but all serve very different purposes. The Tate at London's Millbank houses the country's leading collection of British art, Liverpool exhibits contemporary art, St. Ives concentrates on the St. Ives School of Art, and the new gallery at Bankside will focus on modern art. Having worked first with the Tate gallery in Liverpool, we have now established a long-term relationship with each gallery in the group and have created an identity to help represent the different members of the Tate family in a more relevant way. All the galleries share one Tate name and mark but each has its own exclusive typeface for promotional and marketing materials.

This appears on everything from posters promoting upcoming events to paper bags used in the gift shops. There is a family likeness and consistency but the individual personalities are retained. The identity system is also intended to be as flexible as possible and can be expanded in response to change and growth within the Tate organization.

In 1990 the director of the Tate gallery at Millbank carried out a complete rehanging of the collection – the most radical and extensive since the gallery's opening in 1897. It wasn't just the collection that the Tate wanted to overhaul – it also needed a new corporate identity, sign system, and clearer literature to herald the changes taking place in what had been, until that point, a rather conservative organization.

As we had previously worked on an identity for the Tate in Liverpool, the brief was to develop a low-key, timeless logotype that, while standing out, would not compete with the art being displayed. It also had to use a typeface specially cut for the gallery in the early 1980s by type designers Michael Harvey and Herbert Spencer.

The new logotype appeared on posters, catalogs, and other promotional literature in the Tate's house colors of red and gray. It also played a part in a new identity for the annual Turner Prize. When the prize was first set up in 1984, it was an award for the greatest contribution to art in Britain. In 1991 the criteria were modified, awarding the prize to an outstanding exhibition or presentation by an artist under fifty years of age. We developed a tripartite identity that linked the prize to the gallery and to the sponsor, Channel 4 television. A brochure and four posters were also produced to promote an exhibition of work by each of the four short-listed artists.

It was around this time that we were asked to look at the identity of the Tate in St. Ives. However, with plans for Bankside under way, we suggested that rather than continue to invent new identities we would produce an identity that underscored the individuality of each gallery but also signalled that they were all part of the larger Tate organization.

These separate but interlinked identities have now been applied to everything from signage, literature, and posters to leaflets, invitations, events, and wrapping paper used in Tate gift shops. We have also developed some merchandise for the shops and helped the galleries select the right images for posters promoting exhibitions to make them appeal to as wide a cross section of the public as possible.

For the new Artnow gallery at the Tate Millbank, which provides artists with space for experimental installations, we produced an identity, signage, and a template for catalogs. Much of the art is off the edge, which we have expressed both typographically and by bleeding images in the literature.

The bled-off Artnow logo is used consistently on signage and all associated literature. Although the gallery is part of the main building, it was decided that an individual identity was required to reflect the art appearing there.

artnow
1
artnow
Exhibition Sponsors
1995–6
CDT
Häagen-Dazs
Exhibition Donors
1995–6
artnow

We built as much flexibility as possible into the poster series to allow the differing subject matters and painting styles to express themselves. The consistent elements are the identity and the use of Franklin Gothic heavy and Janson plain as the typefaces.

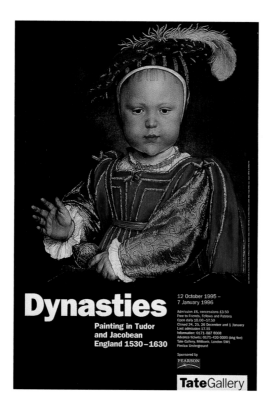

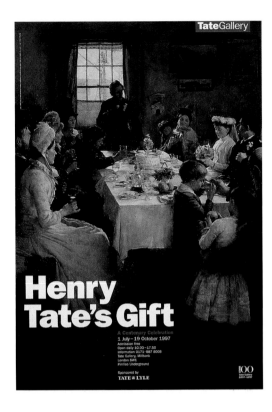

Only painting details are allowed to be bled; when the whole painting is used, it has to float in space. Each poster is reproduced in a variety of sizes, doing double duty as advertisements outside the museum proper and as mementos of the respective exhibitions.

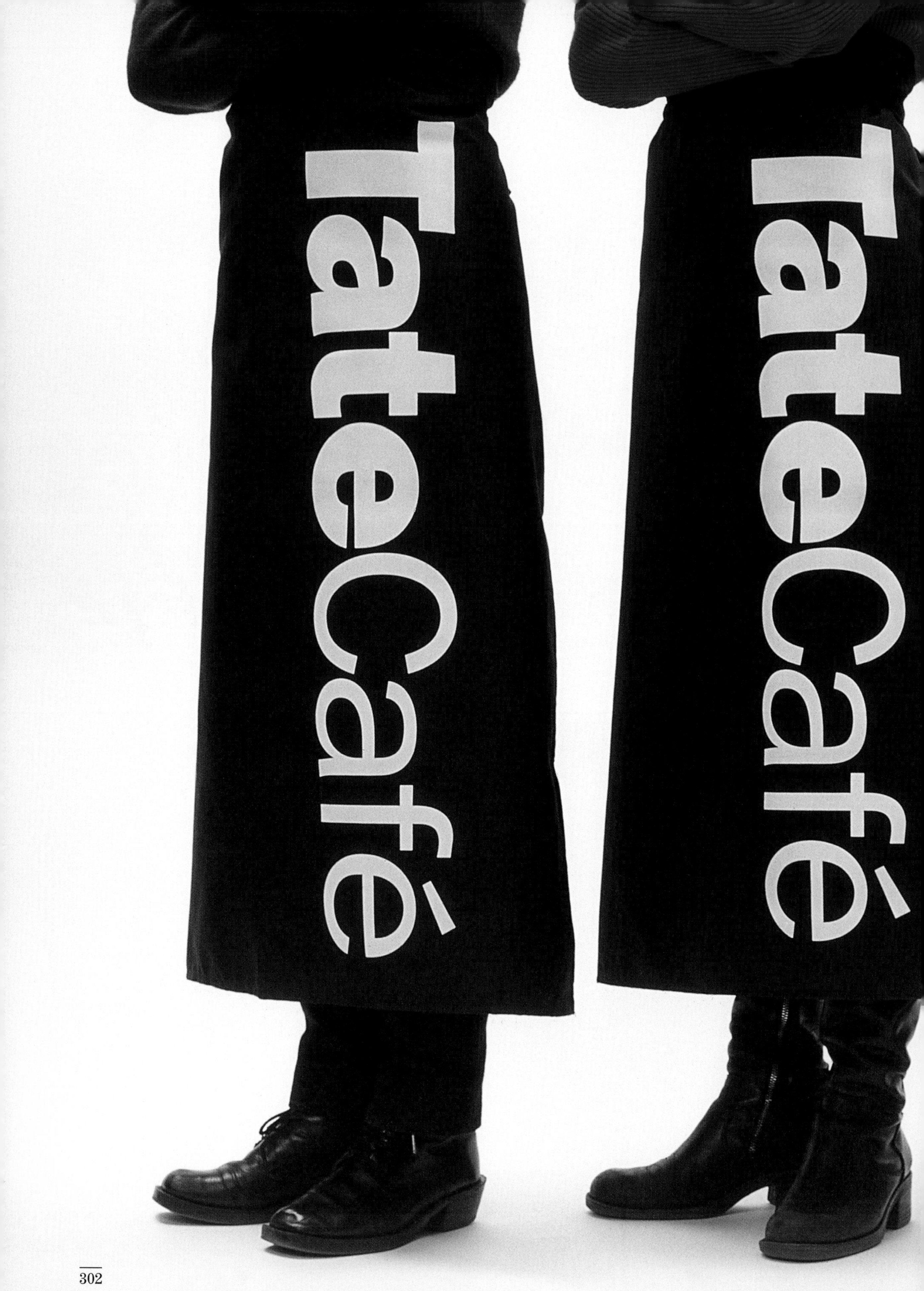
TateCafé
TateCafé

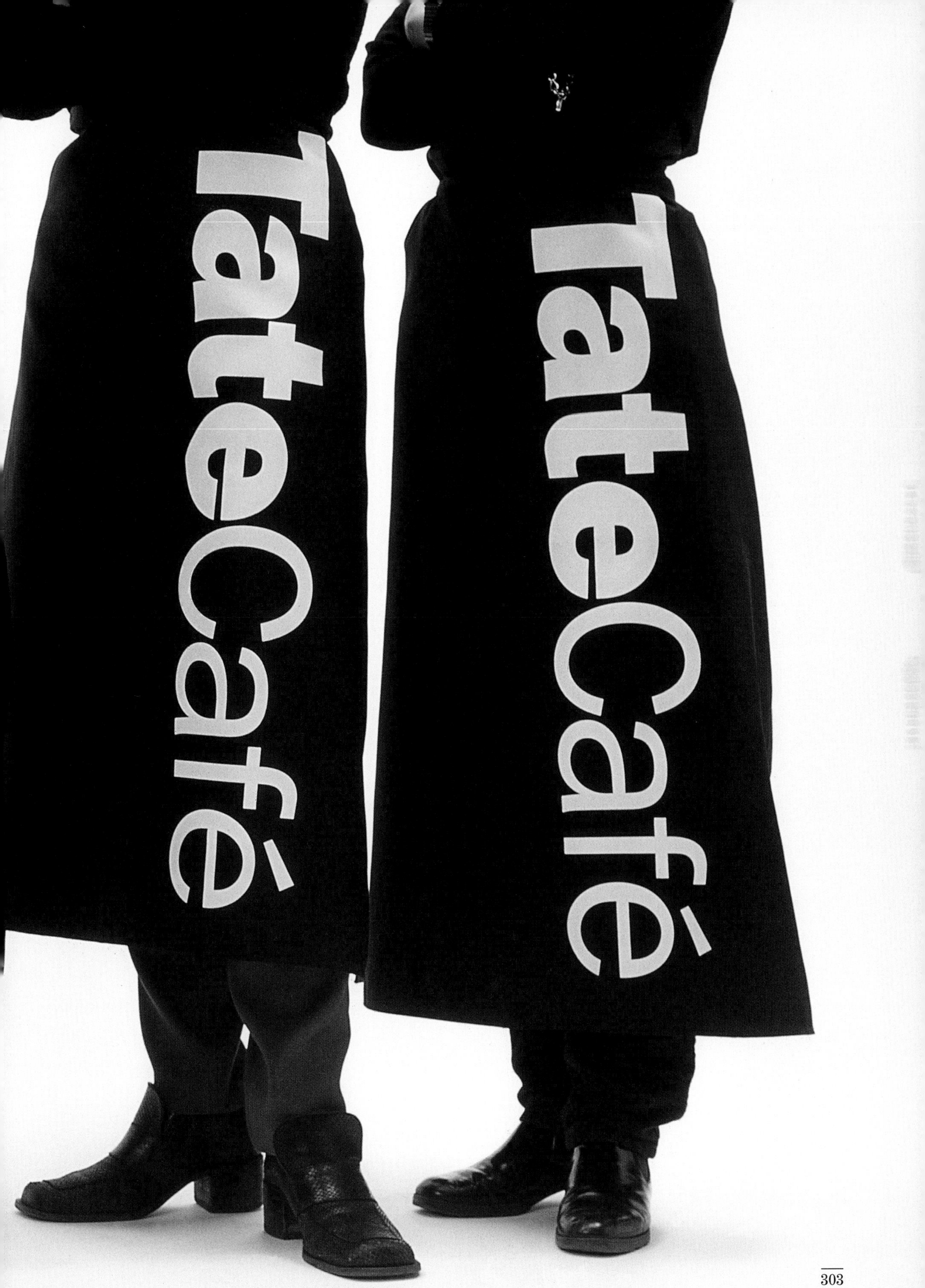
TateCafé
TateCafé

The signage at the Tate required utmost flexibility to cope with the gallery's changing exhibition needs. The freestanding Mondrian sign is an example of the "permanent" signage system, which had to be movable and updatable as well.

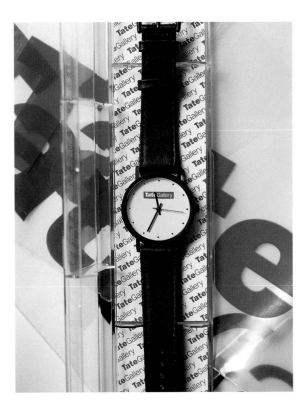

The consistent use of the Tate identity is played out across signage, external and internal, literature, and gift-shop items. The identity for the Tate Café and Restaurant, intended to be noticeable but unobtrusive, encompasses signage, packaging, and uniforms.

A new design identity and publications program sharpens the image of one of the founding colleges of the University of London, necessary with the rapid enlargement of the university system in Britain.

King's College London

King's College London is one of the two founding colleges of the University of London. It is a multifaculty institution with an enviable reputation for research. This is where Maurice Wilkins won his Nobel Prize for work on the structure of DNA, where Charles Wheatstone invented telegraphy, where Desmond Tutu studied theology, where Arthur C. Clarke studied science fact. By the early 1990s, Britain's university system was growing rapidly as part of government education policy. This meant that established universities had more competition, not just for students but also for government and research funding. King's responded with a new design identity that projected the college's senior status and traditions within a new and well-ordered visual presentation. The identity work led to the development of a raft of new publications for external and internal use, headed by the prospectuses for undergraduates and postgraduates and the flagship yearly review. The design program culminated in the transfer of skills and responsibility for its application to in-house designers.

King's College London was reluctant to give up the strong academic traditions represented by its old identity; it was also felt that students wanted to identify with this solid reputation rather than with anything of a more modish style. So the new logotype was designed to represent King's status and aims in a modern context while acknowledging its historical position.

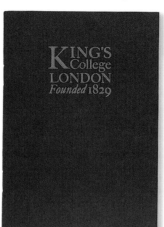

The typeface chosen for the logo was Caslon Old Face, originally cut in the middle of the eighteenth century by William Caslon, who worked in Chiswell Street in the City of London, not far from the main campus of King's in the Strand. The logo includes "Founded 1829," which distinguishes the academic rank of the college, proclaiming its heritage and giving it an edge over newer rivals. An additional identifying element in King's print is the use of the Caslon ampersand instead of the word "and" in titles and headings.

The new logotype, the primary corporate color of red, and the new typography were introduced for stationery. Specifications were also drawn up for other general applications, such as publications, print, and signs. Publications, from student recruitment brochures and prospectuses to annual reviews and alumni magazines, were redesigned to support the overall quality of presentation from the college and to build its characteristic design identity.

The distinctive work of leading photographer Phil Sayer also helped build the unique visual character of the college. The *Report*, which is the yearly review of King's research and teaching achievements, was conceived from scratch with an editorial plan devised by David Gibbs, who became the regular editor. While most university annual reviews ape commercial annual reports, the *Report* was conceived as a magazine. The novel style and editorial platform attracted much attention, and in 1996 the *Report* won the HEIST award for best university review of the year. In the same year, the undergraduate prospectus also won its category in the HEIST awards. Along with its sister publication, the postgraduate prospectus, the approach to the design has been themed on imagery of students.

The most recent application of the design identity has been in signing the college estate. King's has four campuses in London, and with the medical school merging with St. Thomas's and Guy's in 1998, signs have taken on a new importance in promoting and maintaining the King's College identity.

In a world of graphics driven by technology, the decision to stay true to King's College's senior status and tradition is apparent in the intimate booklet documenting the identity philosophy and fundamentals, literature, and signage.

A new design for the King's College logotype is being introduced. This will become the College's prime marque of identity.

The design is part of a more ordered approach being adopted in the overall visual presentation of the College.

The King's College coat of arms and the Fougasse rendition of the College mascot Reggie play a limited role in the new scheme.

Although the coat of arms is to be retained for certain uses, it has been decided that it is not suitable for the prime marque of identity.

Because it is very common for universities and colleges to use their coats of arms as their prime visual representation, King's by following suit suffers from a certain lack of distinctiveness.

The new logotype has been designed to represent *King's College* distinctively, in a way that is sensitive to its identity and in keeping with its status and its aims. It also acknowledges *King's* historical roots. The typeface used for the marque is called *Caslon Old Face.*

Only the form of the marque shown here may be used; any variations would dilute the recognition of the logotype. The last line should always be retained: it adds visual balance to the logotype and distinguishes the academic rank of the College, among the oldest in the land.

KING'S
College
LONDON
Founded 1829

Caslon Old Face, chosen for the new *King's* logotype, has particularly apt connotations. *William Caslon* was one of the greatest of the early English type cutters, working at his foundry in Chiswell Street in the City of London, not far from the Strand site of *King's College.*

Originally cut towards the middle of the eighteenth century, *Caslon Old Face* was *William Caslon's* most famous and popular typeface, and in common use when *King's* was established.

18pt Caslon Old Face
ABCDEFGHIJKLMNOP
QQUQuRSTUVWXYZ
ABCDEFGHIJKLMNOPQRSTUVWXYZ
abcctdefghijklmnopqrstuvwxyz
ff fi fl ffi ffl [(' , ; : . - ? !)]
1234567890 & £ $

Caslon Old Face Italic
ABCDEFGHIJKLMNOPRS
TUVWXYZ
A B C D E G J K M N P
2U 2u R T Y h k v w
abcctdefghijklmnopqrstuvwxyz
ff fi fl ffi ffl (' , ; : . - ? !)
1234567890 & £ $

The new logotype may be used in conjunction with the University of London designation, as shown.

KING'S College
LONDON
Founded 1829

UNIVERSITY OF LONDON

The King's College coat of arms will only be used when suitable on the more formal and official documentation emanating from the College.

By allocating the coat of arms this more exclusive role, it will lend prestige and dignity as appropriate to such items as examination diplomas and certificates as well as acting as a legitimising device on legal and official titles and documents.

Reggie the King's mascot, whose colourful history can be traced back to the early 1920s, is held in great affection by alumni, students and staff.

One of King's famous sons was the illustrator and cartoonist Fougasse, nom de plume of Kenneth Bird. He was an engineering student at King's from 1904 to 1908 and was the first Student President of the University of London Union.

Of the many Fougasse renditions of Reggie, the one shown here may be adopted for less formal, internal use by students and staff, on such items as student magazines and posters. Reggie should not be used, however, in any way as a replacement or additional marque on stationery or publications.

In summary, the new scheme being adopted for visual presentation of King's College has three elements, which are to be used for prescribed applications.

The prime marque of identity is the new logotype for day-to-day use on stationery, publications and other print, as well as on signs and other general applications.

The coat of arms is to be used more exclusively where it will provide an endorsement of status and dignity to formal items.

A particular Fougasse rendition of Reggie may be used for less formal, internal applications by students and staff.

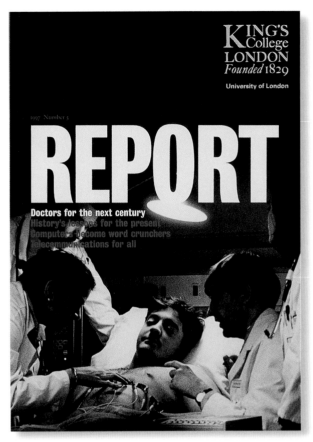

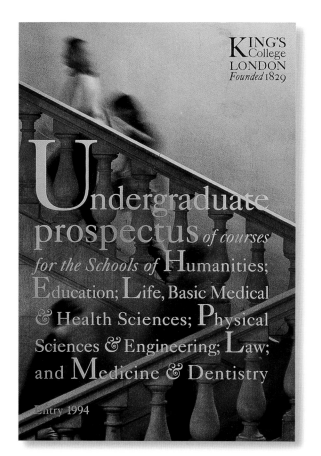

A new graphic system, derived from a company's Yankee heritage and its archives, brings a venerable shoe and apparel maker back from the brink of commodification – and enables the creation of a new product line as well.

G.H. Bass & Company

Every American – well, every boating American, or at least every would-be Kate Hepburn or George Bush – knows G.H. Bass & Co. Its Bass Weejun moccasins have been the boat shoe of choice for generations of New England gentry, not to mention a myriad of other down-easters. By the mid-1990s, however, the American footwear and apparel manufacturer Phillips-Van Heusen Corporation (PVH) was on the verge of destroying the good name of its Bass subsidiary. PVH was flooding retail outlets with Bass shoes, clothing, and accessories in an effort to position it as a value brand. The tactic succeeded only in cheapening the Bass name and its merchandise. "We were harvesting the brands, not investing in them," says Bruce J. Klatsky, PVH's chairman, chief executive, and president. The erosion, which was also evident in the aging of the company's customer base, was reflected in PVH's stock price, which plummeted from forty dollars per share in early 1994 to a low of nine dollars in late 1996. The negligence was apparent in Bass's existing visual communications, which were a mix of unrelated corporate identity elements. In their efforts to distinguish product lines and attributes, internal merchandising groups degraded the overall integrity of the Bass brand. They used disparate imagery and messages, such that consumers could see only isolated fragments of a very blurry corporate image.

Recognizing the problem, PVH in 1995 retained the architects Bergmeyer Associates to redesign the presentation of G.H. Bass & Co. in department stores and outlets. Bergmeyer recommended Pentagram to consult on the treatment of identity and package design. Together, the client, architects, and designers agreed on a thematic direction that came out of Bass's New England past: the general store.

Until the early twentieth century (and to this day in some places), the small-town general store was where rural Americans obtained everything from food and hardware to candy and cloth. These shops were typically spare, displaying goods in plain wrappings on open shelves. Evolving from the refashioned retail environments, the new graphic designs for Bass – on shoe boxes, hang tags, shopping bags, and other packaging – would come out of modern nostalgia for such simplicity.

The graphic assignment was not a simple matter of creating a new logo, tags, and shoe boxes, but a complicated process of developing a unified visual system for a spectrum of communications. Yet, as is typical of a large, contemporary apparel company, the work still had to be produced by various internal design departments and art directors, external advertising agencies, public relations firms, and others. There had to be a certain level of design consistency to rebuild the brand, but enough variety to motivate the creative staff.

Market research showed that Bass's erosion had not advanced beyond the critical point: consumers still had strong recognition of the brand, a familiarity based on its true product heritage. The original Weejun moccasin had been around for 120 years, and people knew that Bass made shoes and

had factories in Maine. These messages had been delivered through a history of communications that focused on New England's outdoor pleasures – camping, fishing, sailing, canoeing, and so on. We recommended that Bass use this Yankee legacy as the defining characteristic of a new visual personality.

With the Bass archive to draw from – almost a hundred years worth of print ads and promotions catalogued by the corporate librarian and proudly displayed in Bass's Maine headquarters – the designers were able to play with historical images. The new G.H. Bass & Co. logotype is a pastiche of bygone typographic treatments freshly rendered in Caslon 540, a classic typeface with a proper British pedigree. The logo is used in combination with icons and tinted photographs that represent the urbane side of down-east life. From a 1990s perspective, some of the images seem naive, even comical, but they treat consumers to a refreshing view of simpler times.

In keeping with the general-store concept, Pentagram also conceived a new line of food, gardening, and gift products made in New England and sold exclusively in Bass stores under the "Spirit of Maine" brand name. Uncomplicated Yankee style is reflected in the restrained graphics and spare package forms: black-and-white maritime photos and Harvard-crimson accents are the only decoration printed on the uncoated white labels. The packaging program has earned several design awards, including a Gold Industrial Design Excellence Award (IDEA) in the prestigious international competition sponsored by the Industrial Designers Society of America and *Business Week* magazine.

In his fourth-quarter 1997 letter to shareholders, PVH Chairman Klatsky pointed to the importance of the company's brand revival. "We understood from the beginning that our game plan of upgrading and repositioning our brands was no simple task and that it would not come without some disappointments along the way," he said. "However, we believe we are on the right course and that the rewards of investing in and building our brands will be substantial."

The packaging for a revitalized G.H. Bass & Co. relies on a classically designed logo-type (in Caslon 540), coupled with black-and-white historical advertising from the G.H. Bass & Co. archives in Wilton, Maine, that has been converted to a pastel color palette.

men's

ular Fit

gh the hip. Tapered to the knees.
, durable denim. 100% cotton.

.H. BASS & CO.
SINCE 1876

PRODUCERS OF QUALITY
SINCE 1876
G.H. BASS & CO.
CASUAL ACCESSORIES

Mens

BAS
MOCCA.

The Ideal
footwear
for all
Sports

UINE MOCCASIN
STRUCTION

The "Spirit of Maine" was invented as a sub-brand of Bass. Products created in Maine, such as jellies, jams, and pancake mix, were packaged and sold as companions to the larger brand in the retail store, keeping with the general-store theme.

A bold and basic identity campaign, carried through from iconography to restroom lighting, signals a motorway service company's confidence in itself, persuading travelers to stop and smell the coffee at places they usually avoid.

Granada Hospitality

Granada Hospitality, a division of the U.K.'s largest leisure and entertainment company, operates thirty-five service areas along Britain's motorway network. After some three decades in the business, the company knew its market – and knew its market was, increasingly, driving right on by. For years, service-area owners had counted on a comfortable monopoly. If drivers needed to stop for refreshment and rest, they had no choice but to accept low standards and poor quality. Granada's properties had deteriorated to such an extent that, at best, they were merely utilitarian; at worst, they were downright scruffy. Even the newer facilities, while cleaner and more modern, lacked consistency and consideration. And therein lay the problem. By the 1990s, cars could go longer distances on a single tank of fuel, more comfortably and quietly than ever. Travelers did not have to stop as frequently. Granada Hospitality needed to show that it could provide drivers with the respite and services they really wanted and needed. That meant challenging the prevailing culture of motorway service areas, proving that they were places where drivers could genuinely remove themselves from their journey for a while, not just to fill their tanks and their stomachs but also to refresh their heads. If Granada could do so, more drivers would stop – a simple yet salutary business concept.

The company decided to use design as the signifier of its new attitude and strategy and was receptive to several quite radical ideas on how to achieve it. In 1996 Granada chose its Stafford motorway service area in England's Midlands as a test site for a comprehensive refurbishment, complete with a new visual identity.

The thrust of the program for Pentagram was to simplify and unify the communicative chaos that had prevailed. The exterior directional signage, for example, was a cacophony of words and pictograms, slapped on haphazardly over the course of many years. But unity itself was not enough. We believed that a bold front – the graphic equivalent of a thrust-out chest – would signal a new and improved self-confidence on Granada's part and make drivers comfortable with the idea of stopping for a spell.

The graphic identity is built around a red G in a circle. The circular theme is picked up in the external signs, where the communications system is based on discs, with each disc limited to a single message. Multiple discs are mounted vertically or horizontally. Words are kept to a minimum; the main messages are represented by internationally recognized pictograms. Along with the new signs, drivers are welcomed by clearly lit, giant pillar signs with the big red G above canopied information points, which give further directions while providing protection from the weather.

The design team paid great attention to architectural and contextual detail throughout the Stafford motorway service area, reasoning that the particulars would project a comfortable assuredness to consumers. Outside, we provided display space for a local museum, which put up plaques with items of interesting regional information. Our idea was to minimize the feeling of limbo in which drivers find themselves at most service stops. Inside, the station's public areas represent our belief that generous design has a noticeable civilizing effect. The patterned carpets that had been installed to disguise dirty floors were done away with. In their stead floors of polished wood and terrazzo were chosen.

No motorway service company in the U.K. had a simple, strong graphic device. Hence Granada's _G_ – which we also thought of as a happy exclamation. Our dream is that customers will eventually talk about visiting "the big G."

A new Granada Coffee Bar was added at Stafford. Fusing together elements of a boulevard brasserie, an American diner, and a Knightsbridge café, the space was created to offer the best coffee, fresh juices, and food with comfort and panache. The bar has no windows, allowing motorists to forget the outside world for a moment. The exterior signage program was extended to the interior, with red upper-case initials, each in a circle, identifying the individual service bays. Fluorescent tubes, which give human skin a ghastly green pallor, were banished; lighting was carefully detailed throughout the architecture, where it spotlit features of the interior. Pentagram also created a new self-service restaurant at Stafford. Glazed tiles, black canopies with white lettering, and down-lit islands give it the resonance of an up-market food hall.

The design team gave toilet areas special consideration. Although rest rooms are typically the traveler's first experience at a service area, they are also the place where companies are prone to seek cuts in cost, thus casting a grim aura around the whole experience. We made each stall wider and replaced the thin boards that had separated the stalls with terrazzo panels. In the women's rest room, we installed multiple mirrors and engraved circles into the glass to give each patron the feeling of looking into a private mirror.

Pentagram attempted to refine not only the design but the services and the way they were offered at Stafford. We asked Granada to give one staff person responsibility for offering free windshield, ashtray, and auto-carpet cleaning to motorists entering the service station. To facilitate this task, Ralph Selby created a mobile unit, based on a three-wheeled industrial scooter. This creation contained a vacuum and water pump. Although the company later decided to abandon this service, it proved a big hit with travelers, who went so far as to give gratuities to the young cleaners.

Granada, too, profited substantially from the new identity program. Corporate research revealed that people using Granada's Stafford motorway services were spending more time and money per person per visit than the average at the company's other locations. With motorway traffic projected to grow in Britain well into the next century, Granada Hospitality is now equipped with a proven formula to increase its share of an expanding market, and has begun applying the design principles established at Stafford to all thirty-five of its sites on the U.K. motorway network.

The coffee bean, in all its glory, was given iconic status at the Granada Coffee Bar. Individual beans were displayed in glass cases, framed by panels of wood and linear stainless-steel trim.

In the Granada Coffee Bar, functional devices and construction elements use contrasting translucent and solid materials to convey privacy, relaxation, quality, even humor. Note the light reflector made out of a baking mold and drinking glass.

When travelers pull into a service area, they are generally looking for something specific, and are often in a hurry. We adopted a pictorial signing system with each graphic element on a separate disk, allowing for different combinations. Where the symbol was directional, we bent the supporting pole to increase the power of the message.

Protective trims and other building details and essentials are geometrically arranged to add rhythm and value to the architecture of the Granada Coffee Bar (above) and the self-service restaurant (right).

By avoiding the obvious – angles, colors, and sizes – a temporary trade-fair exhibit creates a new family of applications, and indeed a new market, for a construction material so familiar as to seem almost traditional.

Dupont Corian

Product design can be described as the art of working with materials to communicate an idea. Some design goes further, asking a series of "what ifs" to challenge assumptions about the nature of a project and the materials it employs. The exhibit that Pentagram created for DuPont Corian, a synthetic solid-surfacing material used pervasively on kitchen and bathroom counters and sinks, at the 1996 International Contemporary Furniture Fair is a good example of this investigative type of design. Corian was an extremely well-known material and brand name, yet it was appearing at the prestigious ICFF for the first time in its thirty-year history. DuPont wanted to grow the market beyond the one Corian had long dominated. Furniture, the company reasoned, was an underutilized application. Having little familiarity with that market, however, DuPont called Pentagram. None of us had very much experience with Corian. So the design team began with questions.

What else could this material do? Could it be jazzed up?

The breakthroughs began in a conversation with Corian's chief engineer, who explained that the material's narrow palette – it was most frequently seen in off-whites and earth tones, or as imitation stone – was predicated not on chemical limitations but on consumer desires in the 1960s, when Corian was coming into its own. The same was true of the way it was manufactured; Corian was made in thirty-inch-wide strips because that was the average width of a countertop-plus-backsplash.

So we decided to play. We avoided all horizontal surfaces, eliminating anything that might suggest the material's familiar applications. The design team built two nine-inch-thick, twelve-foot-high Corian walls, which combine to define a dynamic twenty-by-thirty-foot exhibition space.

The first wall displayed the results of our experiments with color. To show that imitating stone was not the last word for Corian, we developed a custom family of bold, contemporary hues that included violet, an edgy pale green, and a glowing safety orange. The blocks of color spell out "Corian?" – the question we expected would be asked by startled observers at the furniture fair.

The second wall, slightly curved and set perpendicular to the first one, screams the answer: "Corian!" Pushing the design limits in another direction, it narrated our exploration of the material's physical qualities. Here, Corian was subjected to carving, routing, thermoforming, drilling, and sandblasting. The patterns that resulted were flooded with light from behind, revealing the unsuspected translucent beauty of the material and creating an arresting and memorable sight in the crowded exhibition hall.

To highlight even more the versatility of the material, Pentagram built furniture from Corian. Rather than commission new designs that might distract fairgoers' attention from the material, we opted to produce a collection of classic pieces – chairs by Rietveld, Mackintosh, and Jacobsen; tables by Eames, Le Corbusier, and Kiesler. All were built using conventional fabrication techniques.

There were limitations to the way Corian could be used, which the designers discovered during the research. Some solid colors were too easily marked and scratched; a pure black Corian product was not yet feasible. Yet the 1996 ICFF successfully proved that Corian could be taken from the kitchen and assume its rightful place in the living rooms, bedrooms, and offices of discerning customers. Less than two years later, it is no longer a question mark.

Corian baseball bats, milled by Louisville Slugger, proved to be a big hit in the interior-design industry, and a perfect complement to the now famous colorful leather baseballs.

To underline the relevance of Corian for the furniture designers at the ICFF show, the exhibit also included classics of twentieth-century furniture reinterpreted in the material. Black and white were chosen to contrast with the colorful "Corian?" wall.

Translucency, a less well known characteristic of Corian, is explored in virtually every form of manipulation possible, including routing, carving, sandblasting, inlay, drilling, forming, lamination, and shaping. All transformations are displayed in a touchable, illuminated wall.

Utilizing design cues from traditional radios along with familiar handheld electronic products helps fashion a device to guide consumers through the new terrain of radio-on-demand.

Command Audio

In the mid-1990s, while technology and media companies were experimenting with video on demand and interactive TV, an engineer in northern California set out to solve a different problem. How could people caught in captive situations make better use of their time? He was judging from his own experience: he wanted to be able to stay informed, to learn, and to enjoy entertainment programs he wanted when he wanted. So he started Command Audio Corporation, which developed a radio-on-demand service. The company offers hundreds of daily programs in audio form and transmits them wirelessly to a proprietary compact radio receiver. For the first time, continuously updated and personalized information, such as traffic, news, stock quotes, and sports scores, would be available when wanted. All programs would start when the consumer was ready to listen, with a controllable unit that would pause, skip, replay, and even save selections.

Better yet, Command Audio's technology was smart – the receiver would learn a user's preferences and offer other selections expected to be of interest to that listener.

The company engaged Pentagram to design the navigation system, content organization methods, and appearance. The challenges were significant, because the product was mainly for use in the car. Allowing consumers to find the shows they wanted quickly and easily, while driving a car at high speed, was a great challenge. To enable safe usage while in a car, an eyes-free design was imperative. A handheld design was chosen to eliminate the need to install it in the vehicle and to allow use while exercising, gardening, and so forth.

Using a software program, Macromedia Director, we experimented and designed with different kinds of interfaces and feedback methods and then built several prototypes. We wanted to borrow familiar metaphors for the operation of the unit to speed consumer acceptance and reduce learning time. An intuitive metaphor for the playback operation was the transport controls found on CD players, which also carried over to the functions of pausing, skipping, and saving. But the interface also needed to provide a way for the consumer to browse the programs offered on the service and then a method for consumers to select the programs they wanted to receive. Also needed was a way to hear just a subset of programs in a particular order, as well as the ability to enter the names of stocks.

We determined that both audio and display were the useful feedback methods. At each step the listener is prompted by voice and audible cues called earcons – the audio equivalent of a computer screen's visual icons, these enable complete eyes-free use of the product.

The tasks required of a user were segmented by frequency of use and resulted in a separate playback mode for daily use. A program guide mode allows consumers to choose from the content offered, with a set-up menu for entry of stock quotes and other customization options. An LCD display aids content selection and customization, which we believed would generally be done at home or in the office, not while driving. To further emphasize the eyes-free design, a flip cover was added over the display.

A final important area of involvement was the design of the device itself. Our aim was to arrive at a shape that would be easy to use and comfortable to hold while driving, yet also refined and sensual. The design needed to be clearly differentiated from other handheld products such as cellular phones and remote controls.

During the design process, dozens of full-scale foam models were developed. Both handmade and machined by computer-controlled milling equipment, they served as a feedback tool to evaluate size, shape, detail, and control layout quickly as the design was evolving.

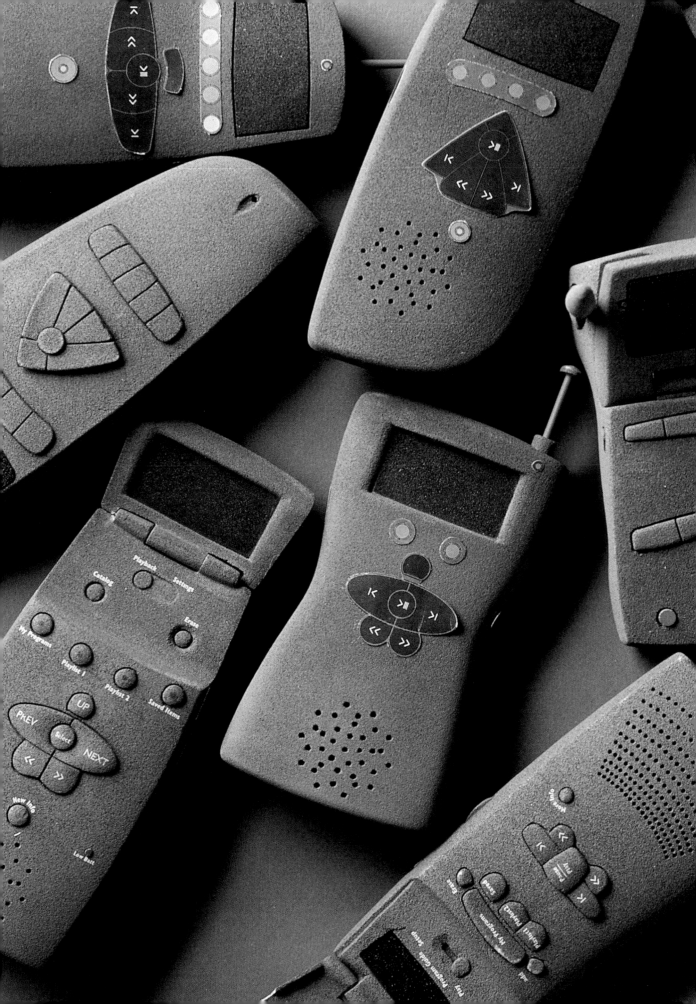

To evaluate and refine the product's operational interface, several working prototypes were built with fully operational display and buttons. The prototypes were cabled to an Apple Macintosh that ran a simulation of the software interface in Macromedia Director.

An imposing, twenty-eight-story headquarters for Japan's largest communications conglomerate is made warm and welcoming, courtesy of whimsical environmental signage that renders the vast space comprehensible.

Fuji Television Network

Renowned architect Kenzo Tange designed the new high-tech home of Fuji Television Network overlooking Tokyo Bay. The titanium-and-aluminum-clad structure encompasses almost half a million square feet and houses twenty-eight stories of offices, studios, public spaces, and parking garages. With its suspended observation sphere and sky corridors, the building projects a fabulous, futuristic vision. In its formal elegance, the architecture satisfies sophisticated design expectations; but in its cool strength, it has a somewhat imposing aspect. Fuji Television, an entertainment and communications company, was concerned that its headquarters be accessible and inviting; not just impressive, but gracious as well. Senior executives sought an appropriate graphic treatment to lend the building warmth and personality. The client's brief called for multiple permutations of twenty-six types of interior and exterior signs. The Pentagram team based the design program on an architectural grid of the two-tower Fuji building and established a limited range of visual and formal elements to reflect different signing purposes. Changes in typography, imagery, color, and material differentiate signs by tower and by floor, by function and form, by business activity and organizational hierarchy.

A strip of squares is the visual motif linking all sign types. Though the pattern was originally derived from Kenzo Tange's fenestration, it also resembles the sprocket holes in film and thereby refers to both the architecture and business activity. Fuji's wide-eyed corporate logo and signature vermilion mark external and general information signs. The bold sans serif typeface Futura Heavy announces information in all public areas, while delicate Garamond lends a reserved tone to executive floor signs. Cathode-ray colors greet actors, anchors, and other broadcast personnel on signs in the media tower, and supergraphics identify voluminous TV stage doors with saturated fields of color. The interior signs of the office tower are smaller in size and visually quieter, fea-

turing smooth, businesslike finishes and minimal use of color. On the uppermost floors, materials are upgraded to etched glass, polished woods, and metals. These choices bow to the customary restraint and formality of executive life.

Fuji employed a project liaison and translator, Kanna Ikebe of International Management Group, to advise the design team on Japanese protocol for seating arrangements, gift giving, and numerous other matters of etiquette. Such courtesies were critical to the flow of communication among designers, clients, architect, and Kajima Corporation, the international design and construction firm. The entire design project, from an initial briefing session to final approvals, was completed in just over fourteen weeks.

When the installation was complete, Fuji formally expressed approval of the program with a festive unveiling ceremony and dinner. But the company's satisfaction was made plain publicly on the brochure announcing the new headquarters: its cover bore a full-color photo of the building with one of its bright new signs, front and center.

The film-strip motif common to all Fuji signage is a visual nod to the company's business as well as to Kenzo Tange's architectural design. The sprocket-like shapes linking all sign types provide warmth and personality in a setting of titanium and aluminum.

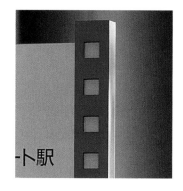

Fuji's sign system encompasses wall-mounted and freestanding panels, room numbers and wayfinding devices, bulletin boards and desktop signs. Twenty-six sign types were developed, although not all were implemented.

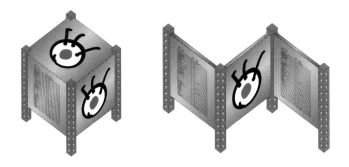

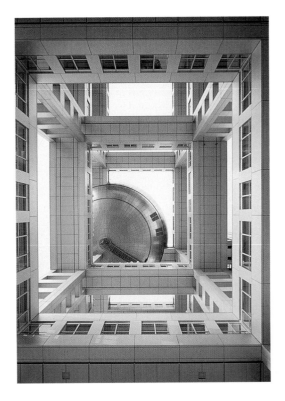

Refashioned retail environments and collateral graphics reflect the cool style of an advertising campaign, lending sophistication and vibrancy to a fabric with a stodgy reputation.

TSE Cashmere

The wool of the wealthy, the warm undercoat fibers of the Kashmir goat have long been associated with aristocratic country clubs and conformist garments unchanged in style. In the late 1980s, Augustine Tse, recognizing the possibilities that cashmere held for an affluent, modern audience, developed his own collection. The epitome of relaxed luxury, the TSE label has blossomed, with five stores in the U.S. – including its flagship store on New York's Madison Avenue – and two in Hong Kong. Yet most customers, especially those in Britain, experience the TSE brand through shops-in-shops, or concessions, at large department stores. While such locations boast prestige, for a young fashion label trying to establish a profile for itself they can be inhibiting places. So TSE's U.K. management set about reconsidering the weak messages its shops were giving out. They thought about utilizing restricted floor space and new ways of displaying their merchandise.

In the past, for example, the clothes had been stacked up on shelving units. Could new fittings reflect the quality and design values of the clothes?

If there was a cue to guide the designs, it was in TSE's U.S. advertising and in its Madison Avenue store. The ads, shot by the noted fashion photographer Bruce Weber, established a tone of elegant minimalism for TSE. That was carried forward in the storefront, where a well-detailed, pared-down but not austere simplicity was articulated by white walls and handmade beechwood fittings.

Various collateral materials were designed to complement Weber's photographic style. To heighten the contrast in these pieces we refined the color scheme used in the U.S., buttressing the warm grays and dull browns with white type on solid black backgrounds.

The company's next request of Pentagram was to transfer this minimalism to U.K. retail environments, each of which presented a different challenge. At the first shop-in-shop, located in London's Harvey Nichols, we exercised more selectivity over the merchandise that was on display, making it light on the ground, and created architectural elements to conceal stock cleverly. For the clothing to breathe, space had to be created around the product. As much merchandise as possible is floated above floor level. Clothes are hung on rails instead of folded, and stock is confined to new cabinets hidden inside changing rooms or concealed within slim mirrored hanging columns.

The subtle detailing of the clothes finds an echo in the craftsmanship and fine materials of the interior. Rich wooden surfaces and etched glass screens are punctuated with exposed metal fittings. The floor is trimmed with a metal inlay, and hard metal trays enhance the sense of value surrounding the warm, soft merchandise.

At the discount outlet we designed in Bicester, the materials are more modest. But to maintain the sense of luxury, the design team chose to be more generous with exposed detailing. Cabinets are edged with the stitchwork of fat dovetails. Louvered light fittings have been handcrafted from plywood. And the shelving units, instead of lying right up against the enclosing walls, taper slightly, giving the illusion that they are leaning inward.

Pentagram's first work for TSE was to translate its minimalist style into various collateral materials. The graphic language we created matched the photographer's visual clarity by limiting text to only one word on a line. Sentences thus became columns.

At the discount outlet, materials are more modest. But to retain a sense of the luxury and other values associated with TSE, exposed detailing in cabinetry, shelving, and light fixtures is more generous.

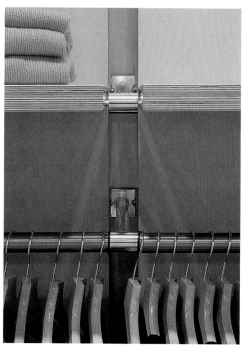

For shop-in-shop environments within large department stores, small architectural spaces, with a distinctive use of crafted joints, help to reflect the craftsmanship and luxury of the garments.

Acropolis, Gre. 75/N3
Actaeon Group (isls.), FrPol. 163/M7
Acton, Ca, US 192/B2
Acton (nbrhd.), Eng, UK 56/C2
Acton, On, Can. 186/S8
Acton, Tx, US 176/K7
Acton, Mt, US 171/K5
Acton Vale, Qu, Can. 187/K2
Actopan, Mex. 199/L6
Actopan, Mex. 199/N7
Açu, Braz. 207/G4
Açude Aratas (res.), Braz. 207/F4
Açude Banabuiu (res.), Braz. 207/G4
Açude Oros (res.), Braz. 207/G4
Acula, Mex. 199/P8
Aculeo (lag.), Chile 214/N8
Acworth, Ga, US 189/L6
Acy-en-Multien, Fr. 56/L4
Ad Dabbah, Sudan 142/F1
Ad Dabbūrah, Sudan 142/G1
Ad Dafīnah, SAr. 126/D4
Ad Dahnā' (des.), SAr. 126/D3
Ad Daljamūn, Egypt 139/B3
Ad Damazin, Sudan 142/G3
Ad Damīr, Sudan 142/G1
Ad Dammām, SAr. 126/F3
Ad Dāmūr, Leb. 131/C1
Ad Daqahliyah (gov.), Egypt 128/B3
Ad Darb, SAr. 126/D5
Ad Dawḩah (Doha) (cap.), Qatar 126/F3
Ad Dilam, SAr. 126/E4
Ad Dilinjāt, Egypt 139/B3
Ad Dīwānīyah, Iraq 129/F4
Ad Du'ayn, Sudan 142/E3
Ad Dujayl, Iraq 129/F3
Ad Duwādimī, SAr. 126/D4
Ad Duwayd, SAr. 128/E4
Ad Duwaym, Sudan 142/G2
Ad-Dakhla, WSah. 136/B5
Ada, Ok, US 179/F3
Ada, Mn, US 182/F4
Ada, Oh, US 186/E4
Ada, Gha. 141/F5
Ada, Yugo. 76/E3
Ādaba, Eth. 144/A4
Adaba, India 121/E2
Adainville, Fr. 56/G5
Adair, Ok, US 179/G2
Adair (cape), NW, Can. 167/J1
Adair, Ia, US 181/G3
Adair (bay), Mex. 175/F5
Adairsville, Ga, US 188/E3
Adairville, Ky, US 188/D2
Adaja (riv.), Sp. 72/C2
Adak (isl.), Ak, US 101/U4
Adam, Oman 127/G4
Adam (mt.), UK 215/E6
Adamantina, Braz. 213/G2
Adamaoua (prov.), Camr. 142/B4
Adamaoua (plat.), Camr., Nga. 133/D4
Adamawa (state), Nga. 142/B3
Adamello (peak), It. 87/G5
Adaminaby, Austl. 159/D3
Adamovka, Rus. 97/L2
Adams, NY, US 187/H3
Adams, Ma, US 187/K3
Adams, Ne, US 181/F3
Adams, Tn, US 188/D2
Adams, Wi, US 181/K2
Adams (mt.), Wa, US 170/D4
Adams (lake), BC, Can. 170/E2
Adams (riv.), BC, Can. 170/E2
Adams (co.), Pa, US 194/A4
Adams Run, SC, US 189/G4
Adamstown (cap.), Pitc. 163/M7
Adamstown, Pa, US 194/B3
Adamsville, Tn, US 188/C3
Adamsville, Tx, US 177/E2
Adamw (plat.), Nga. 141/H5
Aden ('Adan), Yem. 144/C2
'Adan (Aden), Yem. 144/C2
Adana (int'l arpt.), Turk. 128/C2
Adana, Turk. 128/C2
Adana (prov.), Turk. 128/C2
Adanhé, Gabon 146/B3
Adapazarı, Turk. 77/K5
Adarama, Sudan 142/G1
Adare, Ire. 58/B4
Adare (cape), Ant. 216/M
Adarza (peak), Fr. 72/E1
Adaut, Indo. 154/C2
Adavale, Austl. 160/B4
Add (riv.), Sc, UK 59/A4
Adda (riv.), Sudan 142/D3
Adda (riv.), It. 71/H4
Addicks (dam), Tx, US 177/M9
Addicks (res.), Tx, US 177/M9
Addis, La, US 190/C2
Addison, Il, US 193/P16
Addison, Al, US 188/D3
Addison, Tx, US 176/L7
Addison (Webster Springs), WV, US 189/G1
Addlestone, Eng, UK 56/B2
Addo Elephant NP, SAfr. 150/D4
Addy, Wa, US 170/F3
Adelsried, Ger. 84/D6
Aden (gulf), Afr.,Asia 103/D8
Aden (int'l arpt.), Yem. 144/C2
Aden, Ab, Can. 171/J3
Adenau, Ger. 81/F3
Adendorf, Ger. 79/H2
Aderbissinat, Niger 141/G3
Adèrké, Chad 134/C4
Ādēt, Eth. 142/H3
Adh Dhahībāt, Tun. 137/H2
Adh Dhirā', Jor. 130/D4
Adi, D.R. Congo 147/G2
Adi (isl.), Indo. 117/H4
Ādī Ābun, Eth. 144/A2
Ādī Ārk'ay, Eth. 142/H2
Ādī Da'iro, Eth. 126/C6
Ādīs Ābeba (Adekeieh), Erit. 144/A2
Ādī Kwala, Erit. 144/A2
Ādī Tekelezan, Erit. 144/A2
Ādī Ugrī, Erit. 144/A2
Adiaké, C.d'Iv. 140/E5
Adieu (cape), Austl. 157/G5
Ādīgala, Eth. 144/B3
Adige (riv.), It. 93/F1
Adige (Etsch) (riv.), It. 87/G4
Adigeni, Geo. 97/G4
Adigo (Etsch) (riv.), It. 87/G4
Ādīgrat, Eth. 144/A2
Adilcevaz, Turk. 129/E2
Adimo, Nga. 141/F5
Adin, Ca, US 172/C3
Adiora (well), Mali 141/E2
Adīrī, Libya 134/B3
Adirondack (mts.), NY, US 169/L3
Addis Ababa (Ādīs Ābeba) (cap.), Eth. 144/A3
Ādīs Ābeba (Addis Ababa) (cap.), Eth. 144/A3
Ādīs 'Alem, Eth. 144/A3
Ādīs Zemen, Eth. 142/H2
Adisutjipto (int'l arpt.), Indo. 115/E3
Adıyaman, Turk. 128/D2
Adiyaman (prov.), Turk. 128/D2
Adjud, Rom. 77/H2
Adjuntas, de la Presa (res.), Mex. 199/F4
Adler/Sochi (int'l arpt.), Rus. 96/F4
Adlington, Eng, UK 61/F4
Adliswil, Swi. 87/E3
Admiral, Sk, Can. 171/K3
Admirality (isl.), Ak, US 166/C3
Admirality (inlet), NW, Can. 167/H1
Admirality Island Nat'l Mon., Ak, US 166/C3
Admiralty (inlet), Wa, US 193/B2
Admiralty (isls.), PNG 162/D5
Admiralty (gulf), Austl. 154/B3
Admiralty Gulf Abor. Rsv., Austl. 154/B3
Admire, Ks, US 179/F1
Adnan Menderes (int'l arpt.), Turk. 96/C5
Ado (riv.), Japan 109/J5
Ado Ekiti, Nga. 141/G5
Ado Odo, Nga. 141/F5
Adobe Creek (res.), Co, US 178/C1
Adogawa, Japan 109/K5
Adok, Sudan 142/F3
Adolfo López Mateos, Mex. 198/B3
Ādoni, India 121/C3
Adorf, Ger. 85/F2
Adoru, Nga. 141/G5
Adour (riv.), Fr. 92/D2
Adra, India 123/F4
Adra, Sp. 72/D4
Adranga, D.R. Congo 147/G2
Adrano, It. 74/D4
Adrar, Alg. 137/E4
Adrar (phys. reg.), Mrta. 140/B1
Adrar (pol. reg.), Mrta. 140/C1
Adrar (pol. reg.), Alg. 141/F1
Adrar (reg.), Mrta. 136/C5
Adrar (wilaya), Alg. 137/E4
Adrar bou Nasser (peak), Mor. 136/E2
Adrar Sotuf (mts.), WSah. 136/B5
Adré, Chad 142/D2
Adria, It. 89/F3
Adrian, Mo, US 179/G1
Adrian, Mi, US 186/D4
Adrian, Or, US 172/E2
Adrian, Mn, US 181/G2
Adrian, WV, US 189/G1
Adriatic (sea), Eur. 55/F4
Adro, It. 88/C2
Aduana del Sásabe, Mex. 175/G5
Adukrom, Gha. 141/E5
Adulis (ruin), Erit. 144/A2
Adur (riv.), Eng, UK 63/F5
Adutiškis, Lith. 67/M4
Advance, Mo, US 188/C2
Adventure Bay, Austl. 158/C4
Advocate Harbour, NS, Can. 184/E3
Ādwa, Eth. 144/A2
Afek NP, Isr. 131/B4
Aff (riv.), Fr. 70/B3
Affenrücken, Namb. 150/A3
Affoltern im Emmental, Swi. 86/D3
Affric (lake), Sc, UK 59/A2
Affton, Mo, US 181/J4
Afghanistan(ctry.) 103/F6
Afgooye, Som. 145/D1
Afia, Gabon 146/B2
'Afīf, SAr. 126/D4
Afikpo, Nga. 141/G5
Afipskiy, Rus. 99/K5
Afiqim, Isr. 131/D3
Aflou, Alg. 92/D4
Afmadow, Som. 145/C1
Afobaka (dam), Sur. 206/C1
Afogados da Ingàzeira, Braz. 207/G4
Afognak (isl.), Ak, US 168/X13
Afollé (phys. reg.), Mrta. 140/C2
Afonso Bezerra, Braz. 207/G4
Afore, PNG 155/H2
Afragola, It. 92/D6
Afrânio, Braz. 207/F5
Africa(cont.) 133/*
Afrin (riv.), Turk. 130/E1
'Afrīn, Syria 130/E1
Afrique (peak), Fr. 86/A3
Afsluitdijk (dam), Neth. 78/C2
Afte (riv.), Ger. 79/F5
Afton, Ok, US 179/G2
Afton, Wy, US 173/H2
Afton, Ia, US 181/G3
Afton, Mn, US 183/Q7
Afuá, Braz. 206/D3
Afuidich (lake), WSah. 136/B5
'Afula, Isr. 131/C3
Afyon, Turk. 128/B2
Afyon (prov.), Turk. 96/D5
Afzalgarh, India 122/B1
Agadem, Niger 142/B1
Agades (int'l arpt.), Niger 141/G2
Agadez, Niger 141/G2
Agadez (dept.), Niger 137/H5
Agadir, Mor. 136/C3
Agadir (Inezgane) (int'l arpt.), Mor. 136/C3
Agadyr', Kaz. 125/B2
Agago (riv.), Ugan. 142/G5
Āgamani, India 123/G2
Agamor (well), Mali 141/F2
Agaña (cap.), Guam 162/D3
Agano (riv.), Japan 111/F2
Agar, SD, US 180/D1
Āgarfa, Eth. 144/A4
Āgaro, Eth. 142/H4
Agartala, India 123/H4
Agassiz Ice Cap (ice field), NW, Can. 167/T6
Agassiz NWR, Mn, US 182/F3
Agate, Co, US 180/C4
Agate Fossil Beds Nat'l Mon., Ne, US 180/C2
Agats, Indo. 155/E1
Agattu (isl.), Ak, US 101/T4
Agbabu, Nga. 141/G5
Agbor Bojiboji, Nga. 141/G5
Agboville, C.d'Iv. 140/D5
Ağcabädi, Azer. 129/F1
Ağdam, Azer. 129/F2
Ağdärä, Azer. 129/F1
Ağdaş, Azer. 97/H4
Agde, Fr. 70/E5
Agdz, Mor. 136/D3
Agen, Fr. 70/D4
Agency (lake), Or, US 172/B2
Agency, Mo, US 181/G4
Agency, Ia, US 181/H3
Ageo, Japan 109/D2
Ager (riv.), Aus. 85/G7
Ageræk, Den. 66/C4
Āgere Maryam, Eth. 144/A4
Agerisee (lake), Swi. 87/E3
Agersø (isl.), Den. 65/H7
Ageyevo, Rus. 96/F1
Agger (riv.), Ger. 81/G1
Aggteleki NP, Slvk. 76/E1
Āghā Jārī, Iran 129/G4
Aghada, Ire. 58/B6
Aghagallon, NI, UK 60/B3
Aghagower, Ire. 58/A2
Agiabampo, Mex. 198/C3
Ağın, Turk. 128/D2
Aga (aut. okrug), Rus. 104/G1
Aginskoye, Rus. 104/G1
Agivey, NI, UK 60/B1
Agjert, Mrta. 140/C2
Agliana, It. 89/D6
Ağlıköy, Turk. 96/E4
Agly (riv.), Fr. 70/E5
Agna, It. 89/E3
Agnanderón, Gre. 75/G3
Agnes, Tx, US 176/K7
Agnew, Austl. 156/D4
Agnibilékrou, C.d'Iv. 140/E5
Agnita, Rom. 77/G3
Agno (int'l arpt.), Swi. 87/E6
Agno (riv.), It. 89/E1
Agnone, It. 92/D4
Agny (riv.), Fr. 90/B1
Ago(bay) 67/J4
Ago, Japan 109/L7
Ago Are, Nga. 141/F4
Agogna (riv.), It. 71/H4
Agon (pt.), Fr. 82/D3
WSah. 136/B4
Água Branca, Braz. 207/G4
Água Branca, Braz. 207/F4
Agua Buena, Chile 212/B3
Agua Caliente, Az, US 175/F4
Agua Caliente Ind. Res., Ca, US 174/D4
Água Clara, Braz. 213/F2
Agua de Dios, Col. 207/L8
Agua Dulce, Ca, US 192/B2
Agua Dulce, Mex. 200/C2
Agua Fria, NM, US 175/J3
Agua Hedionda (lake), Ca, US 192/C4
Agua Larga, Ven. 204/D2
Agua Prieta, Mex. 175/H5
Agua Vermelha (res.), Braz. 210/C3
Aguachica, Col. 204/C2
Aguadas, Col. 207/K7
Aguadilla, PR 197/M8
Aguadulce, Pan. 204/A2
Aguaí, Braz. 211/K7
Agualeguas, Mex. 177/E4
Agualva-Cacém, Port. 73/P10
Aguan (riv.), Hon. 196/D4
Aguapeí (riv.), Braz. 210/C4
Aguapey (riv.), Arg. 213/E4
Aguaray, Arg. 212/D2
Aguarico (riv.), Peru 204/B5
Aguaro-Guariquito NP, Ven. 197/H6
Águas (hills), Braz. 211/L7
Águas Belas, Braz. 207/G5
Aguas Blancas, Chile 212/B3
Aguas Corrientes, Uru. 215/K11
Águas da Prata, Braz. 211/K6
Águas de Lindóia, Braz. 211/K7
Águas Formosas, Braz. 211/E3
Aguasay, Ven. 205/F2
Aguascalientes (state), Mex. 196/A3
Aguascalientes, Mex. 198/E4
Aguaytía (riv.), Peru 208/C3
Águeda, Port. 72/A2
Agueda (riv.), Sp. 72/B2
Aguelhok, Mali 141/F2
Agûenit, WSah. 136/B5
Aguêraktem (well), Mali 136/D5
Agugliano, It. 89/G6
Agui, Japan 109/L6
Aguié, Niger 141/G3
Aguijan (isl.), NMar. 162/D3
Aguila, Az, US 175/F4
Aguilâl Faï, Mrta. 140/B2
Aguilar, Co, US 178/B2
Aguilar, Sp. 72/C4
Aguilar de Campóo, Sp. 72/C1
Aguilares, Arg. 212/C3
Aguilas, Sp. 72/E4
Aguililla, Mex. 198/E5
Aguja (pt.), Peru 208/A2
Agulhas (cape), SAfr. 150/M11
Agulhas Negras, Pico das (peak), Braz. 211/M7
Agung (vol.), Indo. 115/F3
Agusan (riv.), Phil. 114/D3
Agustín Codazzi, Col. 204/C2
Agutaya, Phil. 114/C3
Agwata, Ugan. 145/A1
Agwok, Sudan 142/F4
Aha (hills), Bots. 148/D3
Ahaggar (mts.), Alg. 137/G5
Ahal (prov.), Trkm. 97/L5
Aham, Ger. 85/F5
Ahar, Iran 129/F2
Ahascragh, Ire. 58/B3
Ahau, Fiji 162/G6
Ahaura, NZ 161/B3
Ahaus, Ger. 78/E4
Aherlow (riv.), Ire. 58/B5
Ahero, Kenya 145/A2
Ahfir, Mor. 138/C2
Ahipara, NZ 161/C1
Ahırlı, Turk. 128/C2
Ahlat, Turk. 128/E2
Ahlen, Ger. 79/E5
Ahlerstedt, Ger. 79/G2
Ahmadābād, India 127/K4
Ahmadnagar, India 121/B2
Ahmadpur East, Pak. 124/A5
Ahmadpur Siāl, Pak. 124/A4
Ahmar (mts.), Eth. 144/B3
Ahmar, 'Erg el (des.), Mali 136/D4
Ahmed (well), WSah. 136/B5
Ahmeyine (well), Mrta. 136/B5
Ahoada, Nga. 141/G5
Ahoghill, NI, UK 60/B2
Ahome, Mex. 198/C3
Ahon (peak), Chad 134/C4
Ahoskie, NC, US 189/J2
Ahr (riv.), Ger. 68/D3
Ahram, Iran 129/G4
Ahraurā, India 122/D3
Ahrensburg, Ger. 79/H1
Ahse (riv.), Ger. 79/F5
Ahuacatitlán, Mex. 199/K8
Ahuacatlán, Mex. 198/D4
Ahuachapán, ESal. 200/D3
Ahualulco, Mex. 199/E4
Ahumada, Mex. 177/A2
Ahun, Fr. 70/E3
Ahunda, Gha. 141/F5
Åhus, Swe. 66/F4
Aḩuzzam, Isr. 131/B5
Aigueblanche, Fr. 90/C1
Aigues (riv.), Fr. 70/F4
Aigües Tortes y Lago de San Mauricio, PN, Sp. 73/F1
Aiguillon, Fr. 70/D4
Aikawa, Japan 111/F1
Aikawa, Japan 109/C2
Aiken, SC, US 189/G4
Ailao (mtn.), China 112/D3
Ailao (mts.), China 112/D4
Aileron, Austl. 157/G2
Aileu, Indo. 154/B2
Ailigandí, Pan. 204/B2
Ailinglapalap (isl.), Mrsh. 162/F4
Aille (riv.), Fr. 90/C6
Aillevillers-et-Lyaumont, Fr. 86/C2
Aillon (riv.), Fr. 90/C1
Ailly-sur-Noye, Fr. 80/B4
Ailsa Craig (isl.), Sc, UK 59/A6
Ailsa Craig, On, Can. 186/F3
Ailuk (isl.), Mrsh. 162/G3
Aimäjärvi (lake), Fin. 65/E3
Aime, Fr. 90/C1
Aimen (pass), China 106/C5
Aimogasta, Arg. 212/C4
Aimorés, Braz. 211/E3
Aimorés, Serra dos (mts.), Braz. 211/E3
Ain (dept.), Fr. 90/B1
Ain (riv.), Fr. 70/F4
'Aïn Beïda, Alg. 138/K7
Aïn Ben Tili, Mrta. 136/C4
'Aïn Beniau, Alg. 138/G4
'Aïn Bessem, Alg. 138/G4
Aïn Chok-Hay Mohammadia (prov.), Mor. 138/A2
'Aïn Defla, Alg. 138/F4
'Aïn Defla (wilaya), Alg. 138/F4
Aïn el Aouda, Mor. 138/A3
'Aïn El Bey (int'l arpt.), Alg. 138/K6
'Aïn El Hammam, Alg. 138/H4
'Aïn el Turk, Alg. 138/D2
'Aïn Fakroun, Alg. 138/K6
'Aïn M'lila, Alg. 138/K6
'Aïn Oulmene, Alg. 138/H5
'Aïn Oussersa, Alg. 138/G5
'Aïn Sefra, Alg. 137/E2
Aïn Taoujdat, Mor. 138/B3
'Aïn Taya, Alg. 138/G4
'Aïn Temouchent, Alg. 138/D2
'Aïn Touta, Alg. 138/H5
Ainaro, Indo. 154/B2
Ainaži, Lat. 67/L3
Aincourt, Fr. 56/H4
Ainos (peak), Gre. 75/G3
Aínos Ethnikós Dhrimós, (nat'l. park), Gre. 75/G3
Ainsdale, Eng, UK 61/E4
Ainslie (lake), NS, Can. 185/G2
Ainsworth, Ne, US 180/E2
Aiome, PNG 155/G1
Aipe, Col. 204/C4
Aiquile, Bol. 212/C1
Aïr (plat.), Niger 137/G5
Air Force (isl.), NW, Can. 167/J2
Airabu (isl.), Indo. 115/D2
Airaines, Fr. 80/A4
Airasca, It. 90/D3
Airbangis, Indo. 115/B2
Airdrie, Sc, UK 59/C5
Airdrie, Ab, Can. 171/G2
Aire (riv.), Eng, UK 61/G3
Aire, Canal d' (canal), Fr. 80/B2
Aire-sur-la-Lys, Fr. 80/B2
Aire-sur-l'Adour, Fr. 70/C5
Airgin Sum, China 104/G3
Airmolek, Indo. 115/C3
Airola, It. 92/D5
Airolo, Swi. 87/E4
Airton, Eng, UK 61/F3
Airuno, It. 88/C2
Airvault, Fr. 70/C3
Aisch (riv.), Ger. 71/J2
Aiseau-Presles, Belg. 81/D3
Aisén del General Carlos Ibáñez del Campo (pol. reg.), Chile 214/B5
Aisne (riv.), Fr. 68/B4
Aïssa (peak), Alg. 137/E2
Aist (riv.), Aus. 85/H6
Aït Ben Haddou, Mor. 136/D3
Aït Ourir, Mor. 136/D3
Aitape, PNG 162/D5
Aith, Sc, UK 57/W13
Aitkin, Mn, US 183/H4
Aitō, Japan 109/K5
Aitolikón, Gre. 75/G3
Aitrach, Ger. 87/G2
Aitrang, Ger. 87/G2
Aitutaki Atoll (isl.), CookIs. 163/J6
Aiuaba, Braz. 207/F4
Aiud, Rom. 77/F2
Aiuruoca (riv.), Braz. 211/M7
Aiuruoca, Braz. 211/M6
Aix (mt.), Wa, US 170/D4
Aix-en-Provence, Fr. 90/B5
Aix-les-Bains, Fr. 90/B1
Aiyang, China 107/C2
Aíyina, Gre. 75/H4
Aiyínion, Gre. 75/H2
Ajigasawa, Japan 108/B3
'Ajjah, WBnk. 131/C4
Ajka, Hun. 76/C2
'Ajlūn, Jor. 131/D4
Ajmer, India 118/B2
Ajnāla, India 124/C4
Ajo, Az, US 175/F4
Ajo, Cabo de (cape), Sp. 70/B5
Ajuchitlán del Progreso, Mex. 196/A4
Ajusco (vol.), Mex. 199/Q10
Ajuy, Phil. 114/C3
Ak-Dovurak, Rus. 125/F1
Aka (riv.), Japan 111/F1
Aka Eze, Nga. 141/G5
Akabane, Japan 109/M6
Akabira, Japan 108/C2
Akabli, Alg. 137/F4
Akademik Obruchev (mts.), Rus. 104/C1
Akagera, PN de l', Rwa. 147/G3
Akaishi-dake (peak), Japan 111/F3
Āk'ak'ī Besek'a, Eth. 144/A3
Akālgarh, Pak. 124/B3
Akalkot, India 121/C2
Akaltara, India 122/D4
Akan (lake), Japan 108/D2
Akan NP, Japan 108/D2
Akana, Congo 146/C3
Akankpa, Nga. 141/H5
Akaroa, NZ 161/C3
Åkarp, Swe. 66/E4
Akarsu, Turk. 128/D2
Akasha East, Sudan 135/F4
Akashi, Japan 109/G6
Akashi (str.), Japan 109/G6
Akaska, SD, US 182/D5
Akbarpur, India 122/D2
Akbarpur, India 122/B2
Akbaytal (pass), Taj. 125/B4
Akbou, Alg. 138/H4
Akçaabat, Turk. 96/F4
Akçakale, Turk. 128/D2
Akçakoca, Turk. 77/K5
Akçaova, Turk. 77/J5
Akçapınar, Turk. 128/D2
Akçay, Turk. 130/A1
Akchâr (phys. reg.), Mrta. 136/B5
Akchatau, Kaz. 100/H5
Akdağmadeni, Turk. 96/E5
Akdar, Al Jabal al (mts.), Libya 93/J4
Akechi, Japan 109/M5
Akeley, Mn, US 183/G4
Akelo, Sudan 142/G4
Akeno, Japan 109/A2
Akeno, Japan 109/E1
Åkers styckebruk, Swe. 65/A1
Åkersberga, Swe. 66/H2
Akershus (co.), Nor. 64/D3
Akershus Castle, Nor. 64/S8
Aketi, D.R. Congo 147/E2
Akhalk'alak'i, Geo. 97/G4
Akhalts'ikhe, Geo. 97/G4
Akharnaí, Gre. 75/N8
Akhaura, Bang. 123/H4
Akhelóos (riv.), Gre. 75/G3
Akhisar, Turk. 96/C5
Akhmeta, Geo. 97/H4
Akhmīm, Egypt 135/F3
Akhnūr, India 124/C3
Akhtopol, Bul. 77/H4
Akhtuba (riv.), Rus. 97/H3
Akhtubinsk, Rus. 97/H2
Akhtyrskiy, Rus. 99/K5
Aki, Japan 110/C4
Aki (riv.), Japan 109/C2
Akiéni, Gabon 146/C3
Akigawa, Japan 109/C2
Akimiski (isl.), On, Can. 167/H3
Akıncı (pt.), Turk. 130/D1
Akıncılar, Turk. 128/D1
Akins, Ok, US 179/G3
Åkirkeby, Den. 66/F4
Akishima, Japan 109/C2
Akita, Japan 108/B4
Akita (pref.), Japan 108/B4
Akitio, NZ 161/D3
Akiyama, Japan 109/C2
Akjoujt, Mrta. 140/B2
Akka, Mor. 136/C3
Akkerhaugen, Nor. 66/C2
Akkeshi, Japan 108/D2
Acre ('Akko), Isr. 131/C3
'Akko (Acre), Isr. 131/C3
Akkrum, Neth. 78/C2
Akkystau, Kaz. 97/K2
'Aklé 'Aouâna (dune), Mrta. 140/D2
Aknīste, Lat. 67/L3
Aknoul, Mor. 138/C2
Akō, Japan 110/D3
Akoabas, Camr. 146/C2
Akobo, Sudan 142/G4
Ākobo Wenz (riv.), Eth. 142/G4
Akoga, Gabon 146/B2
Akok, Gabon 146/B2
Akom II, Camr. 146/B2
Akoma, PNG 155/G1
Akonolinga, Camr. 146/C2
Akora, Pak. 124/B2
Āk'ordat, Erit. 142/H2

The overall look, structural pacing, and pictorial and editorial treatments distinguish the first totally new world-atlas series to come on the market in more than twenty years.

Hammond World Atlases

The process of making maps – a costly manual effort, in which a single map might require forty separate layers of information – had changed little between 1900, when Caleb Hammond founded his eponymous map company, and 1987. That was when C. Dean and Kathleen Hammond embarked on a program to transform cartography. The quality of an atlas is measured by the accuracy of its data. The use of satellite imagery and computer-aided design in recent years has made pinpoint precision in mapmaking attainable and regular updating economically feasible. These possibilities prompted Hammond, Inc., to spend $12 million in a five-year effort to build a computer-based mapping system. The Hammonds put together a team of editors, mathematicians, cartographers, and digital specialists to create a geographic database that would allow the company to make and update maps with unprecedented ease and accuracy.

Africa

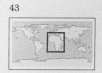

vegetation is densest in the Congo Basin, and decreases away from the Equator. The Sahara, an area of 3.5 million square miles (9.1 million sq. km.), is the largest desert in the world.

In 1990, Hammond asked Pentagram to take the fruits of this effort and design the first collection of world maps generated entirely from a digital database, as well as the context for displaying them in book form.

This would be the first fully revised world atlas on the market in more than twenty years. In approaching its design, Pentagram had two main objectives: create a book that both serious and casual users could navigate with ease and make the pictorial and editorial content visually exciting and understandable.

It was essential to convey the scale and comprehensiveness of data revisions contained in this new series. Yet it was also important to maintain the integrity of the maps and respect cartography's rich visual history. The final product had to continue and build on Hammond's established image as the premier authority in world atlases. Additionally, the series, which embraced a range of price points and functions, was to project a coherent, readily identifiable brand image for Hammond.

Pentagram made recommendations on the use and selection of colors, typestyles, and symbols; graph and chart design; and the visual depiction of the newly developed Optimal Conformal Projection Hammond and physicist Mitchell J. Feigenbaum created based on fractal geometry. Pentagram also designed the editorial sections of the atlas, which provided thematic information about land use, population, vegetation, languages, and natural resources. The flagship atlas included topical essays and a 115,000-entry master index.

The maps, startlingly clear and textural, dominate the presentation. Divider pages signal a change in information (for example, from relief to political to detailed topographic maps), while generous visual guides aid in navigation through the 303-page reference document. A simple, easily accessible index was created to allow for the maximum number of entries and to ease wayfinding by surprinting large letters of the alphabet on the pages. In place of the generic cover design of recent decades – a satellite image of earth known as the "big blue marble shot" – covers use dramatic type, images, and color to distinguish the Hammond series.

Kathleen Hammond says that combining "the best mapmaking with the best graphic design" enabled her company to "redefine the playing field." The critically acclaimed *Hammond Atlas of the World* went on the market in 1992 and sold out in six weeks. Since then, Pentagram has designed several new volumes in the series, a CD-ROM version of the atlas, and a fully revised second edition with new groundbreaking cartography.

Hammond's relief maps were created by photographing hand-sculpted, three-dimensional TerraScape models, which depict the relationships of land and sea forms and their rugged contours.

Cairo at the apex of the delta to the Suez Canal. The entire region is classified as desert (less than 10 inches [25 cm.] of rainfall per year). Desert-like areas are visible southwest of the delta and in the northwestern Sinai. Major rock outcrops (darker areas) are seen encircling the Red Sea. The two bodies of water flanking the southern end of the Sinai Peninsula are the Gulf of Suez and the Gulf of Aqaba.

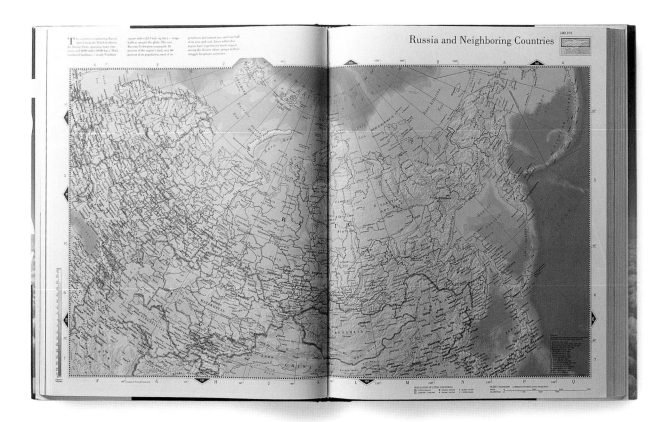

Presenting the curvature of the earth on a flat surface with geographical accuracy has led to hundreds of projection techniques. Hammond's Optimal Conformal Projection, which reduces shifts in scale over an entire region, is the most accurate yet.

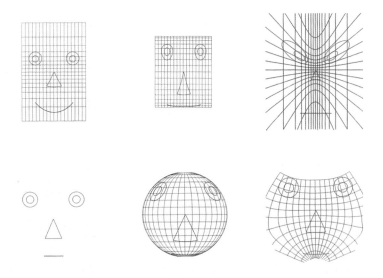

Mapping the same image on different projections will distort it in different ways. Optimal Conformal Projection (shown above at lower right) is the most successful at accurately representing true shapes and distances up to a hemisphere on a map.

Asia

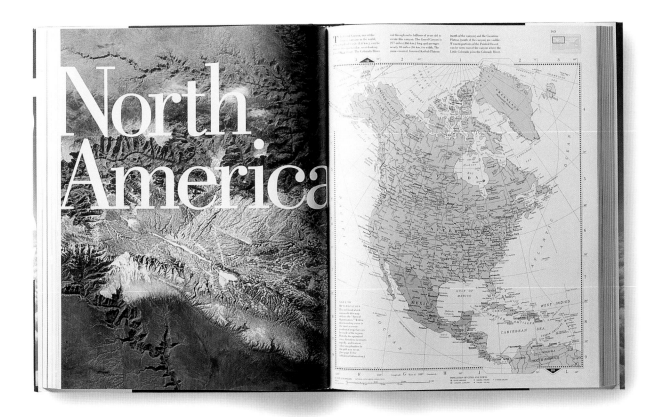

Generated from a computer database that is structured by latitude and longitude, these new maps balance political and topographic detail in a single projection; the historical record is permanently stored in the digital database.

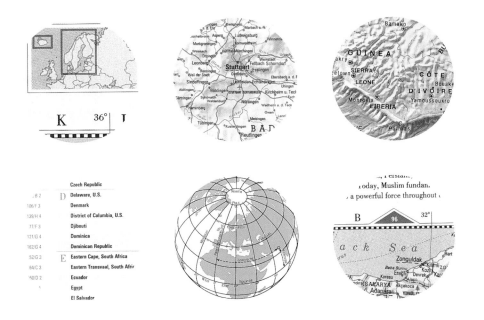

The atlas employs a number of visual and data devices, such as index letters, adjacent-area page numbers, and a quick reference guide, to help direct readers through the numerous types of maps (political, topographic, relational).

Hammond produces many different atlases at a variety of price points to satisfy a wide range of audiences (from children to scholars). What renders the variety feasible are the economics made possible through computer-based mapmaking.

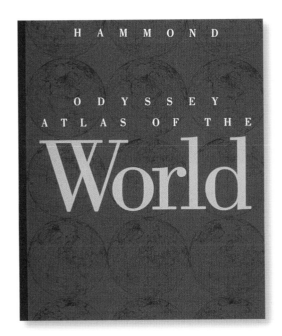

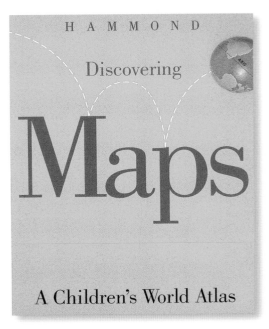

Functioning as an extension of each book in the series, Hammond's CD-ROM atlas adds an entirely new dimension to mapmaking products. It enables its users to find, access, and sort complete cartographic databases.

Halfords Motor Oil

From its roots in selling bicycles, Halfords has become a British retail success story. With more than four hundred stores, a third of them superstores with garages, the British retailer of automotive parts and accessories, with a growing business in car servicing and repair, has achieved substantial market share in all its key sectors. It sells over 30 percent of the U.K.'s bicycles and accessories; it commands a 25 percent share of car-body products and 20 percent of oil. When the business was reviewed in the mid-1990s, however, Halfords knew that maintaining that leadership meant changes – particularly in the oil business. Traditionally the Halfords brand had competed with other own brands of major oil companies, which had an armlock on the premium end of the market. This was constraining profit growth. Halfords needed to upgrade the position of its brand to take on these proprietary products without compromising its traditional market.

The work coincided with a general repositioning of Halfords, which, in a market dominated by negative consumer perceptions, wanted to project an image of honest professionalism. Whalan's assessment was blunt and to the point. "We've got to get out of the furry-dice business," he said when he appointed Pentagram as the company's design consultant.

Halfords' research indicated that the public had a low level of understanding about exactly which motor oil was suitable for which engine type. In fact, about a quarter of all cars were getting the wrong oil. Removing the confusion would benefit both the public and Halfords, when consumers traded up to higher grades. The challenge for designers was to package the new value-added range of oils the company planned to produce in ways that improved drivers' understanding of the different types and enhanced the perception of the Halfords brand. At the same time, the containers had to facilitate ease of pouring, but without adding new production costs. After performing a competitive container review, we drew up a checklist to assess various designs and their evolution that would measure such qualities as shelf impact, aesthetic appeal, ease of manufacture and filling, graphics applications, carrying, spout and cap operation, pouring, and ease of loading, transportation, and unloading. Sketched concept designs were analyzed on a point-scoring system. This analysis revealed twelve possible solutions.

Conceptual designs were primarily focused on a five-liter container, although we were constantly considering the application to a one-liter package. Skeletal models were made in a workshop in order to understand and appreciate how the real forms did or did not diverge from the paper concepts. From this process, three contenders were winnowed, and each was produced as an accurate foam model. Reviewing the analysis and the models, Halfords chose to produce the most radical version of all. The handle is on the broad

In industrial design, Cole Porter comes to mind: anything goes. Typically, the designer will first reach for a pencil to sketch an idea taking shape in his or her mind. Sketched concept designs were analyzed on a point-scoring system.

 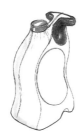   

side, or front, of the container, so the user can position an integral telescopic spout much closer to the engine before beginning to pour. Working with the design firm Lippa Pearce, we researched various forms of labeling, eventually adopting metallic-finish colors to signify the different grades of oil – red for standard, blue for standard plus, green for premium, and black for diesel. A label on the lower left corner of the bottle also communicates clearly the content and its usage. At the final development stage, we coordinated other specialists, including cap makers, patent and marketing consultants, container fabricators, and label manufacturers, to produce the final result.

User trials resulted in positive responses among the three main types of Halfords-oil customers – car enthusiasts, who are highly proficient at servicing tasks; driver dabblers, who carry out only basic servicing; and light users, who rarely do more than top up the oil themselves. Halfords new motor oil was launched in May 1996, fourteen months after the project was briefed. The company says sales volume and profitability all jumped after the introduction, despite an increase in the average price for its motor oils. Surveys have shown that the new container's shape, function, color, and graphics make things easier for the consumer – a main aim of the entire Halfords rebranding program.

Since the completion of the oil-repackaging project, we have continued to work with Halfords as a design-management consultant. Our approach has been to avoid imposing rigid visual rules; however, we have sought to clarify the packaging across Halfords' various businesses, including its own-brand parts, with more than 1,600 different lines. Gray, green, and silver backgrounds now predominate for more technical items. As with the company's new oil containers, we steered the typography toward simple, information-graphic solutions, with sans serif type aligned left, rather than toward a marketing-led design.

Ideas quickly need a physical presence. Concept sketches were translated into skeletal models in our workshop. At the point when something can be touched and handled, the understanding of the human interface truly begins.

Schemes	Halfords	A1	A2	A3	B1	B2	C1	C2	C3	D1	E1	F1	F2	Castrol
Qualities														
Pouring	4	4	4	4	7	6	4	5	5	7	7	7	8	3
Need for a pull-out spout	1	2	2	2	8	3	5	4	6	7	7	3	6	0
Carrying	7	9	9	9	8	9	7	4	6	6	8	5	5	8
Cap Operation	3	6	6	6	6	3	6	6	6	7	6	7	7	3
Moulding (practicality)	7	3	3	3	6	6	8	8	8	8	6	3	3	5
Bulk transporting	5	8	8	6	1	1	6	6	4	6	7	8	0	7
De-palletising	8	8	6	6	1	1	5	5	6	4	2	6	0	7
On line	4	8	4	8	0	0	7	7	8	8	1	7	4	7
Filling	7	8	7	8	1	1	8	8	8	8	6	8	5	8
Packaging (boxing)	7	8	7	7	2	2	7	8	5	7	6	8	5	8
Pallestisation (volume)	4	9	9	7	1	1	4	4	2	6	5	8	9	6
Unique appearance or quality	2	9	8	8	9	9	5	6	5	8	9	9	8	2
Graphics application	4	6	7	4	4	4	7	6	5	8	8	8	6	4
Volume scale - Visistripe	0	7	7	7	5	2	5	6	5	7	3	5	4	3
Translation to 1 litre	0	7	6	6	4	4	7	6	6	8	6	7	6	0
Total	63	102	93	91	63	52	91	89	85	105	87	99	76	71
Rating	11	2	4	5	11	12	5	6	8	1	7	3	9	10

Fantasies become function through frequent experimentation. Favorite ideas are often abandoned at this stage, for the designer's underlying responsibility is to satisfy the client's functional and commercial imperatives.

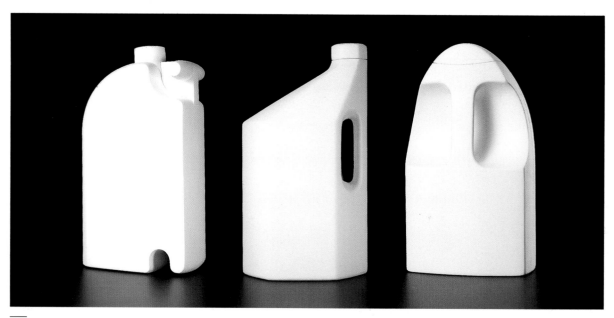

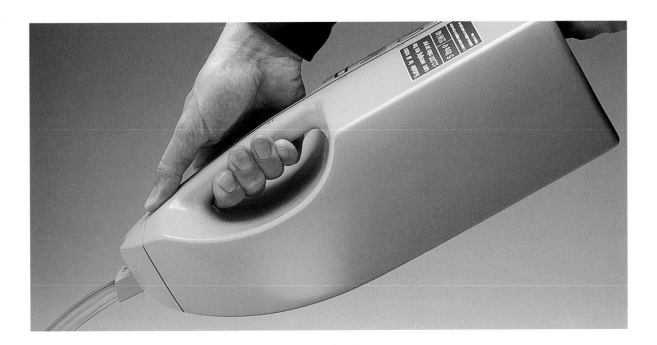

If an unfamiliar product conveys its function at first sight, it is well on the way toward introducing an innovation. Consumers are extremely sophisticated in assessing the how and what of an unfamiliar vessel, as we found when fashioning new containers.

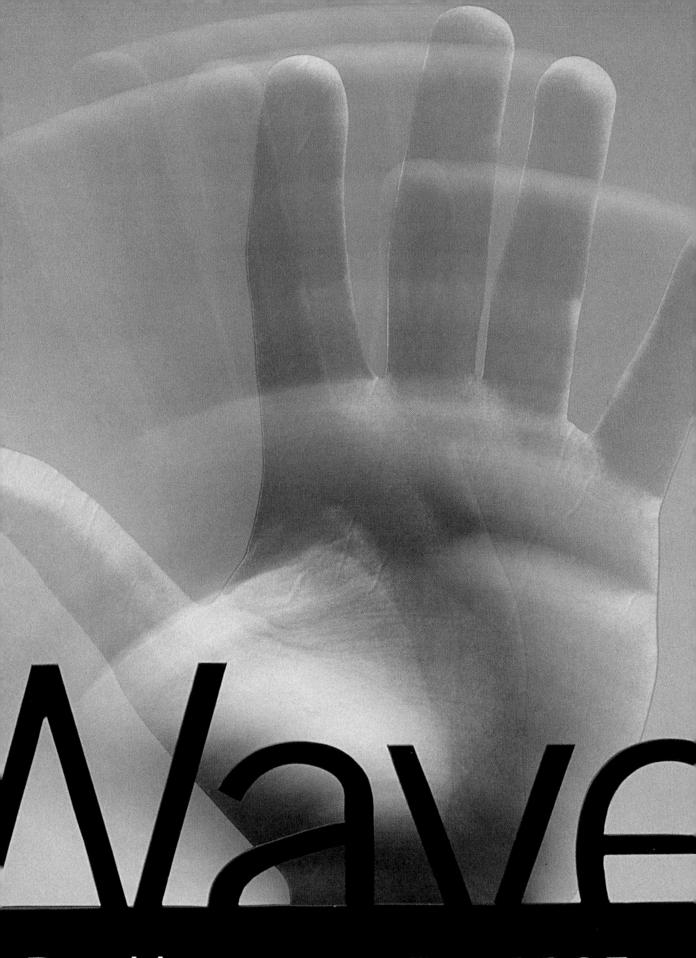

Wave

Brooklyn   The 1995

Brooklyn Academy of Music

The Brooklyn Academy of Music – known to New Yorkers as BAM – suffers a fate familiar to many arts organizations. While the institution is often praised by critics, it is constantly seeking to expand its audience. Housed in a grand but aging beaux-arts theater complex dating from the turn of the century, BAM is off the beaten track for the many performing-arts mavens whose horizons do not extend past lower Manhattan. The exception is BAM's Next Wave Festival, an annual program of experimental theater and music begun in 1981 that has featured such artists as Tom Waits, Robert Wilson, and Trisha Brown. In step with its experimentation in performance, BAM often used a different designer each year for the elaborate program mailings. This shifting identity exacerbated a problem that focus groups had already identified: Next Wave was a hot brand, able to draw crowds to see unknown acts, but its cachet was not rubbing off on BAM as a whole. To address this problem, BAM brought in Pentagram to design a consistent graphic program for Next Wave in 1995. The unspoken goal was to create a graphic identity that could in time expand to encompass all of BAM, leveraging the image of the whole institution on the strength of its most popular production.

Fragments of News Gothic type obscured behind wide stripes became the basis of the Next Wave look, used on all festival posters, advertisements, invitations, and brochures. Practically, this design system allows for the use of very large type, even in cramped applications such as newspaper advertisements. More poetically, the use of type stepping from behind horizontal lines suggests the next big thing coming over the horizon. After the first of the new Next Wave materials were completed, Pentagram extended the same principles to BAM Opera, BAM's spring programs, and a wide variety of special events. The design system proved very resilient: BAM's identity remained identifiable through many manipulations of color and layout. When BAM undertook a major renovation of its historic building in the spring of 1996, it saw the opportunity to extend the new "pan-BAM" graphic image to the building itself. Hugh Hardy, the architect and design consultant on the project, suggested using what he referred to as the Cuisinart typography on all new signage in the building. Our signage program for BAM thus became another step toward bathing the institution in the glow of Next Wave.

BAM's two major theaters, the Opera House and the Helen Carey Playhouse, are entered from a grand ground-floor lobby. Signage for these spaces shares the most with the Next Wave graphic approach. Set in existing panels above the doorways, the brushed aluminum lettering seems to slide in and out of the rich architectural detailing that surrounds it.

By bringing the language and sensibility of the Next Wave Festival into BAM's everyday communications, Pentagram hopes to blur the distinction between the institution and its most popular program, and keep the crowds coming all year round.

BAM's graphic identity has proved to be resilient. Pentagram and BAM's in-house staff have adapted the look to institutional and promotional print materials, advertising, direct mail, and architectural graphics. The big hand waving is a countertop display.

BAM

Brooklyn Acade

1919

Next

Festi

oklyn Aca

BAM

X

Wa

5th Ann

st

Next Wave Festival is

P MORRIS
ANIES INC.

BAMbill

The Brooklyn Academy
of Music

Brooklyn Academy of Music

Brooklyn
Academy
of Music

BAM

BAM

Brooklyn
Academy
of
Music

**BAM's 1995
Next Wave Festival**

Robert Wilson
Tom Waits
Vito Acconci
Kristin Jones & Andrew Ginzel
Ilya Kabakov
Don Byron
Bill Frisell
Vernon Reid
Steven Berkoff
Cloud Gate Dance Theatre
Carl Dreyer
Richard Einhorn
The Camerata Chorale
Brooklyn Philharmonic
Kronos Quartet
Ping Chong
David Rousseve / REALITY
Cheek by Jowl
Mark Morris Dance Group

ee
tickets

to the **15th**
Anniversary of
the BAM Next
Wave Festival

Light

95

gui

Way

Music

Brooklyn
Academy
of
Music

30 Lafayette Avenue
Brooklyn NY 11217
Telephone: 718.636.4122
Fax. 718.857.2021

Stephen P. Millikin
Audience Development Manager

BAM

**Mark Morris
Dance Group**

**Brooklyn Academy of Music
1995 Next Wave Festival
is sponsored by
Philip Morris Companies Inc.**

For tickets call TicketMaster
212.307.4100
For information call BAM
718.636.4100.
BAM Prefers VISA

Brooklyn
Academy
of
Music

30 Lafayette Avenue
Brooklyn NY 11217
Telephone: 718.636.4100
Fax: 718.857.2021

BAM

tickets

while the famous gas lamps are burning
Tues–Sat, 5–7pm, $19.96
Free Valet Parking · Live Piano Music
372 Fulton Street (718) 875-5181
All major credit cards accepted

Based on Alice's
Adventures in Wonderland
and Through the Looking Glass
by Lewis Carroll
(a.k.a. Lewis Carroll)

Brooklyn Academy
of Music
October 6 at 8pm;
October 7 at 8pm;
10 – 14 at 8pm;
October 8 at 3pm

For tickets

pera

A multimedia identity program employs vibrant colors, a unifying logotype, and a chronologically appropriate typeface to suggest the vast scope and deep seriousness of an institution known mostly for its collection of old bones.

American Museum of Natural History

For millions of present and former schoolchildren, mention of the American Museum of Natural History in New York conjures up warm memories of towering dinosaur exhibits and a suspended blue whale. While precious to the soul of an institution, such sentiments hardly do justice to the scholars behind the scenes – or pay the bills. Pentagram worked with the museum as part of a comprehensive institutional reorganization and revitalization plan that aimed at balancing AMNH's scientific ambitions, entertainment requirements, and funding needs. The design team used the museum's 125th anniversary in 1994 to introduce a new institutional image with a vibrant graphic language that made a timely public statement about the museum's new leadership and exhibitions. The serif typeface DeVinne, created by American printer Theodore Low DeVinne within a few years of the museum's founding in 1869, reproduces elegantly and legibly on both

tiny tickets and gigantic banners. A bright color palette, dominated by deep sea blue and tree green with dashes of volcanic red, orange, and yellow, counteracts public misperceptions of the museum as a dreary old place. And a globe functions as a unifying icon that represents the scope of the institution's work in education and research on the natural history of the world.

To maintain consistency from one medium to another, Pentagram established a set of layout rules for how the various graphic elements should be combined. Images and type are aligned to a geometric grid and appear in the same flat plane – never in overlapping layers. Key illustrations and photographs are reproduced as large-scale silhouettes on solid-color backgrounds. These strategies squeeze maximum visual impact from publication budgets that often limit printing to the least expensive one- and two-color processes.

During the 125th anniversary celebrations, the museum introduced the bold new design system on block-wide banners and a parade of flags around its landmark building. AMNH also hung special anniversary ribbons over new interior directional signs and rolled out a series of coordinated invitations, bulletins, posters, and advertising.

When the celebrations subsided, the museum replaced the anniversary flags and banners with announcements proclaiming ongoing exhibitions and removed the ribbons but left the new interior signs in their places. Regular communications representing a variety of departmental voices sustained the consistent visual tone. The change was significant enough to herald a new institutional attitude towards the public, but not so completely radical as to distract critical audiences from the museum's more important educational and scientific objectives.

The American Museum of Natural History's identity consists of a primary color palette, a globe, icons for each division of science, and the typeface DeVinne. The identity was initially introduced to celebrate the museum's 125th anniversary.

American Museum of Natural History

| Ichthyology | Invertebrates | Mammalogy | Ornithology | Vertebrate Paleontology |

Individual icons for each division were added to the identity system two years after the 125th-anniversary identity was introduced. The icons serve to brand each division of science and also to make science accessible to schoolchildren.

American Museum of Natural History

| Anthropology | Astronomy & Planetarium | Earth & Planetary Sciences | Entomology | Herpetology |

The museum identity functions most successfully on its web site. The globe icon appears and spins on the museum's home page. A click on the globe calls up the division icons, all available for exploration.

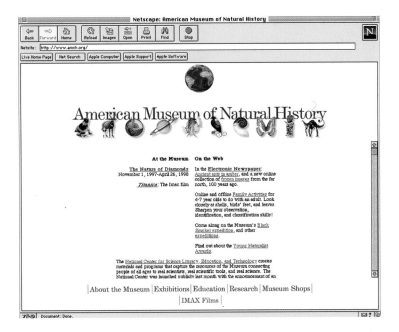

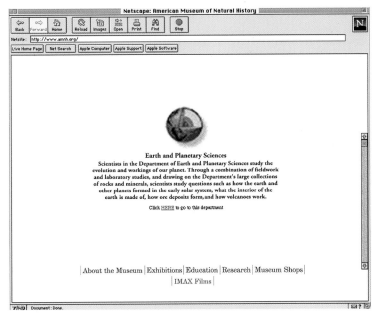

American Museum of Natural History

Herpetology

Anthropology

Pentagram designed products for the museum that used the identity. The products promoted specific exhibits while reinforcing the museum identity. The lines of merchandise also generated funds for the nonprofit institution.

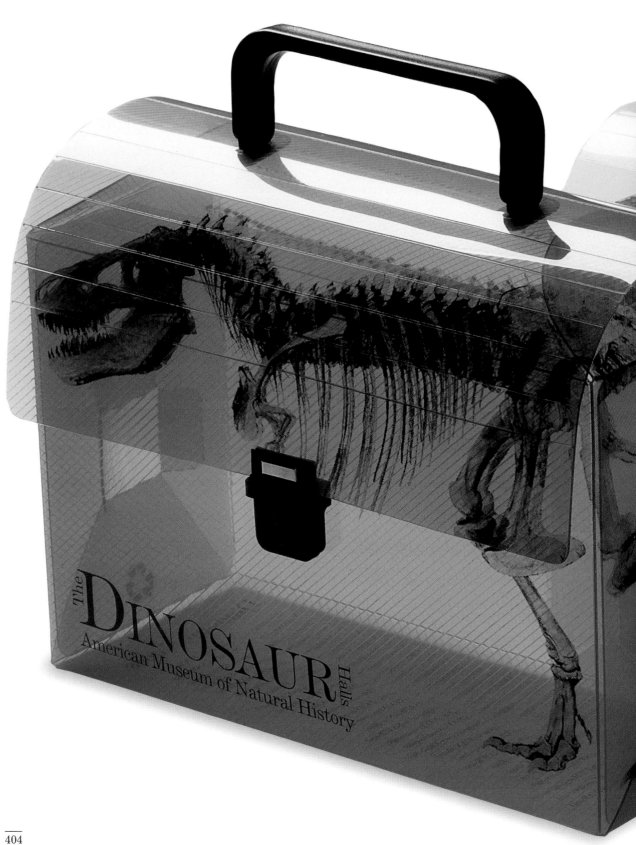

The reopening of the Dinosaur Halls, the museum's most popular exhibit, was the focus of institutional communications for over a year. New products were introduced in a DinoStore gift shop, and a massive, dinosaur-sized banner was mounted on the building facade.

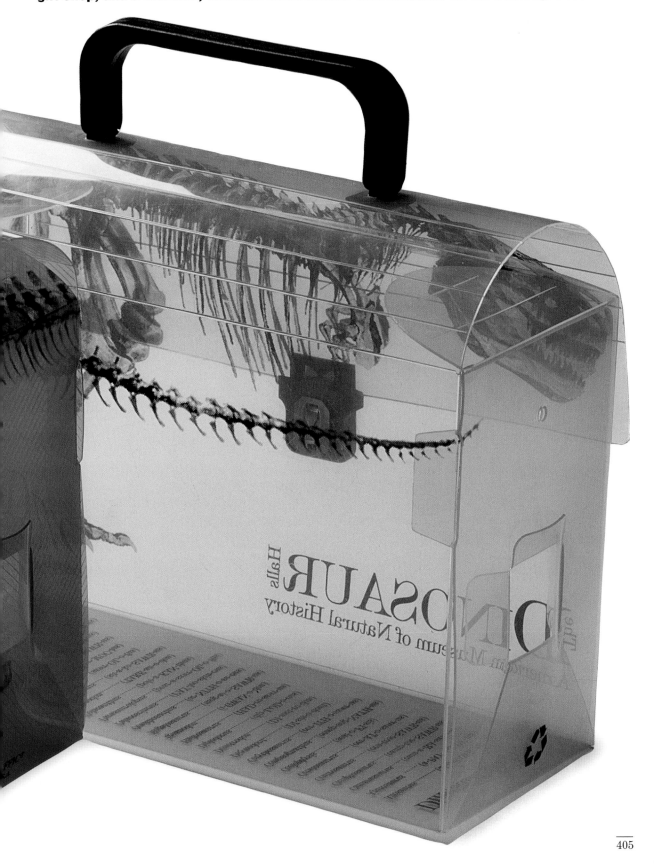

ROOSEVELT
MEMORIAL TO
YOUTH OF AMERICA
THE FAITH OF OUR FATHERS
RIGHTS OF THE PEOPLE
CONSERVATION OF THE PEOPLE
LIFE OF NATURE
AND IN MAN

CLARK

LEWIS

American Museum of Natural History

WILLIAMS-SONOMA

A CATALOG FOR COOKS

FEBRUARY 1994

Direct mail and advertising for Williams-Sonoma, based on the premise that cooking can actually be fun for those who know what they are doing, mimic the Williams-Sonoma retail experience and emphasize individual products.

Williams-Sonoma

It is hard to imagine America's premier purveyor of cookware and gourmet specialty products beginning life as an addendum to a modest, northern California hardware store. But then, it is hard to imagine Chuck Williams, founder of Williams-Sonoma, as a carpenter. That was 1956. Americans were connoisseurs of meat and potatoes, not quiches, soufflés, and homemade pasta. In the ensuing decades, Williams, along with Julia Child, James Beard, Craig Claiborne, and a handful of others, forever changed the way Americans eat. Today, Williams-Sonoma operates 150 stores throughout the United States and is parent to a publicly held "lifestyle" empire. Williams-Sonoma issued its first catalog in 1971, strongly encouraged by Edward Marcus of Neiman-Marcus, which had raised catalog retailing to an art form. Chuck Williams's company sent its first "professional" catalog to a list of about five thousand households. Success was instant.

The following year's catalog adopted a digest size, a format it kept until 1993, when Pentagram was approached by Williams-Sonoma to give its book a new look. The decision to change the design was made with good reason. Sales growth via direct marketing in America has outpaced that of retail stores in recent years, triggering a profusion of catalogs competing for armchair shoppers. Williams-Sonoma could not risk standing pat. Furthermore, the catalog is a major driver of Williams-Sonoma's total sales, including those of its retail stores. Its contents change quarterly, but it goes out monthly. Stores generally experience an upward "spike" in foot traffic and sales soon after each mailing. And when catalog customers enter the stores, they frequently see images drawn from the catalog.

A major facelift was already underway in Williams-Sonoma's retail stores. That interior redesign reorganized product display and used white finishes, light, and natural woods to give the stores a bright, airy feel. We proposed that the catalog mimic the interiors in both feel and flow. How we would do that emerged from a series of meetings in which the design team and the client debated merchandising tactics, asking questions – what exactly is the best way to show a stainless-steel fish poacher or a potato ricer? – for every product in the book. In the old design, the majority of products were displayed in what amounted to a series of group photos. For the new catalog, products were individually photographed and allowed to stand on their own merits, just as they do in the stores. Working with Dallas photographer Pat Haverfield, the photography's tone of voice shifted to more dramatic representations often shot on location – both concepts new to Williams-Sonoma.

For these changes to have the desired impact, the decades-old digest size was replaced by a magazine format. A three-column page grid was set up to help link text with image and also to establish production guidelines for in-house designers.

Williams-Sonoma was an immersion project. To completely re-concept this venerable catalog and art direct as many as fifteen shots a day, we enveloped ourselves in the company's arts – so much so that the members of the design team actually became pretty good cooks! We also inverted the conventional process of designing a catalog, constructing layouts around the best possible photographs rather than filling in the blanks of a preconceived design.

When Williams-Sonoma's millions of mail-order customers received their first Pentagram-designed issue, they responded with enthusiasm. Catalog sales increased by 60 percent from the previous year.

The premise of the reconceived Williams-Sonoma catalog was that shopping at home is little different from shopping in the store. Like the stores, the catalog was remerchandised – broken down into coherent departments and product collections.

Covers were conceived and produced to compete visually with other direct-response advertising, to command attention on their own, and to communicate a special theme or message. Above all, though, covers always promoted a specific product, service, or theme.

A house style for imagery was built on dramatic lighting and engaging composition. Presenting subjects in unexpected scale and perspective contrasted with the literal interpretations found in many catalogs.

Catalog spreads were configured to educate, entertain, inform, and communicate key messages while depicting ten to fifteen products. Description and product always went hand in hand, while function was achieved by showing the products in action.

Nespresso Café Set with Special Bonus
Those who insist on fine, freshly made coffee but regret the fuss and time spent in making it will value this machine. Whether you select regular coffee, espresso or cappuccino, each cup is reliably first-rate, and ready in seconds. The secret? Airtight premeasured capsules of freshly ground, top-quality coffee blends. With the coffee maker comes 20 capsules, 10 of which are decaf. Each capsule makes one cup. (To reorder capsules, there is a toll-free number.) 8' x 9' x 11¼' high, made in Germany.
The set #51-753616 Reg. $350.00 **Special $249.00**

Special Bonus! With the purchase of the Nespresso Café Set, you will receive two porcelain 3-oz. espresso cups and two saucers (retail value $22.00), at no additional cost.

Nonstick Electric Griddle
Vitantonio's electric griddle is large enough to cook five big pancakes, six grilled-cheese sandwiches or a half pound of bacon at a time. And because it automatically maintains the selected temperature, foods cook evenly. Surplus fat is channeled through a groove around the nonstick cooking surface into a concealed drawer for disposal, and the surface wipes clean easily. Set at low temperature, the griddle keeps food nicely warm for leisurely breakfasts. Made in the USA of cast aluminum with a heat-resistant plastic housing. 21' x 14' x 3' high. Black or White. #51-796094 Reg. $90.00 **Special $70.00**

Waffle Iron and Griddle Cleaning Brush
No more waiting for hot waffle-iron grids, griddles or grills to cool down so that between batches you can scrub off those crusty bits. This plastic-handled brush has firm Teflon bristles that can withstand heat up to 500° and won't damage nonstick surfaces. Dishwasher safe. 7' long. Made in the USA.
#51-798298 **$10.50**

Vermont Maple Syrup
Butternut Mountain Farm's Grade A pure maple syrup, produced solely from sap tapped from Vermont sugar maples, is a light and delicate topping for pancakes, waffles, ice cream and plain cakes. It is packaged in a handsome unlabeled glass bottle, with a clamp top, that will find other uses once the syrup is gone. 8½-fl. oz. bottle. #51-699769 **$9.00**

Belgian Waffle Iron and Classic Waffle Iron
Waffles, everyone's favorite breakfast treat, are easy to prepare in both our Belgian waffle iron and Classic waffle iron. For consistent results and desired degree of crispness, each has five thermostatically controlled settings. Silicone-coated baking grids ensure that batter won't stick. Both models are made in the USA by Vitantonio, have chromed steel housings and plastic handles, and a compact design for easy storage. 900W. Recipe included.
Belgian Waffle Iron
This waffle iron makes 5"-square, ¾"-thick waffles with deep pockets to hold lots of butter, syrup or fruit topping. 10¼' x 4¼' high.
#51-633792 **$50.00**
Classic Waffle Iron
The Classic model bakes a 7"-round waffle. 7¼' diam., 4¾' high. #51-607895 **$50.00**

11-Piece Glass Bowl Set
Chuck Williams discovered these nesting tempered-glass bowls in France more than 25 years ago and used them to hold everything from a lone egg yolk to large salads. They range from 2½' diam. to 12' diam. — the largest is a 6-qt. size that's just right for mixing a double batch of pancakes or waffles. Safe for dishwasher and microwave. *The set* #51-536060 **$27.00**

Belgian Waffle and Pancake Mix
A Cordon-Bleu chef developed this flavorful mix from a centuries-old Belgian recipe. Each 18-oz. sack combines wheat and crunchy rice flours, sugar, whole eggs, leavenings and spices to make ten servings of thick Belgian waffles, standard waffles or pancakes. Simply add liquid ingredients.
Set of two #51-795793 **$9.50**

Marionberry Syrup
Only the juice of fresh, hand-picked marionberries — a hybrid of two Oregon blackberries — plus a hint of sugar are used to make this dark, wonderfully fruity syrup. Serve it warmed over waffles, pancakes, French toast or ice cream. 15-oz. bottle. #51-796292 **$6.00**

Stainless Steel Measuring Spoons
It's the little things that count! Well-made stainless steel measuring spoons are meant to last a lifetime. They are precision manufactured with wide, flat rims for accurate measuring from ¼ tsp. to 1 Tbs. Each is approx. 5' long.
The set #51-445437 **$8.00**

Pyrex Measuring Cup Set
Pyrex measuring cups have open handles for nested storage and increments marked in both standard and metric amounts. The green lettering is exclusive to Williams-Sonoma. Oven, microwave and dishwasher safe. 1, 2 and 4-cup cap.
Set of three #51-551200 **$16.00**

Pyrex Accessory Set
The Pyrex accessory set allows you to shred or juice directly into a 4-cup measure (sold separately and in the set above). Made of high-impact plastic, the set includes two citrus reamers, a stainless steel shredder with both coarse and fine holes, plus a plastic lid. Green or White.
Pyrex Accessory Set
#51-736056 **$12.00**
4-Cup Measure only. #51-520560 **$7.00**

Pyrex Batter Bowl
Measure, mix and pour — all in the 2-qt. Pyrex batter bowl, particularly useful for pancake, popover and waffle batters. Oven, microwave and dishwasher safe. #51-520677 **$12.00**

Stainless Steel Measuring Cups
Bakers, who require exact measurements, will particularly appreciate these durable, heavy-gauge stainless steel measuring cups. Their capacities are scientifically calibrated for accuracy, and their rims are perfectly flat for easy leveling of dry ingredients. ¼, ⅓, ½ and 1-cup cap.
The set #51-523167 **$16.00**

Atlas Cookie Press
This durable press forms perfect cookies in 20 delightful shapes and has four tips for pastry decorations and fillings. Each cookie is consistently uniform in size and thickness, so every batch bakes evenly. It's a snap to use and kids love it! Made in Italy of aluminum, 8¾' long. Recipe and instructions included.
#51-602311 **$22.00**

Vanilla Extract and Beans
Whether you use whole beans or an extract, vanilla from orchids grown on Madagascar's Ile de Bourbon is the very finest. Nielsen-Massey's pure vanilla extract, cold processed to preserve the bean's true flavor, has long been the choice of professional bakers and ice cream makers. Flavoring sugar or liquid ingredients with our bourbon vanilla beans makes a noticeable difference in custards and baked goods.
Vanilla Extract, 8-fl.-oz. bottle. #51-14233 **$11.00**
Vanilla Beans, six pods, approx. 8' long, in corked vial to maintain freshness. #51-76570 **$13.00**

Cushionaire Pro Cookie Sheets
These sheets produce baked goods that are browned to perfection because of their unique construction — two layers of high-quality aluminum with an insulating layer in between. The lower layer protects the upper layer from overheating. Warp resistant and dishwasher safe. Made in the USA.
Small, 14' x 9½'. #51-69856 **$10.00** *Catalog only*
Large, 16' x 14'. #51-52893 **$15.00**

KitchenAid Hand Mixer
Matching power with efficiency, the KitchenAid Ultra-Power Plus hand mixer handles heavy batters as easily as it whips cream. A built-in sensor electronically maintains consistent beater speed, and special TurboBeaters promote greater volume. 175W, 7¼' x 3½' x 6½' high. Made in the USA.
7-Speed Mixer (shown) has touch-pad speed control and LED speed readout. #51-523134 **$69.00**
5-Speed Mixer has a speed control switch. #51-659078 **$59.00** *Catalog only*

To show scale, products like muffin tins were represented by their edible offspring at the actual size. To demonstrate varying sizes of doormats, the same small dog was photographed on different mats. Some customers tried to purchase the dog.

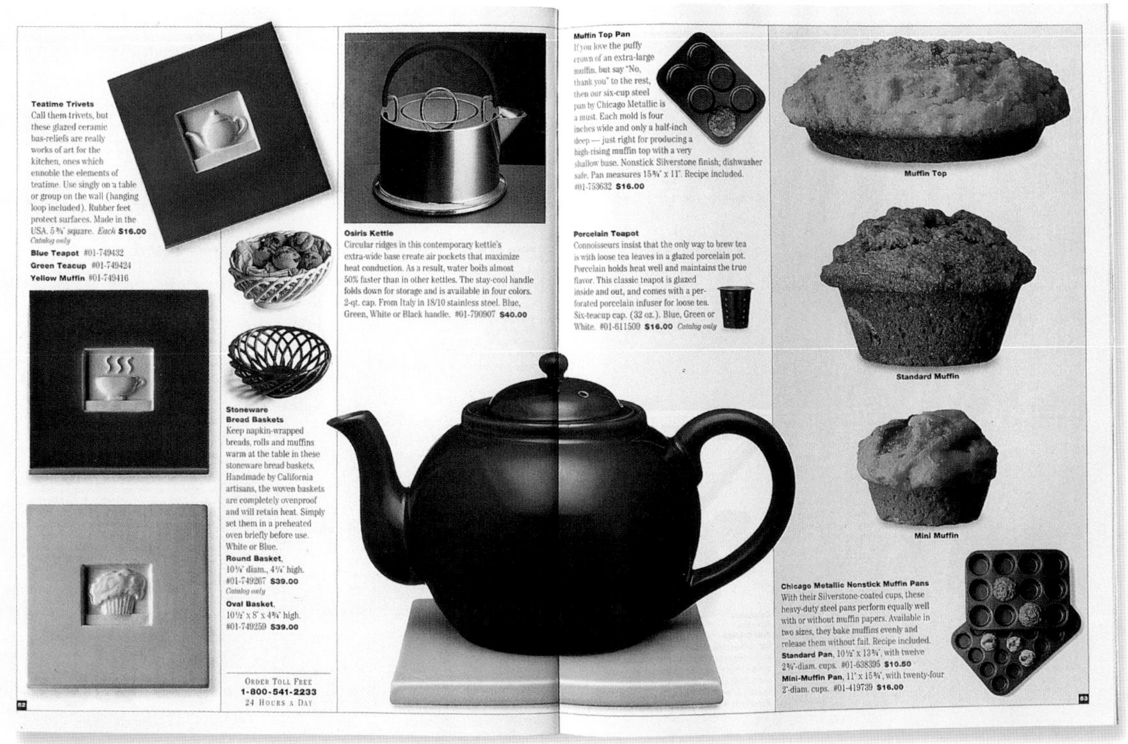

Teatime Trivets
Call them trivets, but these glazed ceramic bas-reliefs are really works of art for the kitchen, ones which ennoble the elements of teatime. Use singly on a table or group on the wall (hanging loop included). Rubber feet protect surfaces. Made in the USA. 5¾" square. *Each* **$16.00**
Catalog only
Blue Teapot #01-749432
Green Teacup #01-749424
Yellow Muffin #01-749416

Stoneware Bread Baskets
Keep napkin-wrapped breads, rolls and muffins warm at the table in these stoneware bread baskets. Handmade by California artisans, the woven baskets are completely ovenproof and will retain heat. Simply set them in a preheated oven briefly before use. White or Blue.
Round Basket, 10¾" diam., 4¼" high. #01-749267 **$39.00**
Catalog only
Oval Basket, 10½" x 8" x 4¾" high. #01-749259 **$39.00**

ORDER TOLL FREE
1-800-541-2233
24 HOURS A DAY

62

Osiris Kettle
Circular ridges in this contemporary kettle's extra-wide base create air pockets that maximize heat conduction. As a result, water boils almost 50% faster than in other kettles. The stay-cool handle folds down for storage and is available in four colors. 2-qt. cap. From Italy in 18/10 stainless steel. Blue, Green, White or Black handle. #01-790907 **$40.00**

Muffin Top Pan
If you love the puffy crown of an extra-large muffin, but say "No, thank you" to the rest, then our six-cup steel pan by Chicago Metallic is a must. Each mold is four inches wide and only a half-inch deep — just right for producing a high-rising muffin top with a very shallow base. Nonstick Silverstone finish; dishwasher safe. Pan measures 15¾" x 11". Recipe included. #01-753632 **$16.00**

Porcelain Teapot
Connoisseurs insist that the only way to brew tea is with loose tea leaves in a glazed porcelain pot. Porcelain holds heat well and maintains the true flavor. This classic teapot is glazed inside and out, and comes with a perforated porcelain infuser for loose tea. Six-teacup cap. (32 oz.). Blue, Green or White. #01-611500 **$16.00** *Catalog only*

Muffin Top

Standard Muffin

Mini Muffin

Chicago Metallic Nonstick Muffin Pans
With their Silverstone-coated cups, these heavy-duty steel pans perform equally well with or without muffin papers. Available in two sizes, they bake muffins evenly and release them without fail. Recipe included.
Standard Pan, 10½" x 13¾", with twelve 2¾"-diam. cups. #01-638395 **$10.50**
Mini-Muffin Pan, 11" x 15¾", with twenty-four 2"-diam. cups. #01-419739 **$16.00**

63

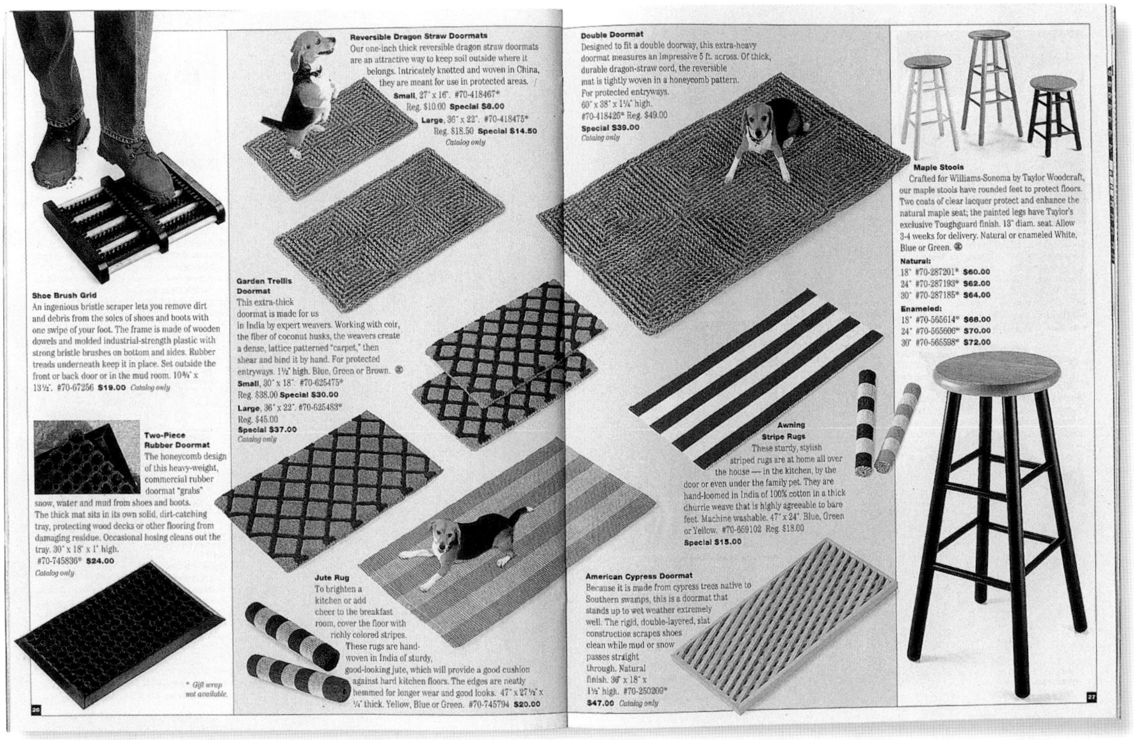

Shoe Brush Grid
An ingenious bristle scraper lets you remove dirt and debris from the soles of shoes and boots with one swipe of your foot. The frame is made of wooden dowels and molded industrial-strength plastic with strong bristle brushes on bottom and sides. Rubber treads underneath keep it in place. Set outside the front or back door or in the mud room. 10¾" x 13½". #70-67256 **$19.00** *Catalog only*

Two-Piece Rubber Doormat
The honeycomb design of this heavy-weight, commercial rubber doormat "grabs" snow, water and mud from shoes and boots. The thick mat sits in its own solid, dirt-catching tray, protecting wood decks or other flooring from damaging residue. Occasional hosing cleans out the tray. 30" x 18" x 1" high.
#70-745836* **$24.00**
Catalog only

* *Gift wrap not available.*

26

Reversible Dragon Straw Doormats
Our one-inch thick reversible dragon straw doormats are an attractive way to keep soil outside where it belongs. Intricately knotted and woven in China, they are meant for use in protected areas.
Small, 27" x 16". #70-418467*
Reg. $10.00 **Special $8.00**
Large, 36" x 22". #70-418475*
Reg. $18.50 **Special $14.50**
Catalog only

Garden Trellis Doormat
This extra-thick doormat is made for us in India by expert weavers. Working with coir, the fiber of coconut husks, the weavers create a dense, lattice patterned "carpet," then shear and bind it by hand. For protected entryways. 1½" high. Blue, Green or Brown.
Small, 30" x 18". #70-625475*
Reg. $38.00 **Special $30.00**
Large, 36" x 22". #70-625483*
Reg. $45.00
Special $37.00
Catalog only

Jute Rug
To brighten a kitchen or add cheer to the breakfast room, cover the floor with richly colored stripes. These rugs are hand-woven in India of sturdy, good-looking jute, which will provide a good cushion against hard kitchen floors. The edges are neatly hemmed for longer wear and good looks. 47" x 27½" x ¼" thick. Yellow, Blue or Green. #70-745794 **$20.00**

Double Doormat
Designed to fit a double doorway, this extra-heavy doormat measures an impressive 5 ft. across. Of thick, durable dragon-straw cord, the reversible mat is tightly woven in a honeycomb pattern. For protected entryways.
60" x 38" x 1¼" high.
#70-418426* Reg. $49.00
Special $39.00
Catalog only

Awning Stripe Rugs
These sturdy, stylish striped rugs are at home all over the house — in the kitchen, by the door or even under the family pet. They are hand-loomed in India of 100% cotton in a thick dhurrie weave that is highly agreeable to bare feet. Machine washable. 47" x 24". Blue, Green or Yellow. #70-659102 Reg. $18.00
Special $15.00

American Cypress Doormat
Because it is made from cypress trees native to Southern swamps, this is a doormat that stands up to wet weather extremely well. The rigid, double-layered, slat construction scrapes shoes clean while mud or snow passes straight through. Natural finish. 36" x 18" x 1½" high. #70-250209*
$47.00 *Catalog only*

Maple Stools
Crafted for Williams-Sonoma by Taylor Woodcraft, our maple stools have rounded feet to protect floors. Two coats of clear lacquer protect and enhance the natural maple seat; the painted legs have Taylor's exclusive Toughguard finish. 13" diam. seat. Allow 3-4 weeks for delivery. Natural or enameled White, Blue or Green.
Natural:
18" #70-287201* **$60.00**
24" #70-287193* **$62.00**
30" #70-287185* **$64.00**
Enameled:
18" #70-565614* **$68.00**
24" #70-565606* **$70.00**
30" #70-565598* **$72.00**

27

Pentagram designed advertising with the objective of identifying Williams-Sonoma close-ly with Thanksgiving. The ads borrowed the instructive voice of the catalogs, focusing on individual products and explaining their relationship to the holiday meal.

Where are you going
for Thanksgiving?

Williams-Sonoma invites
you to visit us first.

In the hectic days before
Thanksgiving, you'll find
it's the little things that will
make a big difference
in your holiday cooking.
The proper tools – and
pertinent tips – are the
secret to stylish success.

Like a length of cotton/
linen twine to truss the
turkey so it's easier to work
with and looks beautiful
when you present it. Let
the turkey rest at least
30 minutes after roasting
so it's easier to carve
and juicier to eat.

WILLIAMS-SONOMA

Butcher Twine
$5.00

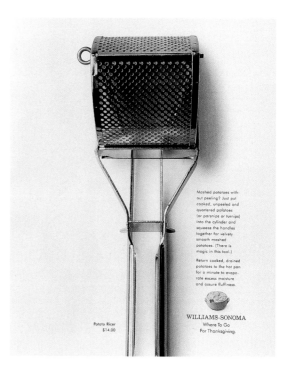

Mashed potatoes with-
out peeling? Just put
cooked, unpeeled and
quartered potatoes
(or parsnips or turnips)
into the cylinder and
squeeze the handles
together for velvety
smooth mashed
potatoes. (There is
magic in this tool.)

Return cooked, drained
potatoes to the hot pan
for a minute to evapo-
rate excess moisture
and assure fluffiness.

WILLIAMS-SONOMA
Where To Go
For Thanksgiving.

Potato Ricer
$14.00

Fat out, flavor in: a
ladle that takes the
frustration out of remov-
ing fat from the broth.
A clever tool with slots
on one side so the fat
flows away and the
flavor remains.

Start broths with cold
water so the full flavor
of the ingredients is
drawn into the liquid.

WILLIAMS-SONOMA
Where To Go
For Thanksgiving.

Fat-off Ladle
$15.00

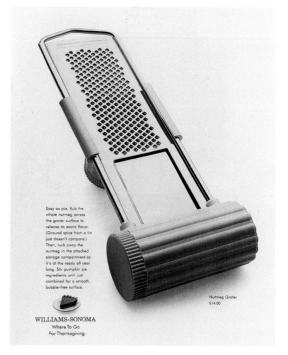

Easy as pie. Rub the
whole nutmeg across
the grater surface to
release its exotic flavor.
(Ground spice from a tin
just doesn't compare.)
Then, tuck away the
nutmeg in the attached
storage compartment so
it's at the ready all year
long. Stir pumpkin pie
ingredients until just
combined for a smooth,
bubble-free surface.

Nutmeg Grater
$14.00

WILLIAMS-SONOMA
Where To Go
For Thanksgiving.

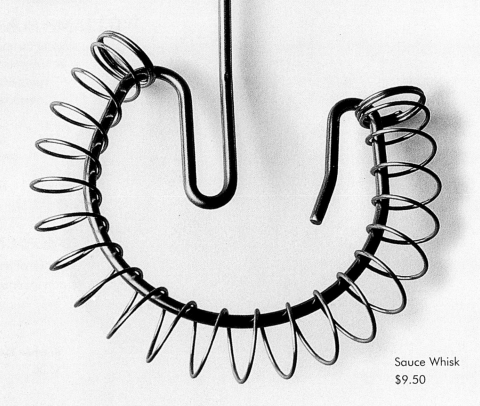

The secret to smooth, elegant gravy: the flat sauce whisk designed especially for stirring, whisking and working all areas of the pan. Balanced and always dependable, it makes the perfect saucier chef.

Heating liquid before adding to other ingredients in the pan helps make your gravy lump-free.

WILLIAMS-SONOMA
Where To Go
For Thanksgiving.

Sauce Whisk
$9.50

To appeal to increasing consumer demand for freedom of choice in selecting casual dinnerware, a retail program packages and displays merchandise to help do-it-yourself retailers and customers make effective, satisfying decisions.

The Pfaltzgraff Co.

The Pfaltzgraff family of German immigrants began making pottery in 1811 in York, Pennsylvania, where the company headquarters still stand. In the 1950s they began producing dinnerware which was first sold by the piece. In the 1960s, with mass production and sophisticated marketing techniques becoming the norm, the company joined others in the industry in prepackaging its dinnerware. Young homemakers, especially, appreciated the convenience and correctness of the four-person china sets sold in housewares departments. Today, a new generation of consumers is returning to the older, more confident ways. Young, independent women and men, single parents, and unmarried couples represent a variety of purchasing, dining, and entertaining habits. Their preferences account for the success of open stock retailers like Crate & Barrel. Pfaltzgraff looked to serve this market by offering mix-and-match lines equivalent in price and quality to its traditional dinnerware sets.

It developed three different patterns within two decorative directions: Cloverhill, with a predominantly green flower-and-trellis theme, and Wyngate, a mostly blue collection with a bold stripe detail. Pfaltzgraff then came to Pentagram, which had earlier created a New York wholesale showroom for the company, to name the line, develop packaging graphics for it, and create display structures that would work in different retail environments.

The name selected, Choices, inspired a logo design incorporating three typefaces, Clarendon, Bodoni, and Futura – a graphic reference to the three-pattern scheme of the dinnerware collections. The logo is used against a field of alternating circles and squares – another iteration of the mix-and-match idea.

For the store displays, Pfaltzgraff wanted the mixing concept to be instantly comprehensible. Furthermore, retailers needed an attractive, compact system that is simple to set up and restock, without a lot of packaging. And consumers, according to research, wanted to have the freedom to handle and intermix product lines, but also to see possibilities. Given a maximum four-by-four-foot tabletop, the designers had to come up with a way to display up to fifty-seven items: nine different serving pieces plus twelve each of the four basic dishes. They had to represent the mix of Cloverhill and Wyngate patterns and show how they might be combined.

Pentagram's graphic and architectural teams devised a set of twelve chipboard box forms that can be piled up to form a honeycombed ziggurat. The display kit also includes a wire-and-printed-cardboard lollipop sign that illustrates the product combinations. The sign works like a three-dimensional flag that can sit atop the ziggurat or stand alone with a smaller selection of product.

The display boxes are printed to match the product packaging, with white details against a plain brown background. The boxes make an economical, efficient backdrop; they let the product stand out but are still attractive enough to be stacked neatly under the table on the selling floor. The rhythm of boxes, squares, and circles gives an impression of order but allows ample room for change.

Additional packaging graphics make the merchandising program almost foolproof. On the sides of the cardboard boxes, silk-screened line drawings of the items inside allow instant product identification. Printed on the bottom of each box – in case the directions enclosed in the shipping carton are discarded – is a plan-o-gram or schematic drawing of the tabletop system.

Pfaltzgraff introduced the Choices line to the public in the spring of 1997 and showcased it to the trade during New York Market Week that fall. "We're really pleased with the results," says Bob Farnsworth, Pfaltzgraff's executive vice president of marketing.

The modular display system we developed for the Choices line of mix-and-match tableware allowed for multiple configurations, from a single tabletop display to a full storefront window, as showcased here at Pfaltzgraff's Fifth Avenue showroom.

Pfaltzgraff and Pentagram first worked together on new showroom interiors, a process that stretched the company's design vision. Three years later, Pfaltzgraff drew upon our multidisciplinary resources to develop the graphic and display strategies for Choices.

the first book of moses, called

genesis

with an introduction by | steven rose

To make the Bible more appealing to modern readers, an Edinburgh publisher presents, for the first time, the books of the New and Old Testaments in separate volumes to be read as individual works of literature.

The Pocket Canon Bible Series

In what the *Guardian* calls "the most radical repackaging of the Bible for decades," Canongate Books Ltd. rethought the format of the holy scriptures in an effort to update their look and attract a mass audience of both religious and secular readers. Drawing upon the seventeenth-century Authorized King James Version of the Bible, the Canongate series consists of twelve volumes (Genesis, Exodus, Job, Proverbs, Ecclesiastes, the Four Gospels, Solomon, Corinthians, and Revelation), reversing the nearly two-thousand-year-old, single-edition, collected-works treatment and presenting each book as it was first written: distinct and separate from the others. In designing the provocative series, Pentagram applied a stark, spare aesthetic to both visual and text treatments, giving the series a compelling look of immediacy, realism, and broadly based relevance. Well before its announced publication date, agreements were reached with additional publishers to produce Greek, German, Australian, Spanish, and U.S. editions. "The point of the series is to republish [the Bible] in a way that makes it accessible as a great work of literature," explains Canongate's Jamie Byng. The Bible "is such a rich text with so many things that are worth thinking about." As part of the contemporizing objective, Byng asked twelve internationally renowned authors and scholars to write introductions for each volume in the series, imparting insight into the original texts, which fall into such distinct categories as law, history, theology, fiction, and poetry. The contributors include Doris Lessing, Louis de Bernières, Will Self, Steven Rose, and Blake Morrison.

Pentagram chose black-and-white photographic and illustrative images for the books' covers. The subject matter is equally modern, from the mushroom cloud of an atomic explosion to the shadowy image of a lone man in dark coat, trousers, and bowler to a ribbon of highway disappearing into the horizon. The objective was to give the books a desirable, intriguing look, one that everyone would be comfortable reading on the subway.

The age-old tradition of beginning each verse on a new line has been replaced with a paragraph format, while a single column of type per page is used instead of the usual two columns. The effect is to create text that is more familiar to today's eye and considerably easier to read.

Previous attempts to restyle the Bible have typically been met with widespread opposition and criticism. This has not been the case with the Pocket Canons. Both religious and literary circles have registered enthusiasm for the new series, thus paving the way for their worldwide distribution and perhaps a resurgence in popularity for biblical storytelling within the general reading public.

Identifying what it calls an "increasing contemporary and premillennial interest in religion," Canongate Books decided to issue its Pocket Canons in hopes of reaching a larger and more varied general readership than have traditional editions of the Bible.

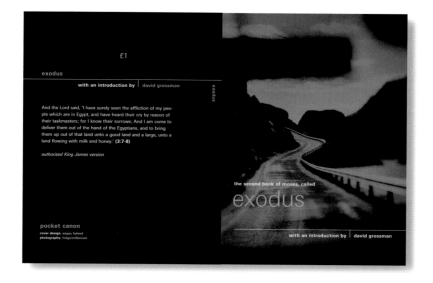

the book of
job

with an introduction by | louis de bernières

proverbs

with an introduction by | charles johnson

ecclesiastes

or, the preacher

with an introduction by | doris lessing

the song of
solomon

with an introduction by | a s byatt

the gospel according to

matthew

with an introduction by | a n wilson

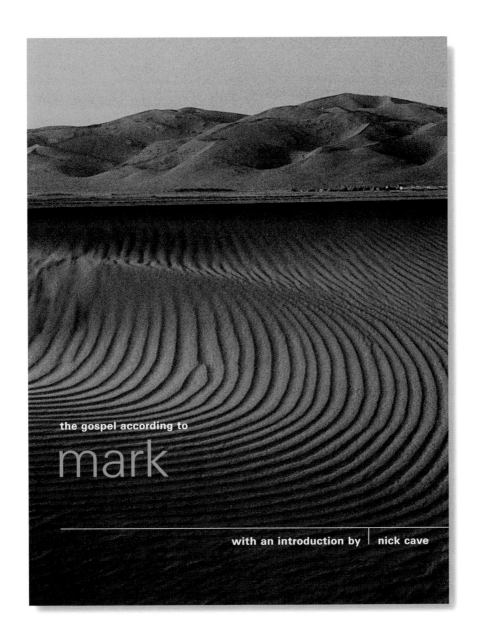

the gospel according to

mark

with an introduction by │ nick cave

the gospel according to

luke

with an introduction by | richard holloway

the gospel according to

john

with an introduction by | blake morrison

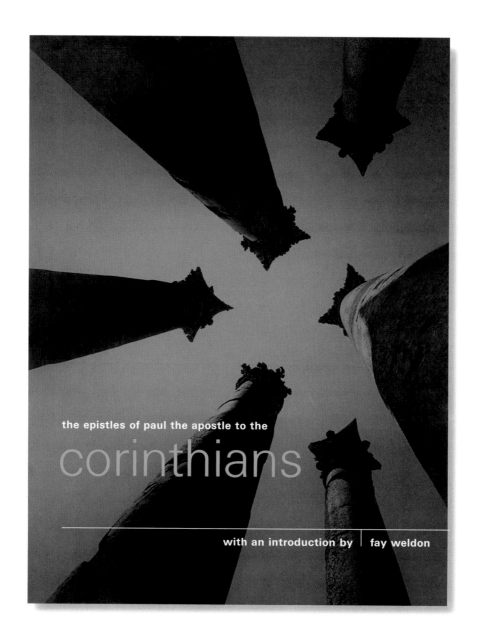

the epistles of paul the apostle to the

corinthians

with an introduction by | fay weldon

revelation

with an introduction by | will self

Packaging, signage, point-of-purchase, and collateral materials reinject ethnicity into a series of products increasingly subject to commodity pricing pressures, transforming them – without the aid of advertising – into a brand family.

Columbus Salame

Good design is about choices. Decisions – serif or sans serif? blue or red? photograph or illustration? – may, after years of experience, be made instinctively and rapidly. But they are nonetheless a learned response, a reaction to a problem in need of important, if simple, solutions. As often as not, that problem is a familiar one. Take the case of the Columbus Salame Company, a successful San Francisco purveyor of delicatessen meats and other prepared foods. Starting with the Italian community in the city's North Beach district, Columbus had, in a generation, built up a strong local following for its mortadellas, prosciuttos, roast beefs, and the like. But by the mid-1990s, the second generation of family management was eyeing a complex future. Having invested deeply in the infrastructure of the company, they were searching for ways to increase their market share and expand their profit margins. They were feeling extreme pressure from both ends of the competitive spectrum.

Above them, nationally advertised brands offered name recognition and distribution clout that were overpowering the supermarket deli counters that were Columbus's main retail venue. Below Columbus, other processors were reducing their prices. If the company followed that route, it would risk lowering its reputation for quality, making retailers even less likely to put it on a shelf with the national wursts.

Columbus came to Pentagram for help in updating its image. At the time, it was seeking something small and discreet: a new logotype that, perhaps, it could apply to the packaging of its primary line of food products.

The logo certainly needed to be changed. A portrait of Christopher Columbus that dated to the 1950s had the kind of neutral, Everyman appearance that was devoid of character and meaning. The old explorer had been Betty Crockerized – turned into a generic American icon – not the sort of image to attract a contemporary consumer with a demand for taste, tradition, craft, and authenticity.

Our design team's first decision was to make Columbus appear more genuine by using a scratchboard illustration that resembled an engraving. While we decided not to eliminate the long-standing color scheme – Columbus

had significant equity in its red-white-blue pattern, and the obvious alternative, the red, white, and green of the Italian flag, was overused – we did add to it. The designers set the illustration against a cream background, which has a depth and warmth and richness that pure white does not. Just as it was important to avoid clichés in the coloring, we wanted to avoid them in the type treatment. The word "Columbus" is thus set in Bodoni bold extra condensed, a serif face with historical European connotations, while descriptive product names are set in Futura, a classic, geometric, Bauhaus-era font that connotes modernity and commerce.

Although leery of conventions, the design team did want to make sure that the company's long European heritage emerged; Christopher Columbus, after all, is as much an Italian as an American symbol. In our research, we had found a lovely old engraved map of Italy. At first, we applied it to the stationery system, ghosting it on the backs of cards and letterhead. But the character was so appealing that we soon added it to the product packaging itself. In the case of dry salamis, the map is used both on the backs of hang tags and printed across the entire wrapping. The

The generic Columbus logo from the 1950s (above) was brought into the present by – ironically – stepping backward to an era of old engravings, muted color palettes, and traditional typography (right).

packaging becomes a point-of-purchase display that hearkens back to the Old World, boosting the image of both the product and the counter that holds it. Yet the cost was roughly the same as before the design change. The client was so pleased with retailers' reaction to the new packaging that, eighteen months later, the company asked Pentagram to take on a second project: a new, premium brand.

Columbus owned a specialty brand already, which carried the name Ticino but bore no marks identifying it with Columbus. We believed that a new name and new packaging would extend the company's brand equity and increase production and distribution of these higher-margin products. Pentagram came up with the name Renaissance. We specifically linked the new brand to Columbus's ownership, expecting that the premium line and the main brand would continually augment each other's value associations.

Our team did two things to distinguish the new Renaissance line from the main Columbus line. We made the background of the labels entirely black, with metallic gold trim and lettering. And we added a four-color Renaissance painting to the labels, a different work for each of four differ-

ent products. Rather quickly, retailers expanded their orders to include the new Renaissance meats; the quality look of the Columbus lines improved the appearance and enriched the atmosphere of their deli departments. In addition, the new look gave the company increased penetration in upscale specialty delicatessens.

The success of the rebranding campaign was also validated by a call to Columbus from Williams-Sonoma, the premium kitchen-product retailer and direct-response marketer. It wanted to include a Renaissance gift pack in all its catalogs. Williams-Sonoma required that the products offered use different packaging than those sold at retail. Pentagram responded with an adaptation of the Renaissance brand packaging: extending one painting, in segments, across the four salamis in the box.

The brand is now being extended to behind-the-counter deli boards, point-of-purchase displays, and calendars. A final, and perhaps the most visible, part of the program is the redesign of the fleet of Columbus trucks. These trucks serve as a series of moving billboards for the company's products, and the new shirts and caps worn by the drivers/salespeople provide a consistent image for the company.

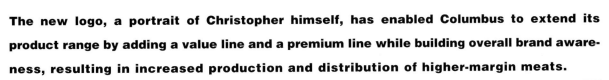

The new logo, a portrait of Christopher himself, has enabled Columbus to extend its product range by adding a value line and a premium line while building overall brand awareness, resulting in increased production and distribution of higher-margin meats.

The number of package sizes, configurations, and materials vary greatly within the Columbus line. A consistent Columbus logo overlays different labels to strengthen the brand identity in the highly competitive deli-case environment.

Giving an opaque color and textured surface to the clear plastic that encases a conventional compact disc provides an iconoclastic band with a global marketing platform.

The Pet Shop Boys

The compact-disc recording format has moved the music industry forward by delivering better recordings than ever before, but the packaging – the conventional jewel box – still speaks the language of vinyl. Whether the Beatles or Beethoven, an individual CD remains distinguishable only by the image on the cover and the tiny typography on the spine. Difficult to open and easy to break, jewel boxes also render any album, once it is stacked on a shelf with others, instantly anonymous. For the launch of the Pet Shop Boys' recording *Very* in 1993, Pentagram developed an alternative packaging concept intended to stand out both in the cluttered retail environment and at home. In the process, we also created a platform for the album's marketing strategy. The band, which delights in defying pop conventions in its music, videos, and performances, wanted a CD case that would transcend its storage function to become an object of desire itself.

The model was a perfume bottle – a package that adds immeasurable perceived value to the fragrance it contains. For the Pet Shop Boys, that meant fashioning something radically different, but still compatible with existing production and distribution processes.

The answer was a traditional jewel case rendered opaque and bright orange in color, studded with a pattern and with the lettering of the album's title raised. The orange plastic cost the same as the transparent plastic normally used on CD cases, while the thickness and pitch of the stud texture were given a final geometry that accommodated the suction pads required for the automated machinery that puts the CD into the case. The texture added another dimension to the musical experience and was intended to give the CD an industrial feel. The color made it stand out dramatically at retail and rendered it instantly recognizable among the stacks of CDs on the audiophile's home shelf.

The packaging was central to the way *Very* was launched. By removing a photographic image and the cultural connotations it inevitably would have carried, we turned what might have been a national product into an international one. The opaqueness and the color allowed retailers around the world to create striking displays of massed orange plastic blocks, which acted as a draw at the point of purchase. The image was prominently featured on publicity posters and was used as a device in the album's promotional video, which depicted the Pet Shop Boys floating on giant orange floor tiles.

At the same time, the band also introduced a dance-music album entitled *Very Relentless* in a limited edition of one hundred thousand. It, too, was packaged in an opaque studded case, but this time the box was actually made of soft plastic, a striking departure from traditional CD packs.

After three years and millions of units sold, demand for *Very* dropped below the point the producer could support the special injection-molding tools needed to manufacture the studded cover. So a follow-up package for the mass market was designed, which featured the traditional clear CD case, but with a cover photograph of the initial version. It underscored the evolution of a design idea directly into a worldwide marketing icon.

The orange case for *Very* was released in 1993; at the same time a dance album, *Very Relentless*, was issued with a soft plastic cover. Three years later, with *Very* still selling but with a lowered demand, the record label went to clear plastic.

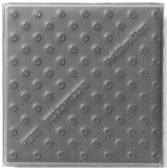

The packaging system was designed from the start to encompass a marketing strategy and enabled the Pet Shop Boys to promote their CD as if it were a perfume bottle, evidenced by its inclusion in the advertising campaign and promotional video.

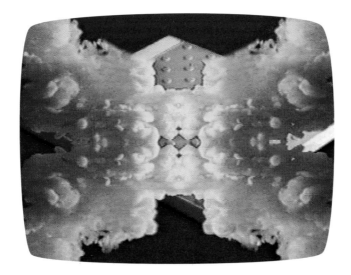

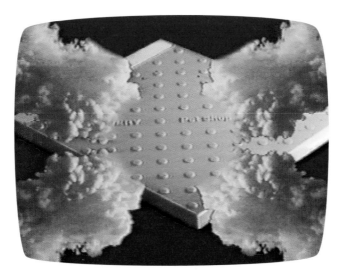

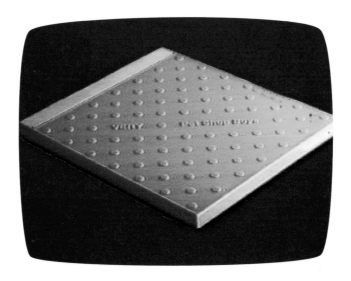

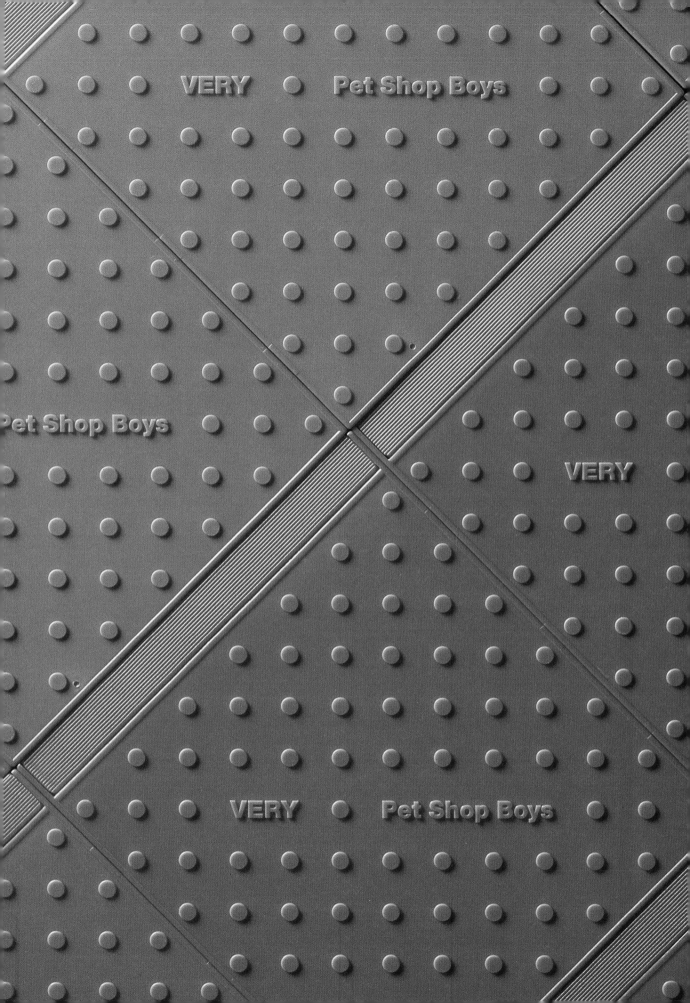

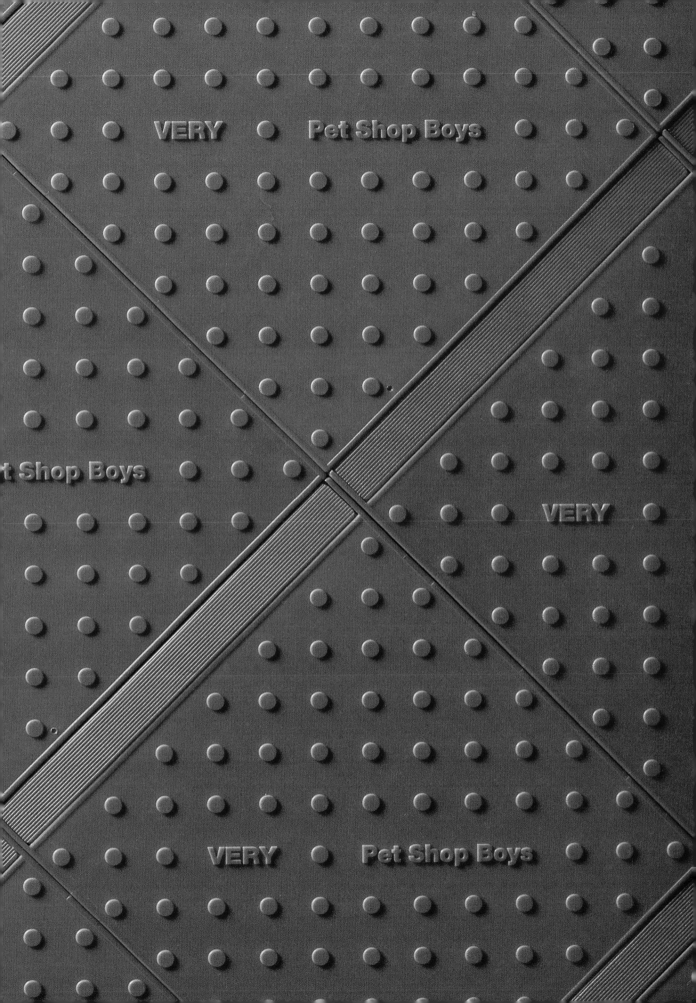

An evocative municipal seal, comprehensive public and retail signage, and a surprising sales center lend an old-fashioned air to a 4,900-acre contemporary planned community near Orlando, Florida.

Celebration, Florida

What does it take to create a real town? There are buildings to build, streets to pave, parks to plant, and residents to recruit, of course. But what about the other elements: the street signs, civic symbols, and commercial marquees that combine to hold a place together and give it character? When The Walt Disney Company assembled some of the most prominent figures in architecture and design to help them turn 4,900 acres of Florida swampland into a suburban utopia just down the road from the Magic Kingdom, Pentagram was given the task of defining the new town's identity, from the town seal to the street numbers on the revival-style houses. In between, we took on every other signage project in town, from Main Street to the movie theater. The design team even got to cook up a custom cast-iron manhole cover to complete the illusion. The origins of Celebration, as the company named the town, were in Walt Disney's long-held personal dream of designing a model community of the future.

Though strains of it exist in Epcot, the Experimental Prototype Community of Tomorrow, Walt's space-age vision was never realized. Still, the idea of building an experimental community for real folks persisted in Disney's corporate memory. Times change. When the plan to develop a town resurfaced during chief executive Michael Eisner's first years at Disney, wide sidewalks, golf courses, and cyberspace had replaced monorails and geodesic domes as hallmarks of the futuristic good life. In response to recent trends in urban design, the town is intended to be an antidote to the lonely car culture that rules most suburbs.

Instead of driving to a strip mall, residents of Celebration can walk to their own self-contained shopping area, intended to evoke the easy charms of a timeless southern seaside town. To bring more life to the lakeside downtown, architects Robert A. M. Stern and Jaquelin Robertson included mixed-use buildings (stores below, apartments above) in their master plan. Other well-known architects, including Michael Graves and the late Aldo Rossi, were commissioned to design the town's showcase public buildings: a post office, bank, town hall, and offices.

Houses in Celebration are designed in one of six approved historical styles, ranging from Colonial Revival to French.

To encourage neighborly interaction, houses are built on very small lots and every one features a front porch. The architects' hope is that residents of the new town will gather on sidewalks and porches to knit together the kind of close community that would be difficult to maintain on streets lined with spaced-out, self-absorbed ranch houses. Underneath the gently curving streets, a fiber-optic network links every home to a profusion of local on-line services and to the Internet beyond.

In the spring of 1993, after the town was planned and the major buildings were distributed to their respective master builders, Pentagram was brought into the project, originally as part of a short design charrette. As the design team's role evolved over the course of that year, our mandate became the creation of the interrelated commercial and corporate identities that would, when expressed in graphic or architectural designs, cement together the real town and Disney's narrative ideal. To achieve this goal, we studied the signage and graphic standards of old-fashioned southern towns and then applied this research to designs that evoke a pleasantly misty past without copying anything. In keeping with the Disney sensibility, we inserted into our work measured wit and large doses of quiet good humor.

Celebration is an ambitious expression of new urban-planning theories that seek to reinvigorate civic life with design principles familiar from small towns. The town seal crystallizes this vision by merging the natural, the human-made, and the human.

Pentagram designed a complete corporate identity for The Celebration Company (the special division of Disney Development that runs the town), its two preview centers (information and sales offices that told the story of the town), street signs, a looming water-tower welcome sign, and 95 percent of all retail signage on the town's commercial streets. In addition, we formatted the *Celebration Pattern Book*, a shrubs-to-chimney guide to approved home-building in Celebration, and the *Retail Guidelines*, a similar codebook for the town's stores.

Large subprojects include signage and identities for the town's golf club, hospital, movie theater, and office buildings; park- and trail-system signage; design of a landmark fountain at the center of town; and – not least – the manhole covers. Pentagram also acted as consultant on the commercial spin-offs: hats, T-shirts, pens, watches, and golf paraphernalia including balls, tees, and clubs. The foundation for many of these projects and products is the town seal, which also serves as the logo of The Celebration Company. Affectionately known as "Tree Girl," the seal is a composition of profiles: an oak tree, surrounded by a picket fence, overarches a girl on an old three-speed, pedaling quickly from a dog nipping at her rear wheel. Tree Girl was originally just one of many designs proposed for the town's manhole covers, but she was adopted by the clients during the design process and elevated to a higher status. This is just as well: the image condenses Celebration's hometown intentions in a form that is instantly recognizable and easily applied elsewhere. On Market Street, the main shopping street, the logo is cut out in pure silhouette and used as a standard on lampposts. The official Celebration watch also creatively reuses the logo: Tree Girl takes a leisurely ride on the minute hand while her dog races by, counting the seconds.

Environmental graphic elements in the town, whether street signs or manhole covers, were manufactured using timeless materials and vintage production techniques. Pentagram designed more than one thousand signs in Celebration.

Celebration's town signs are unified through the consistent use of a single typeface, Cheltenham, and a single color, dark green (this page and opposite). Elements from the town seal, notably the girl and her dog, are often joined by other silhouetted images.

A temporary preview center (overleaf) was established to sell homes while Celebration was still a construction site. Houses were evoked with full-size trompe l'oeil photomurals enlarged from small watercolors.

Even before ground was broken on the town in 1994, the design team sketched its character in the temporary preview center. During its eighteen months of operation in 1994 and 1995, it hosted over one hundred thousand potential residents and curious passersby, until the permanent preview center, which occupies one side of Celebration's well-tended Market Square, replaced it. Sited within view of the busy approach highway, the temporary preview center was conceived as a building and a billboard. Two double off-the-shelf industrial trailers formed its core and housed an inventive exhibit: large aerial perspectives and detailed renderings of street scenes enhanced by real artifacts (tennis rackets, a bike) to show the life to come.

The interior was built with exposed stud-walls and free-standing door frames rising from a full-scale enlargement of the blueprint for the center itself. This witty allusion to the unfinished state of the town united the interior with the exterior concept. To give visitors an idea of the scale and quality of Celebration's houses, three enormous billboards were built around the trailers. Each structure supported a full-size enlargement of a watercolor rendering of a typical Colonial, Coastal, or Victorian house at Celebration. These wafer-thin stage sets were fitted with real porches, mailboxes, and other details and set behind lawns, hedges, and the requisite picket fences.

Inside the temporary preview center's "mirage of homes," several connected trailers were fitted out as an unfinished construction site. In keeping with the work-in-progress ethos, the floor was a full-scale blueprint, complete with architects' dimensions.

Handling all of the official and commercial signage in Celebration gave us an opportunity to shape the overall urban pattern. To allow variation within a unified scheme, the designers chose a single, versatile family of typefaces – Cheltenham, designed in 1896 by architect Bertram Goodhue – for all The Celebration Company signage, including street signs, lot markers, official vehicles, and so forth. In addition to the variety it allows, Cheltenham is one of the few serif fonts that maintains adequate thicknesses for practical use in cut-metal applications.

The commercial signage was treated more freely, but it still follows a few well-considered rules. For instance, every corner store features a larger sign, angled out at forty-five degrees, to punctuate the corner and increase visibility from the converging streets. Complete control of signage also allowed small-scale quality-of-life interventions. The jewelry store, for example, which is adjacent to the cinema, was given a sign with a rotating clock, to reassure theatergoers as they approach the nearby ticket window.

The Celebration Golf Club also demanded its own identity. Here, again, the design is based on the town seal, but in place of the oak tree and picket fence is a smooth 1920s-era golfer in knickers. A tremendous thundercloud, a familiar feature of the Florida landscape, looms behind. The Golf Club is conceived as a sort of renovated barn, and the signage honors this make-believe heritage with allusions to old roadside farm-country motifs.

Today, Celebration is a community of 1,500 residents living in 520 houses and apartments, on its way to a maximum approved build-out of 8,000 residences. Among the earliest residents, there is an understanding of the depth of thought behind their designed environment: they saw the birth of the town from nothing. In the first decades of the twenty-first century, however, the town may reach its estimated maximum population of twenty thousand. Will these future Celebrants be conscious of the intricate design thinking that surrounds them? It is hoped that they will ignore it, just like they would in a real town.

Signs on the town's major buildings reflect each architect's individual style. César Pelli's American modern movie theaters required an Art Deco approach (left); rustic enamel signs decorate Jaquelin Robertson's farmhouse-like Golf Club.

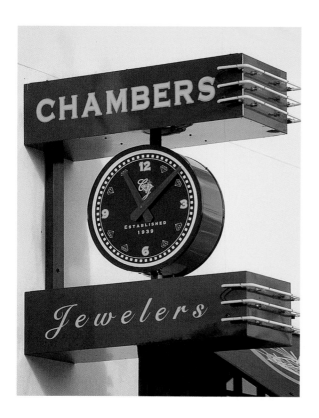

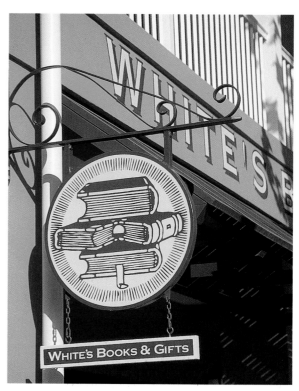

Whereas the town's municipal signs were meant to provide a subtle, consistent background for everyday life, downtown Celebration's retail signs were designed by Pentagram to express the vitality of the classic American Main Street.

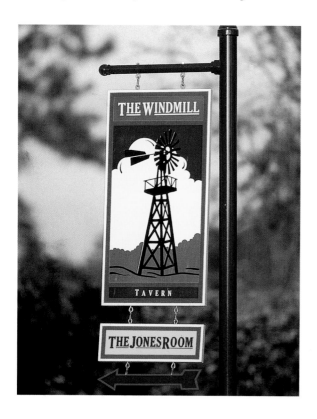

No two retail signs in Celebration are alike. Together, they provide a survey of vintage American sign-making techniques, from simple painted-wood blade signs to more elaborate mechanical signs with animated and electrical elements.

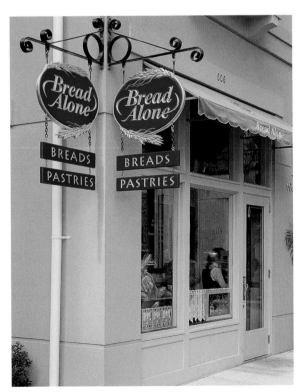

The American Institute
of Architects,
New York Chapter

1995 HERITAGE BALL

Honoring

PHILIP JOHNSON, FAIA

Monday, November 13, 1995

The University Club

1 West 54th Street, NY

Simple, bold iconography and bright primary colors redirect the aesthetics of a graphic program in order to help the AIA's founding chapter renew its image as a leading design force in New York.

American Institute of Architects

The American Institute of Architects' New York Chapter was doing a good job – too good for its own good, in a way. As the national professional organization for licensed architects, the AIA is deeply involved in furthering design excellence, professional development, and civic engagement among members. In New York, where 2,500 members constituted by far the largest AIA chapter, there was concern that the chapter had evolved into primarily a professional practice organization and that its creative leadership position was threatened by other design institutions. This was a particularly sensitive issue given New York's long-standing identification as one of the world's most important centers for design, from architecture to fashion and the arts. To reclaim its creative standing, the chapter enlisted Pentagram to help redirect its internal and external print communication efforts. The AIA had a set of corporate graphics standards

American Institute of Architects, New York Chapter

Thursday May 22, Pier 63, 23rd St. & Hudson River

in place at the national level, which Pentagram was obliged to uphold. The design parameters were simple: the use of the Bodoni typeface and the color red. Building on this foundation didn't require a makeover so much as an "attitude adjustment" harboring a heightened sense of graphic smartness and design awareness. The adjustment was to be the visual signal of an invigorated design emphasis by the New York contingent.

The existing print program included the monthly publication, *Oculus,* and a variety of announcements that went to the design community on a frequent basis, trumpeting exhibitions, speaking programs, and other events, including those honoring luminaries such as Philip Johnson, I. M. Pei, César Pelli, and other world-renowned architects.

Prior to its redesign, *Oculus* had the look and sensibility of an in-house newsletter. Practically produced but lacking a presence, content consisted mostly of news, the who, what, where, and when of the membership.

Pentagram reshaped *Oculus,* elevating it to magazine status. Editorially, it would delve into substantive issues affecting the practice and future of architecture. The content was given pacing, with major and secondary stories and regular departments. A masthead and dramatic cover graphics devoted to each issue's lead story gave it a newsstand aesthetic. The interior was loosely formatted to create a measure of consistency and familiarity but with the opportunity to surprise.

Considerable attention was also paid to poster art, long a significant communications and creative medium in New York, and an art form greatly appreciated by architects. Here, however, there was far less structure, the operative considerations dealing primarily with vivid colors and striking, often whimsical iconography intended to focus attention and spread the word in a world besieged by data. If *Oculus* tended to a more serious debate, the announcements, especially the posters, would balance the demeanor of the program with humor, irony, and metaphor.

The poster, one of New York City's favorite forms of communication, used powerful images that were also familiar, from Philip Johnson's distinctive round eyeglasses (previous page) to the AIA acronym and landmark architecture.

The American Institute of Architects, New York Chapter 1997 Heritage Ball Honoring **I.M.PEI** Monday, November 13, 1997 The University Club 1 West 54th Street, NY Black Tie

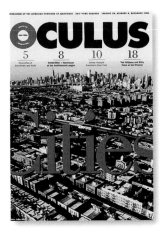

Whether through poster art or the monthly magazine *Oculus*, graphic boldness is the element most used to establish visual continuity in the print program. Coincidentally supporting the architectural design concept that less is more, the simple, visually bold

graphics make it possible to reduce production costs by, for instance, the limited use of color. These graphic signposts are more than merely decorative, they help direct the reader to the publication's message and content.

When an entity is as readily identifiable by an acronym as by its full name – the case for both the American Institute of Architects and New York – typography often can be made to work harder and more effectively than other visual images.

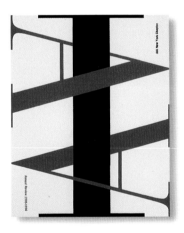

The print materials typically distributed by the AIA's New York chapter take many forms, from posters and calendars to announcements, directories, invitations, and other communication pieces, all of which rely heavily on typographic treatment.

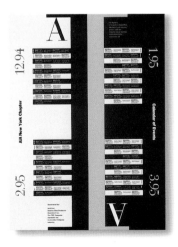

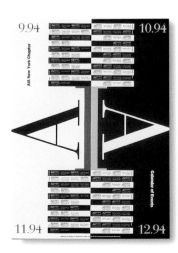

Elegant but low-key interior design serves as a subtle merchandising stage for Sculpture, a sophisticated new shop dedicated solely to lingerie, swimwear, and outerwear.

Sculpture

Product is as much a part of the interiors of Sculpture as the finishes, fixtures, and geometry of this exclusive intimate-apparel store in central London. Shot-silk covered panels, subdued recessed lighting, limestone and glass countertops and shelves, and sparingly displayed merchandise create an appearance more closely resembling an art gallery than a retail establishment. There is no hint of one of the building's previous incarnations: home to rock music icon Jimi Hendrix. From the outset, Pentagram's intent was to instill a degree of sensuousness and intimacy befitting the nature of the apparel. To this end, the elongated, one-hundred-forty-square-meter space has been animated by curved, built-in display cabinetry and angled suspended ceilings that draw customers through the store along a gently meandering route. The entire experience, from the traditional navy blue shopfront to the sales desk set unobtrusively at the back

of the store, is quiet and unhurried, as discreet in its sales approach as the merchandise on display.

The first shop in the U.K. dedicated solely to La Perla Fashion Group's brands, Sculpture is in the heart of London's famed Bondstreet fashion district. While the location has unsurpassed cachet, it presented the design team with some challenges. For example, the building is relatively small and very linear, limiting design options. It is also Grade One Listed, meaning that the historic exterior and overall proportions could not be altered.

The result is a classic facade that leads buyers into an elegantly modern retail setting appropriate to one of the most exclusive fashion lines in the world. From geometry and materials to display methods, Sculpture relies on minimalism to complement rather than compete with its product in much the same way that an art gallery uses light and space to frame its exhibits.

Instead of racks, highly polished stainless-steel rails are suspended from the ceiling or cantilevered from walls to give the lingerie the appearance of floating in space. Panels of ochre-colored, Jim Thompson Thai silk provide backdrops that blend with rich maple flooring at ground level, while on the lower level, silver-toned silk panels blend naturally with smooth limestone floors. Thick glass display shelves and mirrors help to bring a sense of light and depth into the narrow space.

Sculpture was an immediate commercial success. The store continually attracts widespread praise in the fashion industry and from the press.

Part of Sculpture's design objective was to reflect a spirit of generosity and repose in the face of the tight confines of space and a frenetic surrounding environment. The store feels bigger than it is and luxuriously quiet.

**Polaroid
Professional
Photography**
Ausgabe 9

The goal of building stronger relationships between Polaroid and professional photographers was achieved through the conception of a magazine based on a simple premise – always meeting and promoting photographers' interests first.

Polaroid's *P* Magazine

Consumer instant photography may be the high-profile part of Polaroid's activities, but in fact the corporation's professional products represent the larger part of its overall business. So the Polaroid Corporation needed a vehicle to help build a more creative and better technical relationship with its professional customers in Europe, especially photographers and art directors. In order to develop a more sophisticated approach to these people, Polaroid asked Pentagram to make proposals for a magazine aimed specifically at them. (Pentagram had been consultants for Polaroid's consumer and business markets outside North America since 1985.) *P* magazine was the result, launching as a biannual in 1990. The *P* title signifies "Polaroid Professional Photography" as well as "peel apart," the idea behind the logo. The editorship is rotated around Europe, and each issue centers on a particular theme, such as portraiture, still life, and so on, with regular features on technique, Polaroid materials, and photographers' profiles. The visually literate readership of photographers and art directors has taken to the magazine impressed by design, photographic, and production values maintained at the highest level.

Few constraints were imposed on the development of the magazine. The idea was that it should do the job not just of keeping photographers abreast of new product developments but also of building stronger relationships with them. So, working from an editorial concept devised by David Gibbs, the magazine was designed and produced on the basis of always meeting and promoting photographers' interests first.

The first hurdle was the choice of a title. The *P* is internationally recognized and has no language problems. The *P* logo is also particularly appropriate for the professional market because professional Polaroid film, which is available in eight-by-ten, four-by-five, and two-by-two-inch sizes, is still all "peel apart." The design development picked up on what makes Polaroid photography distinctive. Photographers' work is always shown "same size" (thirty-five-millimeter transparencies are reduced or enlarged), and the typographic grid of the magazine is based on an eight-by-ten ratio. *P* magazine has thirty-two pages plus the cover and is printed in five languages. Printing is carried out in seven colors: the four-color process, a second black, one special color, and varnish. Type is overprinted in the second black and there is rarely any dropped-out text because of the different languages. Text lengths allow for German, which runs 25 percent longer than the average.

The format has proved remarkably durable and only a few refinements have been made over the years. After the first ten issues, a third display face, chosen to suit the particular theme of each issue, supplements *P's* original two typefaces. New regular features include advertising campaign stories and the use of Polaroid pictures as final art.

The magazine has also introduced a biannual European photographic competition, which is featured in each and every issue. Judging is carried out at Pentagram's London offices, and the winning entries are published in a special regular supplement of *Creative Review*. Prizes include use of the only twenty-by-twenty-four-inch Polaroid camera in Europe, which is kept in Prague. Entries have grown from a hundred to a thousand since the competition started.

To ensure maximum benefit also accrues to Polaroid itself, the management of *P* magazine is rotated around the European Polaroid businesses so that there is no full-time dedicated manager and all learn and appreciate the tasks involved. The necessary continuity is provided by Pentagram and *P's* regular writer, Peter Lester.

P magazine's bold identity is carried out from issue to issue not through a traditional masthead but with a unique-to-Polaroid "peel apart" P logo; its position can vary on each cover.

Polaroid
Professional
Photography
Fashion
Issue 11

Polaroid
Professional
Photography
Black and White
Issue 12

Polaroid
Professional
Photography
Editorial
Issue 14

Polaroid
Professional
Photography
Location
Issue 15

Some people claim that they dream in colour, others believe their dreams are manifested in black and white. William Ropp dreams in subtle shades of mysterious grey. Through the black arts of photography, his dreams are reincarnated as cryptic images of a world populated by unquiet souls.

WILLIAM ROPP

French photographer William Ropp is thirty-five years old and lives in Nancy. The pictures shown here are chosen from a recently published book, *William Ropp*, Fabbiani del Mosso, Italy, 1995, containing a collection of his remarkable, and frequently alarmic, black and white photographic images.

Remarkable in many ways, especially when you take into account that he is completely self-taught and has only been involved seriously in photography since 1986. Before that time, he devoted himself to writing fantasy and science fiction novels, as well as writing and directing plays. An obsession with fantasy is still very evident in his photographic work.

Ropp describes himself as self taught in everything he does. 'I don't have my culture, and I know hardly anything about the genres I have chosen to work in. Therefore I have to rely completely on my own imagination.'

Like many photographers, Ropp finds it difficult, if not impossible, to talk in depth about what inspires his work. In fact, he regards analysis of the creative process as potentially destructive. 'I am still delighted and quite surprised when something I aim to achieve with photography is a success. My work is a process of turning dreams into images. My subconscious is the source of all my images and I want it to stay that way. I don't want the process to become too considered because this will destroy the freshness, and perhaps even close the door in my dreams.'

Ropp's ability to get in touch with this inner source of inspiration has led to the creation of some prodigious photography. His work has the peculiarly macabre quality that you find in Eastern European folk tales. Indeed a story seems to lurk behind each of these enigmatic images, perhaps a tale of hauntings, of magic or even of madness.

It is a style that has a strangely powerful attraction however, as proven by the many exhibitions he has been invited to take part in all over Europe, the great number of prints he has sold, and the important collections his work has been accepted into.

Although self taught, Ropp is very particular about his working methods. He always uses large format cameras, and prefers to use Polaroid Type 55 4x5" Positive/Negative film. I use a hand-held flash light to illuminate the subjects. Sometimes I position the subjects in front of mirrors and photograph their distorted reflections. Both of these techniques rely on experiment, so it is extremely useful to be able to see an instant proof. And when the final proof shows that I have what I want, I can either use the negative from that same shot, or make another exposure with the minimum of camera movement.' Ropp also favours the unique tonality of Polaroid Type 55 negatives which, he says, produce a print that matches perfectly the mystical mood of his images.

Profile 3

The design direction and editorial content emphasize what makes Polaroid photography distinctive. Photographers' work is always shown at actual size, and the basic typographic grid is eight-by-ten.

Karmen Janusch
Germany
Type 809
Contact No:
49 171 312 1115

Friedrun Reinhold
Germany
Film: Type 669
Contact No:
49 40 439 9118

26 Gallery

P magazine is an international showcase for images which illustrate the unique qualities and advantages of Polaroid instant films. Gallery comprises a selection of excellent individual photographs, picked from your submissions which, viewed together, demonstrate the diversity of work produced on Polaroid films.

If you would like your work to be considered for inclusion in any section of P magazine, check the back cover to see what themes are coming up and send examples, along with brief background details, to your nearest Polaroid contact – there is an address list elsewhere in this issue.

24 Gallery

Tim Bowden UK. Type 55, 5x4" black and white positive/negative film. Contact No: 0171 490 2600.

_P_ magazine is printed in five languages. Type is overprinted in a second black and is rarely dropped-out. The design format allows for text that varies greatly in length, such as the German translation.

Acknowledgments

This book would not have been possible without the contributions of a number of people from both inside and outside Pentagram – clients, writers, photographers, archivists, and support staff.

We graciously acknowledge the fifty clients who not only allowed us to tell their respective stories but who, in many cases, participated in developing those stories.

We are grateful to Randall Rothenberg for his herculean diligence and ability to put into a single essay sixteen very different points of view.

Thanks are due to several writers for capturing the essence of Pentagram and the exhibited work. They are Mark Burton, Michael Evamy, Delphine Hirasuna, Helen Jones, Paul Kunkel, Martina Margetts, Jeremy Meyerson, Philip Nobel, and Paul Pendergrass. Special thanks to David Gibbs, Sarah Haun, and JoAnn Stone, whose efforts extended well beyond their storytelling to editorial collaboration.

We also wish to express our appreciation for all the photographers of Pentagram's work, in particular, David Grimes and his colleague Will Phillips, both of Austin, who are responsible for 275 images included here.

The assistance of the coordinators and archive staff from within each Pentagram office, most notably that of Kurt Koepfle and Julia Wyatt, was invaluable.

We are forever grateful to the team in Austin – Diane Baker, Bill Carson, Julie Hoyt, Marc Stephens, and Jeff Williams. Their time, patience, abilities, and attitudes made *Pentagram Book Five* reality.

Our final and warmest thanks go to Gianfranco Monacelli, Andrea Monfried, and Steve Sears for their editorial counsel, production expertise, and, above all, for keeping us on track.

Pentagram Partners